ARCO

ACCOUNTANT/ AUDITOR

9th edition

Edited by

Deborah L. Byrne, MBA

THOMSON
ARCO

Australia • Canada • Mexico • Singapore • Spain • United Kingdom • United States

THOMSON
ARCO

An ARCO Book

ARCO is a registered trademark of Thomson Learning, Inc., and is used herein under license by Peterson's.

About The Thomson Corporation and Peterson's

With revenues of US$7.2 billion, The Thomson Corporation (www.thomson.com) is a leading global provider of integrated information solutions for business, education, and professional customers. Its Learning businesses and brands (www.thomsonlearning.com) serve the needs of individuals, learning institutions, and corporations with products and services for both traditional and distributed learning.

Peterson's, part of The Thomson Corporation, is one of the nation's most respected providers of lifelong learning online resources, software, reference guides, and books. The Education Supersite℠ at www.petersons.com—the Internet's most heavily traveled education resource—has searchable databases and interactive tools for contacting U.S.-accredited institutions and programs. In addition, Peterson's serves more than 105 million education consumers annually.

For more information, contact Peterson's, 2000 Lenox Drive, Lawrenceville, NJ 08648;
800-338-3282; or find us on the World Wide Web at www.petersons.com/about.

ISBN 0-7689-0851-5

Printed in the United States of America

10 9 8 7 6 5 4 3 2 1 04 03 02

CONTENTS

PART 4: SAMPLE PRACTICE EXAMINATIONS

PART 5: CAREER INFORMATION RESOURCES

APPENDIX

WHAT THIS BOOK WILL DO FOR YOU

Arco has followed testing trends and methods ever since the line was created. We specialize in books that prepare people for tests. Based on this experience, we have prepared the best possible book to help you score high.

To write this book, we carefully analyzed every detail surrounding the forthcoming examination including:

- the job itself;
- official and unofficial announcements concerning the examination;
- all the previous examinations, many not available to the public;
- related examinations; and
- technical literature that explains and forecasts the examination.

CAN YOU PREPARE YOURSELF FOR YOUR TEST?

You want to pass this test. That's why you bought this book. Used correctly, this book will act as a "self-tutor" and will show you what to expect and will give you a speedy brush-up on the subjects tested in your exam. Some of these are subjects not taught in schools at all. Even if your study time is very limited, you should

- become familiar with the type of examination you will have.
- improve your general examination-taking skill.
- improve your skill in analyzing and answering questions involving reasoning, judgment, comparison, and evaluation.
- improve your speed and skill in reading and understanding what you read—an important part of your ability to learn and an important part of most tests.

This book will:

Present the type of questions you will see on the actual test. This will help you feel at ease with the test format.

Pinpoint your weaknesses. Once you know the subjects in which you're weak, you can get right to work and concentrate on those areas. This kind of selective study yields maximum test results.

Supply practice with sample tests. Almost all our sample and practice questions are taken from actual previous exams. On the day of the exam, you'll see how closely this book follows the format of the real test.

Give you confidence *now*, while you are preparing for the test. It will build your self-confidence as you proceed and will prevent the kind of test anxiety that can cause low test scores.

Focus on the multiple-choice type of question because that's the kind you'll encounter on your test. You must not be satisfied with merely knowing the correct answer for each question. You must find out why the other choices are incorrect. This will help you remember information you thought you had forgotten.

After testing yourself, you may find that you are weak in a particular area. You should concentrate on improving your skills by using the specific practice sections in this book that apply to you.

HOW DO I USE THIS BOOK?

If you already know what type of career you wish to pursue, this book will help you prepare for any of the major exams. If you don't know what type of job you'd like to apply for, this book will also help you. Not only will you be able to prepare for your exam, but you will also find information here about various types of careers, and perhaps it will narrow down your choices.

PART ONE

There are five parts to this book. Part One covers the major employment sectors: federal, state, and local (or municipal) careers. Each sector has its own requirements and tests. However, as you will see, there are certain types of questions that will appear on most of these exams, regardless of the type of test you will take.

This section also contains important information on test-taking techniques. You will be given guidelines to help you prepare for the actual test, pointers on how to make the most of the information in this book, and tips on how to become a master test taker. Since feeling anxious before you take a test is a normal reaction, we provide you with helpful tips on feeling relaxed and comfortable with your exam so you can get a great test score.

PART TWO

Part Two is an overview of the various types of careers available. If you haven't already been in the field, you will be surprised by the number of different job opportunities as well as the varied jobs within an area.

If you are beginning your career or job shopping at this time, you should read this section carefully. It will help introduce you to the different jobs and the many opportunities that await you. We hope you will be inspired and excited and will be motivated to apply for, study for, and land one of those jobs. If this section helps you narrow your area of interest, you can then concentrate on the exams that will help you prepare for the job you want.

PART THREE

That leads us into Part Three of this book. Part Three is a review section that supplies you with practice on a variety of different question types. We suggest you complete this part to get an idea of where your strengths lie and what weaknesses you'll have to deal with on the actual test.

This review section contains previous exam questions that are classified by subject matter, which will also help you determine your strengths and weaknesses and where you need additional practice.

PART FOUR

In Part Four, there are sample real examinations closely patterned on the actual exams. Timing, level of difficulty, question styles, and scoring methods all closely conform to the examinations for which they are meant to prepare. And a special feature of this book is that there are answer explanations included for three of the practice exams.

When you take the sample exams, try to set aside the full measure of time to take the exam at one sitting. Time yourself accurately (a stopwatch or a kitchen timer will work well) and stop working when the time is up. If you have not completed all of the questions when time expires, stop anyway. Check your answers against the provided correct answers and score your paper. Then, complete the remaining questions so you get in all the practice you can. Study all of the answer explanations carefully, even those explanations for questions that you answered correctly. By reading all of the explanations, you can gain greater insight into methods of answering questions and the reasoning behind the correct choices.

One very important suggestion: we strongly believe that regardless of the test that you think you're planning to take—or the career path you want to follow—try to take *all* of the exams in this book. It may seem like a lot of extra work, but you never know where you may end up. You may think you're interested in a job with the local city government and end up instead in a private company. Or, the exam you were hoping to take is not being given for another year, but some other test is being given next month. It is always better to be prepared.

PART FIVE

Part Five contains civil service career information resources. Here you will find out how to look for available jobs. Important addresses, phone numbers, and Web sites that will help you pursue your career in civil service are also provided in this section.

The most important thing you can do is to *use* this book. Reading through all of the sections, reviewing question types, and taking the practice exams, will help you use what you learned here to the best of your ability to succeed in your intended career path.

APPENDIX

In the Appendix, a list of accounting and bookkeeping definitions is provided. Be sure to review this section as it contains some of the language you are likely to encounter on your exam.

PART ONE

So You Want to Work for the Government

Government service is one of the nation's largest sources of employment. About 1 in every 6 employed people in the United States is employed in some form of civilian government service. Of those government employees, 5 out of 6 workers are employed by state or local governments, and the remainder work for the federal government.

As you can see, government employees represent a significant portion of the nation's workforce. The employment opportunities cover practically every skill and profession in our complex modern society. Note that every year, thousands of new jobs are created and tens of thousands of replacements are needed on existing jobs.

WHERE THE JOBS ARE: FEDERAL AND STATE CIVILIAN EMPLOYMENT

The federal government is the nation's largest employer, with almost 3 million civilian workers in the United States and an additional 130,000 civilian workers in U.S. territories and foreign countries. The headquarters of most government agencies and departments are in the Washington, D.C., area, but only 1 of 8 federal employees works there.

The executive branch is the largest part of the federal government, with the Office of the President, the cabinet departments, and many independent agencies, commissions, and boards. This branch administers federal laws, handles international relations, conserves natural resources, treats and rehabilitates disabled veterans, delivers the mail, conducts scientific research, maintains the flow of supplies to the armed forces, and administers many programs to promote the health and welfare of the people of the United States.

The largest department is the Department of Defense, which includes the Departments of the Army, Navy, and Air Force. It employs about 1 million civilian workers. The Departments of Agriculture, Health and Human Services, and the Treasury are also large employers. The two largest independent agencies are the U.S. Postal Service and the Veterans Administration.

Federal civilian employment is also available in the legislative branch. Congress, the Government Printing Office, the General Accounting Office, and the Library of Congress are all components of the legislative branch of government. The smallest employer of the three branches is the court system, also known as the judicial branch.

THE MERIT SYSTEM

More than nine out of ten jobs in the federal government run under a merit system. The Civil Service Act, administered by the U.S. Office of Personnel Management, covers six out of ten federal titles. This act was passed by Congress to ensure that federal employees are hired on the basis of individual merit and fitness. It provides for competitive examinations and the selection of new employees from among the most qualified applicants.

Some federal jobs are exempt from civil service requirements either by law or by action of the Office of Personnel Management. However, most of these positions are covered by separate merit systems such as the Foreign Bureau of Investigation, the Nuclear Regulatory Commission, and the Tennessee Valley Authority.

GENERAL PAY SCHEDULE

More than half of all federal workers are paid under the General Schedule (GS), a pay scale for workers in professional, administrative, technical, and clerical jobs and for workers such as guards and messengers. General Schedule jobs are classified by the U.S. Office of Personnel Management in one of fifteen grades, according to the difficulty of duties and responsibilities and the knowledge, experience, and skills required of the workers. GS pay rates are set by Congress and apply to government workers nationwide. They are reviewed annually to see whether they are comparable with salaries in private industry. They are generally subject to upward adjustment for regions that have a very high cost of living. In low cost areas, the GS pay scale may exceed that of most private sector workers.

Most employees receive within-grade pay increases at one-, two-, or three-year intervals if their work is acceptable. Within-grade increases may also be given in recognition of high-quality service. Some managers and supervisors receive increases based on their job performance rather than on time in grade.

High school graduates who have no related work experience usually start in GS-2 jobs, but some who have special skills begin at the GS-4 level. Most people with bachelor's degrees appointed to professional and administrative jobs, such as statisticians, economists, writers and editors, budget analysts, accountants, and physicists, may enter at grades GS-5 or GS-7, depending on experience and academic record. Those who have a master's degree or Ph.D. or the equivalent education or experience may enter at the GS-9 or GS-11 level. Advancement to higher grades generally depends on ability, work performance, and the availability of job openings at higher-grade levels.

FEDERAL WAGE SCHEDULE

About one quarter of federal civilian workers are paid according to the Federal Wage System. Under this system, craft, service, and manual workers are paid hourly rates established on the basis of "prevailing" rates paid by private employers for similar work in the same locations. As a result, the federal government wage rate for an occupation varies by locality. This commitment to meeting the local wage scale allows the federal wage earner to bring home a weekly paycheck comparable to that which he or she would earn in the private sector and to enjoy the benefits and security of a government job at the same time. The federal wage earner has the best of all possible worlds in this regard. Federal government employees work a standard 40-hour week. Employees who are required to work overtime may receive premium rates for the additional time or compensatory time off at a later date. Most employees work 8 hours a day, five days a week, Monday through Friday, but in some cases, the nature of the work requires a different workweek. Annual earnings for most full-time federal workers are not affected by seasonal factors.

Federal employees earn 13 days of annual (vacation) leave each year during their first three years of service; 20 days each year until the end of fifteen years; after fifteen years, 26 days each year. Workers who are members of military reserve organizations are also granted up to 15 days of paid military leave a year for training purposes. A federal worker who is laid off, though federal layoffs are uncommon, is entitled to unemployment compensation similar to that provided for employees in private industry.

Other benefits available to most federal employees include a contributory retirement system, optional participation in low10-cost life and health insurance programs that are partly supported by the government (as the employer), and training programs to develop maximum job proficiency and help workers achieve their highest potential. These training programs may be conducted in government facilities or in private educational facilities at government expense.

GENERAL SCHEDULE PAY

As of January 1, 2002, basic pay under the General Schedule or GS pay plan is as follows:

GS Rating	*Grade 1*	*Grade 10*
GS-1	$14,757	$ 18,456
GS-2	$16,592	$ 20,876
GS-3	$18,103	$ 23,530
GS-4	$20,322	$ 26,415
GS-5	$22,737	$ 29,559
GS-6	$25,344	$ 32,949
GS-7	$28,164	$ 36,615
GS-8	$31,191	$ 40,551
GS-9	$34,451	$ 44,783
GS-10	$37,939	$ 49,324
GS-11	$41,684	$ 54,185
GS-12	$49,959	$ 64,944
GS-13	$59,409	$ 77,229
GS-14	$70,205	$ 91,625
GS-15	$82,580	$107,357

Please note that General Schedule pay is adjusted geographically and that the majority of jobs pay a higher salary. Locality payments in the continental United States range from 8.64 percent to 19.04 percent. Pay rates outside the continental United States are 10 percent to 25 percent higher. Also, certain hard-to-fill jobs, usually in the scientific, technical, and medical fields, may have higher starting salaries. Exact pay information can be found on position vacancy announcements. Check the Office of Personnel Management's Web site for Locality Pay Charts at www.opm.gov.

FEDERAL BENEFITS

The nation's number one employer is our own U. S. government. The excellent benefits are one of the reasons why. The following list of benefits applies to permanent, tenured, full-time employees.

- **Pay Comparability:** Salaries are based on comparison with the private sector.
- **Job Security:** Federal jobs are very secure. Layoffs are rare because federal workers need to provide government services.
- **Annual Pay Increases:** Yearly raises are keyed to Employment Cost Index (ECI).
- **Step Increases Within-Grade:** Increases in pay are based on time on the job and good job performance. As you go from Step 1 to Step 10, your salary increases.
- **Merit Promotion System:** Compete for merit increases in pay.
- **Health Insurance Coverage:** The government shares in the cost of health benefits and gives a choice of more than 300 HMOs and fifteen fee-for-service plans. There is no waiting period, no preexisting condition clause, and no medical exam.
- **Life Insurance Benefits:** The government makes matching contributions and cost of living adjustments.
- **Retirement Benefits:** Workers receive retirement benefits from both the Federal Employees Retirement System and Social Security.
- **Holidays:** There are ten paid holidays every year.
- **Vacation/Sick Days:** Accrue 13-20-26 days per year vacation with 30-day Carry Over. Also, workers earn thirteen days sick leave every year.
- **Training:** Employees receive government-paid training and tuition reimbursement.
- **Alternative Work Schedules:** Flexible work hours and compressed workweeks are available programs, as well as telecommuting from home or a center.

TEST-TAKING TECHNIQUES

Many factors enter into a test score. The most important is the ability to answer the questions, which indicates the ability to learn and perform the duties of the job. Assuming that you have this ability, knowing what to expect on the exam and being familiar with techniques of effective test taking should give you the confidence you need to do your best.

There is no quick substitute for long-term study and development of your skills and abilities to prepare you for doing well on tests. There are some steps you can take when getting ready for and taking a test. These steps fall into four major areas:

(1) be prepared

(2) avoid careless errors

(3) manage your time

(4) guess

BE PREPARED

Don't make the test harder than it has to be by not preparing yourself. You are taking a very important step in preparation by reading this book and taking the sample tests that are included. This will help you to become familiar with the tests and the kinds of questions you will have to answer.

As you use this book, carefully read the sample questions and directions for taking the test. When you take the sample tests, time yourself as you will be timed in the real test.

When you are working on the sample questions, don't look at the correct answers before you try to answer them on your own. This can fool you into thinking you understand a question when you really don't. Try it on your own first, then compare your answer with the one given.

On your examination day, allow the test itself to be the main attraction of the day. Do not squeeze it in between other activities. Be sure to bring your admission card, identification, and pencils, as instructed. Prepare these the night before so that you are not flustered by a last-minute search. Arrive rested, relaxed, and on time. In fact, plan to arrive a little bit early. Leave plenty of time for traffic or other complications that might upset you and interfere with your test performance.

In the test room, the examiner will hand out forms for you to fill out. He or she will give you the instructions that you must follow in taking the examination. The examiner will tell you how to fill in the grids on the forms. Time limits and timing signals will be explained. If you do not understand any of the examiner's instructions, *ask questions*.

Follow instructions exactly. Fill in the grids on the forms carefully and accurately. Incorrect gridding may lead to loss of veteran's credits to which you may be entitled or misaddressing of your test results. Do not begin until you are told to begin. Stop as soon as the examiner tells you to stop. Do not turn pages until you are told to do so. Do not go back to parts you have already completed. Any infraction of the rules is considered cheating. If you cheat, your test paper will not be scored, and you will not be eligible for appointment.

The answer sheet for most multiple-choice exams is machine scored. You cannot give any explanations to the machine, so you must fill out the answer sheet clearly and correctly.

AVOID CARELESS ERRORS

Don't reduce your score by making careless mistakes. Always read the instructions for each test section carefully, even when you think you already know what the directions are. It's why we stress throughout this book that it's important to fully understand the directions for these different question-types *before* you go into the actual exam. It will not only reduce errors, but it will save you time—time you will need for the questions.

What if you don't understand the directions? You will have risked getting the answers wrong for a whole test section. As an example, vocabulary questions can sometimes test synonyms (words that have similar meanings), and sometimes test antonyms (words with opposite meanings). You can easily see how a mistake in understanding in this case could make a whole set of answers incorrect.

If you have time, reread any complicated instructions after you do the first few questions to check that you really do understand them. Of course, whenever you are allowed to, ask the examiner to clarify anything you don't understand.

MANAGE YOUR TIME

Before you begin, take a moment to plan your progress through the test. Although you are usually not expected to finish all of the questions given on a test, you should at least get an idea of how much time you should spend on each question in order to answer them all. For example, if there are sixty questions to answer and you have 30 minutes, you will have about one-half minute to spend on each question.

Keep track of the time but do not focus on the amount of time remaining. You need to answer the questions, but do not spend too much time on any one question. If you find yourself stuck, either guess and mark the question in the question booklet or skip the question entirely. If you skip the question, be sure to mark it as a skip and take care to skip the answer space on the answer sheet. If there is time at the end of the exam or exam part, you can check back for skip marks and give those questions another try.

SHOULD YOU GUESS?

One of the questions you should ask in the testing room is what scoring method will be used on your particular exam. You can then guide your guessing procedure accordingly.

The decision to guess depends on the scoring method for the particular examination part. The two main types of scoring and guessing tips for each are:

Rights Only. One point is given for each correct answer and no subtraction for wrong answers. If this is the scoring for the section you are working on, then you should guess. Do this by reading the question and all of the answer choices carefully. Eliminate those answer choices that you are certain are wrong. Then guess from among the remaining choices. You cannot gain a point if you leave the answer space blank; you may gain a point with an educated guess or even with a lucky guess. It is foolish to leave any spaces blank on a test that counts "rights only." If it appears that you are about to run out of time before completing such an exam, mark all the remaining blanks with the same letter. According to the law of averages, you should get some portion of those questions right.

Rights Minus Wrongs. A point is deducted for each wrong answer and counts heavily against you. If this is the scoring for the section you are working on, *do not guess.* Work as quickly as possible while concentrating on accuracy. Do not rush to fill answer spaces randomly at the end. Keep working carefully until time is called; then stop and leave the remaining answer spaces blank.

MULTIPLE-CHOICE QUESTIONS

Almost all of the tests given on civil service exams are multiple-choice format. This means that you normally have four or five answer choices. There is a basic technique to answering these types of questions. Once you've understood this technique, it will make your test taking far less stressful.

First, there should only be one correct answer. Since these tests have been given time and again, and the test developers have a sense of which questions work and which questions don't work, it will be rare that your choices will be ambiguous. They may be complex and somewhat confusing, but there will still be only one right answer.

The first step is to look at the question without looking at the answer choices. Then select the correct answer. That may sound somewhat simplistic, but your first choice is usually the correct one.

With math questions, you should first solve the problem. If your answer is among the choices, you're probably correct. Don't ignore things like the proper function signs (adding, subtracting, multiplying, and dividing), negative and positive numbers, and so on.

Suppose you don't know the correct answer. You then use the *process of elimination.* It's a time-honored technique for test takers. There is always one correct answer. There is usually one answer choice that is totally incorrect—a "distracter." If you look at that choice and it seems highly unlikely, then eliminate it. Depending on the number of choices, you've just cut down the number of choices to make. Now weigh the other choices. If they seem incorrect, eliminate them. You've now increased your odds at getting the correct answer.

In the end, you may be left with only two choices. At that point, you can select the answer you feel is correct. With only two choices left, you now have a 50 percent chance of getting it right.

HOW TO MARK YOUR ANSWER SHEET

1. Blacken your answer space firmly and completely. ● is the only correct way to mark the answer sheet. ◐, ⊗, ✓, and ⊘ are all unacceptable. The machine might not read them at all.
2. Mark only one answer for each question. If you mark more than one answer, you will be considered wrong, even if one of the answers is correct.
3. If you change your mind, you must erase your mark. Attempting to cross out an incorrect answer like this ✖ will not work. You must erase any incorrect answer completely. An incomplete erasure might be read as a second answer.
4. All of your answering should be in the form of blackened spaces. The machine cannot read English. Do not write any notes in the margins.
5. MOST IMPORTANT: Answer each question in the right place. Question 1 must be answered in space 1; question 52 in space 52. If you should skip an answer space and mark a series of answers in the wrong places, you must erase all those answers and do the questions over, marking your answers in the proper places. You cannot afford to use the limited time in this way. Therefore, as you answer *each* question, look at its number and check that you are marking your answer in the space with the same number.
6. For the typing tests, type steadily and carefully. Just don't rush, since that's when the errors occur. Keep in mind that each error subtracts 1 wpm from your final score.

SCORING

If your exam is a short-answer exam such as those often used by companies in the private sector, your answers will be graded by a personnel officer trained in grading test questions. If you blackened spaces on the separate answer sheet accompanying a multiple-choice exam, your answer sheet will be machine scanned or will be hand scored using a punched card stencil. A raw score is then calculated using the scoring formula that applies to that test or test portion. Raw scores on test parts are then added together for a total raw score.

The civil service testing authority, Postal Service, or other testing body converts raw scores to a scaled score according to a formula of its own. The scaling formula allows for slight differences in difficulty of questions from one form of the exam to another and allows for equating the scores of all candidates. Most civil service clerical test scores are reported on a scale of 1 to 10. Note that the entire process of conversion from raw to scaled score is confidential information.

SUMMARY OF TEST-TAKING TIPS

1. Get to the test center early. Make sure you give yourself plenty of extra time to get there, park your car, if necessary, and even grab a cup of coffee before the test.
2. Listen to the test monitors and follow their instructions carefully.
3. Read every word of the instructions. Read every word of every question.
4. Mark your answers by completely darkening the answer space of your choice. Do not use the test paper to work out your answers.
5. Mark only ONE answer for each question, even if you think that more than one answer is correct. You must choose only one. If you mark more than one answer, the scoring machine will consider you wrong.
6. If you change your mind, erase completely. Leave no doubt as to which answer you mean.
7. If your exam permits you to use scratch paper or the margins of the test booklet for figuring, don't forget to mark the answer on the answer sheet. Only the answer sheet is scored.
8. Check often to be sure that the question number matches the answer space, that you have not skipped a space by mistake.
9. Guess according to the guessing suggestions we have made.
10. Stay alert. Be careful not to mark a wrong answer just because you were not concentrating.
11. Do not panic. If you cannot finish any part before time is up, do not worry. If you are accurate, you can do well even without finishing. It is even possible to earn a scaled score of 100 without entirely finishing an exam part if you are very accurate. At any rate, do not let your performance on any one part affect your performance on any other part.
12. Check and recheck, time permitting. If you finish any part before time is up, use the remaining time to check that each question is answered in the right space and that there is only one answer for each question. Return to the difficult questions and rethink them.

PART TWO

The Kind of Work You Will Be Doing

Accountants and auditors help to ensure that firms are efficiently run, records are kept accurately, and taxes are paid properly and on time. An expanded variety of business and accounting services are provided to clients who support these vital functions. These services exist in all the sectors of accounting—including public, management, and government accounting, as well as internal auditing. The broadening range of services being provided by accountants and auditors includes budget analysis, financial and investment planning, information technology consulting, and limited legal services. Note that many people with accounting backgrounds work for the public sector.

NATURE OF THE WORK

Managers must have up-to-date financial information to make important decisions. Accountants prepare and analyze financial reports that furnish this kind of information.

Three major fields are public, management, and government accounting:

- *Public accountants* have their own businesses or work for accounting firms.
- *Management accountants*, also called industrial or private accountants, handle the financial records of their company.
- *Government accountants* examine the records of government agencies and audit private businesses and individuals whose dealings are subject to government regulations.

Accountants often concentrate on one phase of accounting. For example, many public accountants specialize in auditing. Others specialize in tax matters, such as preparing income tax forms and advising clients of the advantages and disadvantages of certain business decisions. They often help develop estate plans that will have high benefits and low taxes. Still others specialize in management consulting and give advice on a variety of matters. They might develop or revise an accounting system to serve the needs of clients more effectively or give advice about the design data-processing systems. Forensic accounting is a specialty of investigating and interpreting bankruptcies and other complex financial transactions. Others may audit financial statements for assurance to investors and authorities that statements have been accurately prepared. Most Public Accountants are Certified Public Accountants (CPAs) and typically work for public accounting firms or have their own private practices.

Other types of accountants include:

- *Management accountants* provide the financial information executives need to make sound business decisions. Usually, management accountants are part of executive teams involved in strategic planning or new product development. They may work in areas such as taxation, budgeting, costs, or investments. Internal auditing, a specialization within management accounting, is rapidly growing in importance. Accountants who work as internal auditors examine and evaluate their firm's financial systems and management control procedures to ensure efficient and economical operation.

- *Government accountants* and auditors maintain and examine the records of government agencies and audit private businesses and individuals for compliance with government regulations or taxation. Accountants employed by the Federal, State, and local government certify that revenues are received and expenditures made are in accordance with laws and regulations. A significant number of government accountants are employed with the Federal Government as Internal Revenue Service agents or are involved in financial management, financial institution examining, and budget administration.
- *Internal Auditors* verify the accuracy of their organization's records and check for mismanagement, waste, or fraud. There have evolved many highly specialized areas of auditing—electronic data processing, environmental, engineering, legal, insurance premium, bank, and health-care auditors.

Computers are rapidly changing the nature of work for most accountants and auditors. As a result, many accountants and auditors have extensive computer skills. Personal and laptop computers enable accountants and auditors to be more mobile and to use their clients' computer systems to extract information from large mainframe computers. With the aid of computer software, accountants can summarize transactions in formats that are helpful in presenting financial analysis. This greatly reduces the tedious nature of manual work associated with data management and record keeping.

Accountants staff the faculties of business and professional schools. As educators, they may teach accounting as well as finance, marketing, management, and related fields; some are primarily researchers or administrators. Many accountants teach part time, work as consultants, or serve on committees of professional organizations.

WORKING CONDITIONS

Most accountants work in offices and have a standard 35- or 40-hour work schedule. Accounting teachers, on the other hand, with more flexible schedules, divide their time among teaching, research, and administrative responsibilities. Self-employed accountants, who may set up offices at home, work as many hours as the business requires.

Tax accountants work long hours under heavy pressure during the tax season. Accountants employed by large firms may travel extensively to audit or work for clients or branches of the firm.

PLACES OF EMPLOYMENT

Approximately 976,000 people worked as accountants and auditors in 2000. They were employed throughout private industry and government, but almost 25 percent of accountants worked for accounting, auditing, or bookkeeping firms. Approximately 3 out of 25 accountants or auditors are self-employed.

The federal government is the largest employer in the country, with almost 3 million employees nationwide. State and local governments employ an additional fifteen million people with 75 percent of these jobs in local government. Examples of local government employers would be counties, municipalities, towns, and school districts.

Many accountants and auditors are unlicensed management accountants, internal auditors, or government accountants and auditors; however, many are licensed Certified Public Accountants. Other accountants work for federal, state, and local government agencies, and some teach in colleges and universities.

Accountants are found in all business, industrial, and government organizations. Most, however, work in large urban areas where many public accounting firms and central offices of large businesses are concentrated, such as Chicago, Los Angeles, New York, and Washington, D.C.

TRAINING, OTHER QUALIFICATIONS, AND ADVANCEMENT

TRAINING

Training is available at colleges and universities, accounting and business schools, and correspondence schools. Although many graduates of business and correspondence schools are successful, most public accounting and business firms require applicants for accountant and internal auditor positions to have at least a bachelor's degree in accounting or a closely related field. Many employers prefer those with a master's degree in accounting. A growing number of large employers prefer applicants who are familiar with computers and their applications in accounting and internal auditing. For beginning accounting positions, the federal government requires four years of college (including 24 semester hours in accounting or auditing) or an equivalent combination of education and experience. However, applicants face competition for the limited number of openings in the federal government. For teaching positions, most colleges and universities require at least the master's degree or the Certified Public Accountant certificate.

Previous experience in accounting can help an applicant get a job. Many colleges offer students an opportunity to gain experience through summer or part-time internship programs conducted by public accounting or business firms. Such training is invaluable in gaining permanent employment in the field.

Professional recognition through certification or licensure is also extremely valuable. Anyone working as a "certified public accountant" must hold a certificate issued by a state board of accountancy. All states use the four-part Uniform CPA Examination, prepared by the American Institute of Certified Public Accountants, to establish certification. The 2-day CPA examination is very rigorous, and candidates are not required to pass all four parts at once. Only about a quarter of those who take it each year pass every part they attempt. However, most states require candidates to pass at least two parts for partial credit. Although the vast majority of states require CPA candidates to be college graduates, some states substitute a certain number of years of public accounting experience for the educational requirement. Most states require applicants to have some public accounting experience for a CPA certificate. For example, bachelor's degree holders most often need two years of experience while master's degree holders most often need no more than one year. Based on recommendations made by the American Institute of Certified Public Accountants, a few states now require or are considering requiring CPA candidates to have a bachelor's degree plus 30 additional semester hours. This trend is expected to continue in the coming years.

For a "public accountant" or "accounting practitioner" license or registration, some states require only a high school diploma while others require college training. Information on requirements may be obtained directly from individual state boards of accountancy or from the National Society of Public Accountants.

The Institute of Internal Auditors, Inc., confers the Certified Internal Auditor (CIA) upon graduates from accredited colleges and universities who have completed three years' experience in internal auditing and who have passed a four-part examination. The National Association of Accountants (NAA) confers the Certificate in Management Accounting (CMA) upon candidates who pass a series of uniform examinations and meet specific educational and professional standards.

QUALIFICATIONS

People planning a career in accounting should have an aptitude for mathematics and be able to quickly analyze, compare, and interpret facts and figures and make sound judgments based on this knowledge. They must question how and why things are done and be able to clearly communicate the results of their work, orally and in writing, to clients and management.

Accountants must be patient and able to concentrate for long periods of time. They must be good at working with systems and computers as well as with people. Accuracy and the ability to handle responsibility with limited supervision are important.

Perhaps most important, because millions of financial statement users rely on the services of accountants, the public expects accountants to have the highest standards of integrity.

ADVANCEMENT

A growing number of states require both CPAs and licensed public accountants to complete a certain number of hours of continuing education before licenses can be renewed. Increasingly, accountants are studying computer programming so they can adapt accounting procedures to data processing. Although capable accountants should advance rapidly, those having inadequate academic preparation may be assigned routine jobs and find promotion difficult.

Junior public accountants usually start by assisting with auditing work for several clients. They may advance to intermediate positions with more responsibility in 1 or 2 years and to senior positions within another few years. Those who excel may become supervisors and managers; open their own public accounting firm; or transfer to executive positions in management accounting or internal auditing in private firms.

Beginning management accountants often start as ledger accountants, junior internal auditors, or as trainees for technical accounting positions. They may advance to chief plant accountant, chief cost accountant, budget director, or manager of internal auditing. Some become controllers, treasurers, financial vice presidents, or corporation presidents. Many corporation executives have backgrounds in accounting and finance. In the federal government, beginners are hired as trainees and usually are promoted in a year or so. In college and university teaching, those having minimum training and experience may receive the rank of instructor without tenure; advancement and permanent faculty status depend upon further education and teaching experience and are increasingly difficult to attain.

EMPLOYMENT OUTLOOK

Employment in accounting and auditing, according to projections made by the Bureau of Labor Statistics in the *Occupational Outlook Handbook,* is expected to grow about as fast as the average for all occupations through the year 2010. Accountants and auditors who have earned professional recognition through certification or licensure should have the best job prospects. Certified Public Accountants should have a wide range of available job opportunities due to the more stringent state requirements to have 150 hours of college course work, which makes it more difficult to obtain this certification.

Proficiency in accounting or auditing computer software, or expertise in specialized areas such as international business, specific industries or current legislation, also can help job seekers in the accounting field. Government legislation to monitor business activity also is expected to add to the demand for accountants. Legislation and regulations regarding pension reform, tax reform, revenue sharing, funding of elections, financial disclosure, and other matters should create many jobs for accountants. The changing role of accountants and auditors also should spur demand for accountants. In response to market demand, these financial specialists will offer more financial management and consulting services as they take on a greater advisory role and develop more sophisticated and flexible accounting systems. Also, internal auditors will increasingly be needed to discover and eliminate waste and fraud.

It is important to note that in response to these growing trends, as well as the use of accounting software, the demand for traditional services will decrease. Accountants will spend less time doing routine audits due to liability and shift away from income tax preparation because of the popularity of tax preparation firms and computer software. As computer programs become more simplified, some routine accounting-related tasks may be assigned to clerical staff.

College graduates will be in greater demand for accounting jobs than applicants who lack this training. Opportunities for accountants without a college degree will occur mainly in small businesses and accounting firms.

Many employers prefer graduates who have worked part-time in a business or accounting firm while in school. In fact, experience has become so important that some employers in business and industries seek people with one or two years' experience for beginning positions.

The increasing use of computers and electronic data processing systems in accounting should stimulate the demand for those with this type of expertise.

RELATED OCCUPATIONS

Accountants design and control financial records and analyze financial data. Others for whom training in accounting is invaluable include appraisers, budget officers, loan officers, financial analysts, bank officers, actuaries, underwriters, FBI special agents, securities sales workers, and purchasing agents.

THE JOB ANNOUNCEMENT

Information on job opportunities for government accountants and auditors is generally distributed in the form of official job announcements. When a position is open and a civil service examination is to be given for it, a job announcement is drawn up. This generally contains just about everything an applicant has to know about the job.

The announcement begins with the job title and salary. A typical announcement then describes the work, the location of the position, the education and experience requirements, the kind of examination to be given, and the system of rating. It may also have something to say about veteran preference and the age limit. It tells which application form is to be filled out, where to get the form, and where and when to file it.

Note that each city and state has unique features to their announcements, so be sure to read you own announcement very carefully. The announcement will also answer many of your questions and help you decide whether you like the position and are qualified for it.

Listed below are descriptions of the main sections of a job announcement:

WHERE THE JOB IS LOCATED

If the job is a state job, be sure you are willing to work in the area indicated. There is no point in applying for a position and taking the examination if you do not want to move. If you are not willing to move, study other announcements that will give you an opportunity to work in a place of your choice.

A civil service job close to your home has as an additional advantage—the fact that local residents usually receive preference in appointments.

THE DUTIES

The words *Optional Fields*—sometimes just the word *Options*—may appear on the front page of the announcement. You then have a choice to apply for that particular position in which you are especially interested. This is because the duties of various positions are quite different even though they bear the same broad title. A public relations *clerk*, for example, does different work from a payroll *clerk*, although they are considered broadly in the same general area.

Not every announcement has options. But whether or not it has them, the precise duties are described in detail under the heading: *Description of Work*. Make sure that these duties come within the range of your experience and ability.

THE DEADLINE

Most job requirements give a deadline for filing an application. Others bear the words *No Closing Date* at the top of the first page; this means that applications will be accepted until the needs of the agency are met. In some cases a public notice is issued when a certain number of applications have been received.

No application mailed past the deadline date will be considered.

EDUCATION AND EXPERIENCE

Every announcement has a detailed section on education and experience requirements for the particular job and for the optional fields. Make sure that in both education and experience you meet the minimum qualifications. If you do not meet the given standards for one job, there may be others open where you stand a better chance of making the grade.

VETERAN PREFERENCE

If the job announcement does not mention veteran preference, it would be wise to inquire if there is such a provision in your state or municipality. There may be none or it may be limited to disabled veterans. In some jurisdictions widows of veterans are given preference. All such information can be obtained through the agency that issues the job announcement.

WHY YOU MAY BE BARRED

Applicants may be denied examinations and eligibility appointments for any of the following reasons:

- intentional false statements;
- deception or fraud in examination or appointment;
- reasonable doubt concerning loyalty to the United States;
- use of intoxicating beverages to excess;
- criminal, infamous, dishonest, immoral, or notoriously disgraceful conduct.

THE TEST

The announcement describes the kind of test given for the particular position. Please pay special attention to this section. It tells what areas are to be covered in the written test and lists the specific subjects on which questions will be asked. Sometimes sample questions are given. *The test and review material in this ARCO book are based on the requirements as given in this section as well as on actual tests.*

Usually the announcement states whether the examination is to be assembled or unassembled. In an *assembled* examination, applicants *assemble* in the same place at the same time to take a written or performance test. The *unassembled* examination is one where an applicant does not take a test; instead he is rated on his education and experience and whatever records of past achievement he is asked to provide.

Two sample job announcements are printed on the following pages. Note the differences in each announcement and the two parts to the New Jersey announcement (a vacancy listing and a job specification).

(Taken from the State of New Jersey Web site)

Department of Personnel Job Vacancy

ACCOUNTANT

Title: ACCOUNTANT

Last Date for Filing: April 2, 2002

Symbol: M0116D

Jurisdiction Using List: WOODBRIDGE

Existing Vacancies: 1

Salary: $28,000.00 – $52,000.00

Open to Residents of: WOODBRIDGE

Location: WOODBRIDGE TWP.

Work week: 35 hours per week

Description of Job and Requirements: See Job Specification 00004.

Filing Information:
M0116D—OPEN TO RESIDENTS OF WOODBRIDGE TWP. YOUR APPLICATION MUST BE POSTMARKED BY THE LAST DATE FOR FILING—04/02/02.

To file an application for this announcement, print, complete, and mail the APPLICATION (PDF 70K), along with the five dollar ($5.00) Credential Review Fee to:

NJDOP
PO Box 321
Trenton, NJ 08625-0321
EEO & ADA

Please note: Documents with the (PDF #K) indicator are in Adobe Acrobat format. PDF formatted documents appear the same as the original printed forms or documents. To view and print these forms and documents, you must have a PDF viewer, which is available free from Adobe. Click here to learn more about Adobe Acrobat or to download the latest version of the Adobe Acrobat viewer from the Adobe Web site.

IMPORTANT: All applicants must meet the specific residency requirements of this Job Vacancy identified in the **Open to Residents of** and **Filing Information** sections above on or before the **Last Date for Filing**.

NOTE: For additional information on How to Be a More Successful Candidate, please see the FAQ's section of the DOP Home Page.

(Taken from the State of New Jersey Web site)

Department of Personnel

JOB SPECIFICATION 00004

You are reading our New Jersey Department of Personnel Job Descriptions used to describe groups of jobs with similar characteristics. This is **not** a Job Vacancy Announcement.

ACCOUNTANT

DEFINITION

Under direction, performs the routine accounting work involved in preparing financial statements and in maintaining an accounting system; does other related duties.

NOTE: The examples of work for this title are for illustrative purposes only. A particular position using this title may not perform all duties listed in this job specification. Conversely, all duties performed on the job may not be listed.

EXAMPLES OF WORK

- Performs the routine accounting work involved in the installation, operation, and auditing of accounts.
- Reviews varied financial transactions and records for conformance with regulations and established accounting procedures.
- May assign and supervise the work of employees performing clerical accounting and other support functions.
- Compiles financial and other statements and reports using basic data.
- Conducts routine investigations, examinations, and audits of books and financial records, and prepares reports thereof.
- Prepares the routine accounting and statistical tabulations.
- Assists in preparing budget requests; prepares current statements of allocations and disbursements of budgeted funds.
- May design, revise, and install accounting systems.
- Performs the routine work involved in auditing and recording expense invoices and prepares, audits, and edits reports of costs and other financial summaries and statements.
- Checks disbursements for adherence to contractual obligations.
- Prepares accounting reports containing findings, conclusions, and recommendations.
- Maintains accounting records and files.
- Will be required to learn to utilize various types of electronic and/or manual recording and information systems used by the agency, office, or related units.

REQUIREMENTS

EDUCATION

Graduation from an accredited college or university with a bachelor's degree including or supplemented by twenty-one (21) semester hour credits in professional accounting subjects.

NOTE: Applicants who have satisfactorily completed (21) semester hour credits in professional accounting courses at an accredited college or university may substitute accounting experience in work involving the installation, operation, and keeping of large scale systems of accounts for the remainder of the above educational requirement on a year-to-year basis with 30 semester hour credits being equal to one (1) year of experience.

NOTE: Possession of a valid certificate as a Registered Municipal Accountant or Certified Public Accountant, issued by the New Jersey State Board of Certified Public Accountants or as a Certified Municipal Finance Officer issued by the New Jersey Department of Community Affairs, Division of Local Government Services, may be substituted for the above educational requirement.

LICENSE

Appointees will be required to possess a driver's license valid in New Jersey only if the operation of a vehicle, rather than employee mobility, is necessary to perform the essential duties of the position.

KNOWLEDGE AND ABILITIES

- Knowledge of modern accounting principles, methods, and procedures.
- Knowledge of the methods used in the installation, operation, and maintenance of accounts.
- Knowledge of the methods used to prepare accounting and other financial reports.
- Ability to analyze accounting problems.
- Ability to review varied financial transactions for conformance with established accounting procedures.
- Ability to provide technical assistance to those who maintain financial records.
- Ability to apply established accounting methods, procedures, interpretation, and facts.
- Ability to prepare and interpret financial statements.
- Ability to establish and maintain records and files.
- Ability to learn to utilize various types of electronic and/or manual recording and information systems used by the agency, office, or related units.
- Ability to read, write, speak, understand, or communicate in English sufficiently to perform the duties of this position. American Sign Language or Braille may also be considered as acceptable forms of communication.

People with mental or physical disabilities are eligible as long as they can perform the essential functions of the job after reasonable accommodation is made to their known limitations. If the accommodation cannot be made because it would cause the employer undue hardship, such people may not be eligible.

CODE: 00004 DJ 9/9/00

This job specification is for local government use only.

(print below notice on separate page in a box)

Typical Notice of Examination
Accountant
Qualification Requirements

MINIMUM REQUIREMENTS:

(A) Graduation from an accredited college with a baccalaureate degree including or supplemented by 24 credits in accounting including at least one course each in advanced accounting, auditing, cost accounting, and principles of United States taxation; or

(B) A New York State CPA license.

Candidates who were educated in countries other than the United States must file an "Application for Evaluation of Credentials" with their Experience Paper Form A for this examination. Foreign education will be evaluated by the Department of Personnel to determine comparability to education received in domestic accredited educational institutions to determine the extent to which it will be credited toward meeting the minimum requirements for this examination.

DUTIES AND RESPONSIBILITIES:
Under supervision, performs professional accounting work of moderate difficulty and responsibility internally in departments and agencies or in conducting field audits and investigations; works independently or with others in executing responsible accounting assignments following prescribed rules of procedure; performs related work.

EXAMPLES OF TYPICAL TASKS:
Examines the accuracy of the returns of taxpayers that have filed under various City tax laws, determines tax liabilities, and assesses tax payments. Makes field investigations and audits of the books of various types of enterprises, including housing, to determine conformance with City tax laws or City regulations. Prepares working papers, schedules, financial statements, payroll lists, and inventory records. Maintains cost records and prepares reports. Reviews requests for the allocation of capital funds. Assists in preparation and analyses of budgets. Assists in the audit of accounts of City departments and agencies for receipts under franchises, leases, and permits. Checks and verifies entries, footings, and extensions for accuracy. Maintains control of accounts and funds and reserves. Prepares journal entries and adjusting entries. Meets and confers with representatives of both agencies and City taxpayers involved in audits. Prepares written and financial reports. Makes recommendations based on audit findings. Conducts audits at taxpayers place of business, which may be outside New York City. Supervises employees performing work of lower responsibility.

Test Information

Written, weight 100, 70% required; oral, qualifying, 70% required. Only candidates who pass the written test will be summoned to the qualifying oral.

The written test will be of the multiple-choice type and may include questions on internal and external audit procedures; preparation of audit programs; city, state, and federal tax laws; administrative tax codes; assessments on personal income taxes, partnerships, unincorporated business taxes, and corporate taxes; preparation of written reports; research techniques; collection and interpretation of statistics and raw data; preparation and use of financial records and statements; comprehension of and compliance with generally accepted accounting principles, guidelines, and contracts; computer utilization in an accounting system; standards of employee conduct; supervision; and related areas.

The factors in the qualifying oral test will be speech, manner, and judgment in job situations.

People eligible will be required to pass a qualifying medical test prior to appointment. An eligible will be rejected for any current medical and/or psychiatric impairment that impairs his or her ability to perform the duties of the class of positions.

Promotion Opportunities

Employees in the title of Accountant are accorded promotion opportunities, when eligible, to the title of Associate Accountant.

THE APPLICATION FORM

Having studied the job announcement and having decided that you want the position and are qualified for it, your next step is to get an application form. If you are able to use a computer, applications can either be filled out and submitted on line or are available to print from:

http://staffing.opm.gov/vacancies/applyonline.asp

The information will also be marked on the job announcement.

On the whole, civil service application forms differ little from state to state and locality to locality. The questions, which have been worked out after years of experimentation, are simple and direct, designed to elicit a maximum of information about you.

Many prospective civil service employees have failed to get a job because of slipshod, erroneous, incomplete, misleading, or untruthful answers. Give the application the serious attention it must have as the first important step toward getting the job you want.

Here, along with some helpful comments, are the questions usually asked on the average application form, although not necessarily in this order.

THE QUESTIONS

Name of examination or kind of position applied for. This information appears in large type on the first page of the job announcement.

Optional job (if mentioned in the announcement). If you wish to apply for an option, simply copy the title from the announcement. If you are not interested in an option, write "None."

Primary place of employment applied for. This would pertain to a statewide job. The location of the position was probably contained in the announcement. You must consider whether you want to work there. The announcement may list more than one location where the job is open. If you would accept employment in any of the places, list them all; otherwise list the specific place or places where you would be willing to work.

Name and Address. Give in full, including your middle name if you have one and your maiden name as well if you are a married woman.

Home and Office phones. If none, write "None."

Legal or voting residence. List the state in which you vote here.

Married or single. If you are a widow or widower, you are considered single.

Birthplace. Changes in the borders of European countries make it difficult for many foreign-born American citizens to know which country to list as the land of their birth. One suggestion is to set down the name of the town and the name of the country that now controls it, together with the name of the country to which it belonged at the time of your birth.

Date of birth. Give the exact day, month, and year.

Lowest grade or pay you will accept. Although the salary is clearly stated in the job announcement, there may be a quicker opening in the same occupation but carrying less responsibility and thus a lower basic entrance salary. You will not be considered for a job paying less than the amount you give in answer to this question.

Will you accept temporary employment if offered you for (a) one month or less, (b) one to four months, (c) four to twelve months? Temporary positions come up frequently and it is important to know whether you are available.

Will you accept less than full-time employment? Part-time work comes up now and then. Consider whether you want to accept such a position while waiting for a full-time appointment.

Were you in active military service in the Armed Forces of the United States? Veterans' preference, if given, is usually limited to active service during the following periods: 12/7/41–12/31/46; 6/27/50–1/31/55; 6/1/63–5/7/75; 6/1/83–12/1/87; 10/23/83–11/21/83; 12/20/89–1/3/90; 8/2/90 to end of Persian Gulf hostilities; during the Gulf War, from August 2, 1990 through January 2, 1992; or in a campaign or expedition for which a campaign medal has been authorized, including El Salvador, Grenada, Haiti, Lebanon, Panama, Somalia, Southwest Asia, and Bosnia.

Do you claim disabled veterans credit? If you do, you have to show proof of a war-incurred disability. This is done through certification by the Veterans Administration.

Considerable space is allotted on the form for the applicant to tell about all his past employment. Examiners check all such answers closely. DO NOT embroider or falsify your record. If you were ever fired, say so. It is better for you to state this openly than for the examiners to find out the truth from your former employer.

Special qualifications and skills. Even though not directly related to the position for which you are applying, such information as licenses and certificates obtained for teacher, pilot, registered nurses, and so on is wanted. Also, list your experience in the use of machines and equipment, and any other skills you have acquired. Published writings, public speaking experience, membership in professional societies, honors, and fellowships received should also be included.

Education. List your entire educational history, including all diplomas, degrees, and special courses taken in any accredited or Armed Forces school. Also, give your credits toward a college or a graduate degree.

References. List the names of people who can give information about you—their occupations and business and home addresses are often requested.

Your health. Questions are asked concerning your medical record. You are expected to have the physical and psychological capacity to perform the job for which you are applying. Standards vary, of course, depending on the requirements of the position. A physical handicap will not bar an applicant from a job that he can perform adequately.

To give you an idea of a standard application form, here is a copy of the New York City application. Note that we have included a Federal Job Application (OF612) in the appendix of this book.

DEPARTMENT OF CITYWIDE ADMINISTRATIVE SERVICES
DIVISION OF CITYWIDE PERSONNEL SERVICES
1 Centre Street, 14th floor New York, NY 10007

APPLICATION FOR EXAMINATION

(Directions for completing this application are on the ***back*** of this form. Additional information is on the Special Circumstances Sheet)

Download this form on-line: nyc.gov/html/dcas

FOLLOW DIRECTIONS ON BACK
Fill in all requested information clearly, accurately, and completely.

The City will only process applications with complete, correct, legible information which are accompanied by correct payment or waiver documentation.

All unprocessed applications will be returned to the applicant.

1. EXAM #: ☐☐☐☐

Check One: ☐ Open Competitive ☐ Promotion

2. EXAM TITLE: ____

3. SOCIAL SECURITY NUMBER: ☐☐☐ - ☐☐ - ☐☐☐☐

4. LAST NAME: ____

5. FIRST NAME: ____

6. MIDDLE INITIAL: ☐

7. MAILING ADDRESS: ____

8. APT. #: ☐☐☐☐

9. CITY OR TOWN: ____

10. STATE: ☐☐

11. ZIP CODE: ☐☐☐☐☐ - ☐☐☐☐

12. PHONE: ☐☐☐ - ☐☐☐ - ☐☐☐☐

13. OTHER NAMES USED IN CITY SERVICE: ____

Questions 14 & 15: Discrimination on the basis of sex, sexual orientation, race, creed, color, age, disability status, veteran status or religious observance is prohibited by law. The City of New York is an equal opportunity employer. The identifying information requested on this form is to be used to determine the representation of protected groups among applicants. This information is voluntary and will not be made available to individuals making hiring decisions.

14. RACE/ETHNICITY (Check One):
- ☐ White
- ☐ Black
- ☐ Hispanic
- ☐ American Indian/Alaskan Native
- ☐ Asian/Pacific Islander

15. SEX (Check One):
- ☐ Male
- ☐ Female

16. ARE YOU EMPLOYED BY THE HEALTH AND HOSPITALS CORPORATION? (Check One) ☐ YES ☐ NO

17. CHECK ALL BOXES THAT APPLY TO YOU: (Directions for this section are found on the "Special Circumstances" Sheet)
- ☐ I AM A SABBATH OBSERVER AND WILL REQUEST AN ALTERNATE TEST DATE (Verification required. See Item A on Special Circumstances Sheet)
- ☐ I HAVE A DISABILITY AND WILL REQUEST SPECIAL ACCOMMODATIONS (Verification required. See item B on Special Circumstances Sheet).
- ☐ I CLAIM VETERANS' CREDIT (For qualifications see item C on Special Circumstances Sheet)
- ☐ I CLAIM DISABLED VETERANS' CREDIT (For qualifications see item C on Special Circumstances Sheet)

18. Your Signature: ____________________ **Date:** __________

RUDOLPH W. GIULIANI
Mayor

WILLIAM J. DIAMOND
Commissioner

NOTE: You should apply for an examination **only** if you meet the qualification requirements set forth in the Notice of Examination. Read the Notice of Examination carefully before completing the application form.

Fill in all requested information clearly, accurately, and completely. **The City will only process applications with complete, correct, legible information which are accompanied by correct payment or waiver documentation. All unprocessed applications will be returned to the applicant.**

Included in this material is a voter registration form. If you take this opportunity to register to vote, please mail the postage-paid form directly to the Board of Elections. The provision of government services is not conditioned on being registered to vote.

When appropriate the City will issue a refund for unprocessed applications after the close of the filing period.

DIRECTIONS FOR SUBMITTING APPLICATION FOR EXAMINATION

FORMS All required forms which are listed in the upper-right-hand corner of the Notice of Examination must accompany your application. Failure to include these forms may result in your disqualification and you will not receive test scores.

FEE The amount of the fee is stated in the Notice of Examination. Only a ***MONEY ORDER*** made out to ***D.C.A.S. (EXAMS)*** is acceptable payment (check or cash **are not** accepted). On the front of the money order you must clearly write your ***full name***, ***social security number*** and ***the exam number.*** Keep your Money Order receipt as proof of filing.

FEE WAIVER A filing fee is not charged if you are a New York City resident receiving public assistance from the New York City Department of Social Services. To have the fee waived, you **must** enclose a legible photocopy of your current Benefit Card (**formerly known as the Medicaid Card**) with your application. **The Food Coupon Photo Identification Card is *unacceptable*.** You must write your ***social security number*** and the ***exam number*** on the front of the photocopy of the Benefit Card. The name on your application must exactly match the name printed on your Benefit Card.

APPLICATION SUBMISSION Your application must be postmarked no later than the last day of the application period indicated on the Notice of Examination. Mail the completed application, supporting documents, and required filing fee or fee waiver to:

DCAS Applications Section
1 Centre Street, 14th Floor, New York, NY 10007
C/O ***Exam #, Exam Title***

INSTRUCTIONS FOR COMPLETING APPLICATION FORM PROPERLY

To ensure proper processing of Application print all information *CLEARLY*. Failure to do so will delay or disqualify your application.

1. EXAM NO. / EXAM TITLE See the Notice of Examination prior to filling in the exact exam number and exam title. Check either the Open Competitive (OC) or Promotion (PRO) box to indicate the type of examination you are applying for.

2. - 12. GENERAL INFORMATION

- The address you give will be used as your mailing address for all official correspondence.
- Only one (1) address for each person is maintained in the files of this Department.
- If you change your mailing address after applying, see the Change Of Address section on Special Circumstances Sheet.

13. OTHER NAMES USED If you have worked for a New York City agency under another name, write the other name in this section. If you have not used other names, skip this section.

14. - 15. ETHNICITY / SEX Completing this information is voluntary. This information will not be made available to individuals making hiring decisions.

16. HHC EMPLOYEE If you are employed by the Health and Hospitals Corporation, check the **YES** box in this section.

17. SPECIAL CIRCUMSTANCES (Sabbath/Religious Observers, Special Accommodations because of a Disability, or Veterans' Credit) Please see the "Special Circumstances" direction sheet for qualifications and definitions associated with this section.

18. SIGNATURE Signing the application indicates that all statements you provided on this form and all other forms required for this examination are true and subject to the penalties of perjury.

Applicants who do not receive an admission card at least **4 days** prior to the tentative test date must obtain an admission card by coming to the Examining Service Section, NYC Department of Citywide Administrative Services, 1 Centre Street, 14th Floor.

Rev. 8/28/2000

The City of New York
Department of Citywide Administrative Services

Division of Citywide Personnel Services -- Applications Section
1 Centre Street, 14th Floor New York, New York 10007

Internet: nyc.gov/html/dcas

APPLICATION SUPPLEMENT

RETURN THIS SUPPLEMENT WITH YOUR APPLICATION FOR CIVIL SERVICE EXAMINATION.

Section 50-b of the New York State Civil Service Law requires that all applicants for Civil Service examinations be asked the following questions:

1. Do you have any loans made or guaranteed by the New York State Higher Education Services Corporation which are currently outstanding?

   CHECK ONLY ONE: YES ☐ NO ☐

2. If so, are you presently in default on such loan?

   CHECK ONLY ONE: YES ☐ NO ☐

- -

SOCIAL SECURITY NUMBER:				■			■				

PLEASE PRINT CLEARLY:

FULL NAME: ____
(Last Name, First Name, Middle Initial)

ADDRESS: ____
(Include Apartment Number and In Care of- C/O, if applicable)

CITY, STATE, ZIP: ____

EXAM TITLE: ______________________________________ **EXAM NO:** ______

COMPLETE THIS AFFIRMATION: I affirm under penalties of perjury that all statements made on this application and all supplementary information are true.

Signature: ______________________________________ **Date:** ____________

DP-2512A (Rev. 08/28/2000)

THE EXAMINATION

When you have filled out the application form as completely as possible, sign it and send it to the address given on the form. If your examination includes a written test, you must wait until it is scheduled. Shortly before it is to be held, you will be notified where and when to report.

YOU ARE TESTED

Sometimes the date of the written test appears on the job announcement. Sometimes it does not, so you must simply wait until you receive notification of the time and place.

The period between the filing of the application and the taking of the test can be of immense value to you. If you use it wisely, it will help you score high.

The most important step you can take in preparing for your test is to study questions on previous tests—or questions similar to those asked on previous tests. The purpose of this book is to acquaint you with the kinds of questions that will be asked and to provide you with review material in the subjects that will be covered. A thorough knowledge of the forms of the actual test as well as the subject matter will give you a great advantage. There are no substitutes for experience and familiarity.

THE DAY OF THE TEST

The importance of knowing beforehand exactly how to reach the test center and how to get there cannot be stressed enough. Lateness will bar you from taking the test. There is nothing more nerve-wracking than to find yourself in a traffic jam or on the wrong bus with little time to spare. If the test is to take place some distance from your house, make the trip a few days earlier to make sure you know how to get there. On the all-important day, give yourself more than enough time. In this way you will avoid the risk of an upsetting experience under circumstances that may affect your final score.

THE ELIGIBILITY LIST

When all the parts of the examination have been rated (this may include education, experience, and suitability along with the written test), you are notified of your *numerical* rating. If this is high enough to give you a passing mark, you are placed on the eligible list. Appointments are made from this list.

PART THREE

Review with Previous Exam Questions Classified by Subject Matter

BOOKS OF ACCOUNT

1. Does a trial balance of the ledger taken before the books are closed differ from a trial balance taken immediately after the books are closed?

2. If the assets of a business exceed the liabilities, is the business solvent or insolvent?

3. If the cost of merchandise sold exceeds the sales, the result would be a gross profit or loss. Which is correct?

4. Does the Profit and Loss Account show the total proprietary interest (or proprietorship) in the business?

5. Does the exchange of one asset for another of equal value affect the proprietary interest (or proprietorship)?

6. Should the amount of fuel consumed during an accounting period be entered in the Profit and Loss Statement as an expense?

7. Would the use of several books (or journals) of original entry reduce the number of postings to be made at the end of a period?

8. At the close of each period, is the interest income (interest earned) account closed into the Notes Receivable Account?

9. If the proprietor's drawing (personal) account shows a debit balance at the close of a period, would it appear in the:

   (A) Balance Sheet (financial statement) as a liability?
   (B) Balance Sheet (financial statement) as an asset?
   (C) Balance Sheet (financial statement) as a deduction from the Proprietor's Investment (capital) account?
   (D) Profit and Loss Statement as an income?
   (E) Profit and Loss Statement as an expense?

10. After a ledger has been closed, P. & L. shows a credit balance. What kind of item is this if it is not an operating item?

11. If you find the P. & L. Balance on the debit side, what kind of item is it if it is not in the Trading Account?

12. For paying his bill promptly, William Jones receives an allowance of $10. What does he call it?

13. What does the man who makes the allowance call it?

14. Name three common financial expenses:

    (A) __________
    (B) __________
    (C) __________

15. Which of the above is brought onto the books through an adjustment entry?

16. Make a type entry for writing off a bad debt.

17. Is Sales Discount in favor of the buyer or of the seller?

18. Make a type entry for closing the three financial expenses.

19. Make a type entry for two common financial incomes.

20. In what account is inventory shown in the ledger?

21. In what account is initial inventory closed?

22. Is it debited or credited to this account?

23. Through what kind of an entry is final inventory brought onto the books?

24. What two accounts are affected when final inventory is debited?

25. Which account is debited?

26. Which account is credited?

27. Which of the two accounts remains open after the books have been closed?

28. Is initial inventory added to or subtracted from net purchases?

29. Is final inventory added to or subtracted from net purchases?

30. What is the guide to be followed in placing a value on items of merchandise inventory?

31. Does initial inventory increase or decrease cost of sales?

32. Does final inventory increase or decrease cost of sales?

33. Mr. X finds his expired insurance is $20. His office supplies used $10. Make an adjusting entry.

34. His depreciation on copy machines used in preparing advertising material is $40. Make an adjusting entry.

35. His depreciation on delivery equipment is $50. Make the entry.

36. Gross Trading Margin is $2,000. Net Trading Profit is $600. What can you determine?

37. Give the amount.

38. Operating costs total $800. Gross Trading Margin is $1,500. What can you determine?

39. Give the amount.

40. Operating Costs total is $1,200. Trading Profit is $900. What can you determine?

41. Give the amount.

42. I own an automobile for which I paid $1,200. The automobile has depreciated $400. For what amount is the Automobile Account debited if a reserve for depreciation of Delivery Equipment is used?

43. For what amount is the reserve account credited?

44. What is the book value of the automobile?

45. Make Journal entries for the following, but do not post: I sell the automobile for cash, $800.

46. I sell the automobile for cash, $900.

47. I sell the automobile for cash, $700.

48. I trade for a new automobile costing $2,000. I get a trade allowance of $900 and pay cash for the balance.

49. Assume that the trade-in allowance is $800 instead of $900.

50. In the Accounts Receivable Ledger it is found that John Jones owes $40. His account is considered worthless and written off. Make the Journal entry, assuming there is an account "Reserve for Bad Debts."

51. James Ryan owes me on a note, $100. I decide it is uncollectible. Make the entry.

52. John Jones and James Ryan have paid their respective obligations, which I had written off. Make one entry for the two settlements, crediting Bad Debt recoveries.

53. In a given entry, Reserve for Depreciation is credited. What kind of entry is it?

54. An automobile account shows a debit of $1,400. What value does that show?

55. The "Book Value" of the account is $800. From the facts in Question #54, the value of what account may you determine?

56. If the volume of posting is to be reduced, what three special journals are usually necessary?

57. What two ledgers are used in conjunction with the above?

58. If the Sales Journal has only one money column, to what accounts are the totals posted?

59. If the Cash Receipts Journal has four money columns, to what accounts are the totals of three of them posted?

60. If the Cash Payment Journal has four money columns, to what accounts are the totals of three of them posted?

61. If the General Journal has four money columns, to what accounts are the totals of two of them posted?

62. The following summary entry is on X's books: Accounts Receivable, $2,130; Sales, $2,130. In what journal are the total sales on account found?

63. To what ledger are the detailed items that make up the sales of $2,130 posted?

64. What other ledger is affected for the debit?

65. Do the amounts in the Purchase Journal increase or decrease "cost of goods sold"?

66. How do they affect trading margin?

67. I hold James Duke's three months note for $300, dated May 26, 2001. I discount it the same day at 12%. I receive the proceeds in cash, $291. Make the entry.

68. The note was paid by James Duke at maturity. Make the entry.

69. Name a common form of contingent liability.

70. What journal feature is a requirement when subsidiary ledgers are used?

71. When subsidiary ledgers are used, what kind of account is required in the main ledger that is not necessary where there are no subsidiary ledgers?

72. What account title is given to this account for accounts owing us?

73. What must be the relationship between the subsidiary ledger and its control account?

74. By what method may this be determined?

75. What two accounts involving subsidiary ledgers appear in the trial balances and in the balance sheet?

76. Name the two most universal control accounts for which subsidiary ledgers are provided.

77. In case a subsidiary ledger is broken up into a number of divisions, what is the most common basis for the divisions?

78. On what other basis are subdivisions sometimes made?

79. What kind of entries, other than current entries made at the beginning of a period, are usually included in the trial balance?

80. After adjustments are made, into what sections of the Working Sheet are all items extended?

81. In a given period, the net sales are $20,000. The cost of sales is 80%, operating expenses, 17%. Give the amount of:

    (A) cost of sales
    (B) operating expenses
    (C) trading profit

82. What is the gross income?

83. What is the percentage to net sales?

84. Assume that a given firm's sales average $15,000 per month. What are the annual sales?

85. If there are three partners in a certain business concern, how many capital accounts are kept?

86. A partnership consists of three equal partners: Smith, Jones, and Brown. Make the entry for distributing the profits of $3,000; assuming that they are closed direct into the partners' capital accounts.

87. What is the governing body in a corporation?

88. In what ledger are accounts with individual stockholders kept?

89. What is its main ledger control account?

90. Corporation X is organized with assets of $20,000, liabilities of $3,000, and capital stock of $15,000. What can you determine?

91. What is the amount?

92. Corporation Z is organized with assets of $10,000, liabilities of $1,000, and surplus of $1,500. What can you determine?

93. What is the amount?

94. In corporation X, the net income for a given year is $2,000. Make the entry for closing out the Profit & Loss Account.

ANSWER KEY

1. Yes
2. Solvent
3. Gross Loss
4. No
5. No
6. Yes
7. Yes
8. No
9. (A) No
   (B) No
   (C) Yes
   (D) No
   (E) No
10. Net Profit
11. Net Loss
12. Cash Discount
13. Sales Discount
14. Interest Cost, Sales Discount, and Provision for Bad Debts
15. Provision for Bad Debts
16. Dr. Reserve for Bad Debts
    Cr. Accounts Receivable
17. Buyer
18. Dr. Profit & Loss
    Cr. Interest Cost
    Cr. Sales Discount
    Cr. Provision for Bad Debts
19. Dr. Interest Earned
    Dr. Purchase Discount
    Cr. Profit & Loss
20. Merchandise Inventory
21. Purchases
22. Dr.
23. Adjustment entry
24. Merchandise inventory and purchases
25. Merchandise inventory
26. Purchases
27. Merchandise inventory
28. Added to
29. Subtracted from
30. Market or Cost (whichever is lower)
31. Increase
32. Decrease
33. Dr. Profit & Loss
    Cr. Insurance
    Cr. Expense
34. Dr. Depreciation of Furniture & Fixtures
    Cr. Reserve for Depreciation of Furniture & Fixtures
35. Dr. Depreciation of Delivery Equipment
    Cr. Reserve for Depreciation of Delivery Equipment
36. Operating Expenses
37. $1,400
38. Net Trading Profit
39. $700
40. Loss
41. $300
42. $1,200
43. $400
44. $800
45. Dr. Cash $800
    Dr. Reserve $400
    Cr. Automobile $1,200
46. Dr. Cash $900
    Dr. Reserve $400
    Cr. Profit & Loss $100
    Cr. Automobile $1,200
47. Dr. Cash $700
    Dr. Reserve $400
    Dr. Profit & Loss $100
    Cr. Automobile $1,200
48. Dr. Automobile $2,000
    Dr. Reserve $400
    Cr. Cash $1,100
    Cr. Profit & Loss $100
    Cr. Automobile $1,200
49. Dr. Automobile $2,000
    Dr. Reserve $400
    Cr. Cash $1,200
    Cr. Automobile $1,200

50. Dr. Reserve for Bad Debts $40
Cr. John Jones—Acc. Receivable $40
Control, General Ledger

51. Dr. Reserve for Bad Debts $100
Cr. Notes Receivable (James Ryan) $100

52. Dr. Cash $140
Cr. Bad Debts recovered $140

53. Adjusting entries

54. Cost value

55. Reserve for Depreciation of Delivery Equipment $600

56. Cash Journal, Sales Journal, and Purchase Journal

57. Accounts Receivable Ledger, Accounts Payable Ledger

58. Dr. Accounts Receivable
Cr. Sales

59. Dr. Cash
Dr. Discount
Cr. Accounts Receivable

60. Dr. Accounts Payable
Cr. Cash
Cr. Discount

61. Accounts Receivable and Accounts Payable

62. General Journal

63. Accounts Receivable Subsidiary Ledger

64. The General Ledger

65. Increase

66. Decrease

67. Dr. Cash $291
Dr. Discount $9
Cr. Notes Rec. discounted (James Duke) $300

68. Dr. Notes Receivable discounted $300
Cr. Notes Receivable $300

69. Endorsement of a customer's note

70. Special columns

71. Controlling account

72. Accounts Receivable Controlling Account

73. They must be in agreement.

74. A Trial Balance of Subsidiary Ledger

75. Accounts Receivable and Accounts Payable

76. (A) Accounts Receivable
(B) Accounts Payable

77. Alphabetical

78. Departmental or Territorial

79. Adjusting entries

80. Profit and Loss or Balance Sheet

81. (A) $16,000
(B) $3,400
(C) $600

82. $4,000

83. 20%

84. $180,000

85. Three

86. P. & L. $3,000
To Smith—Capital Account—$1,000
To Jones—Capital Account—$1,000
To Brown—Capital Account—$1,000

87. The Board of Directors

88. Stockholder's Ledger

89. Capital Stock

90. The amount of surplus

91. $2,000

92. The capital stock issued

93. $7,500

94. P. & L. $2,000
To Surplus $2,000

JOURNAL ENTRIES

DIRECTIONS: Using the numbers in front of each account title, make the journal entries for the following transactions. Do not write the names of the accounts; simply indicate the number of the account titles to be debited or credited. Always give the number of the account to be debited first; then give the number of the account to be credited. For example: if cash is to be debited and sales is to be credited, write in the answer space 1; 35.

For any transaction, a series of journal entries arises. To determine the correct journal entries:

1. Determine the accounts affected.
2. Determine what effect each of these accounts has on the Balance Sheet.
3. An account is debited when:
   (A) it increases an account on the assessed (left) side; or
   (B) it decreases an account on the liability and net worth (right) side.
4. An account is credited when:
   (A) it increases an account on the liability and net worth (right) side; or
   (B) it decreases an account on the asset (left) side.
5. Note: Since income accounts increase the net worth (right) side, they are credited with any increase. Since expense accounts decrease the net worth (right) side, they are debited with any increase.
6. Since (all other things being equal) a greater purchase account will decrease the net worth (right) side, any increase in purchases is debited.

EXAMPLES:

(A) We receive $100 cash in payment of account from a customer. The accounts involved are: Cash $100; Accounts Receivable $100. In this case, the Cash $100 increases the left side of the balance sheet and the Accounts Receivable $100 decreases the left side of the balance sheet. Therefore debit Cash and credit Accounts Receivable.

(B) We sell $100 merchandise on account. The accounts involved are Sales $100; Accounts Receivable $100. In this case, Accounts Receivable $100 represents an increase of the left side and Sales represents an increase of the right side, Net Worth. Therefore debit Accounts Receivable and credit Sales.

(C) We issue $100 note to a creditor. The accounts involved are Notes Payable $100; Accounts Payable $100. In this case, Notes Payable represents an increase in a right side account and Accounts Payable represents a decrease in a right side Account. Therefore debit Accounts Payable and credit Notes Payable.

(D) Set up an accrual of wages of $100. The accounts involved are Wages $100; and Accrued Wages $100—the former being an expense account and the latter a liability account, which increases the right side. Therefore, debit Wages and credit Accrued Wages.

JOURNALIZING BY ACCOUNT NUMBERS

DIRECTIONS: Using the numbers in front of each account title, make the journal entries for the following transactions. Do not write the names of the accounts; simply indicate the number of the account titles to be debited or credited. Always give the number of the account to be debited first; then give the number of the account to be credited. For example: if cash is to be debited and sales is to be credited, write in the answer space 1; 35.

Numbered Ledger Account Titles

1. Cash
2. Accounts Receivable
3. Reserve for Bad Debts
4. Notes Receivable
5. Notes Receivable Discounted
6. Inventory
7. Real Estate
8. Reserve for Depreciation (Real Estate)
9. Equipment
10. Reserve for Depreciation (Equipment)
11. Sinking Fund
12. Goodwill
13. Legal Expense
14. Interest Expense
15. Delivery Expense
16. Rent Expense
17. Depreciation Expense
18. Bad Debts
19. Selling Expense
20. Purchases
21. Purchases Returned
22. Purchases Discount
23. Accounts Payable
24. Notes Payable
25. Accrued Expenses
26. Dividends Payable
27. Mortgages Payable
28. Bonds Payable
29. Capital Stock
30. Reserve for Sinking Fund
31. Reserve for Contingence
32. Capital Surplus
33. Earned Surplus
34. Profit and Loss
35. Sales
36. Sales Returns
37. Sales Discount
38. Interest Income
39. Miscellaneous Income

1. Cash sales of $2,250 are made.
2. An invoice for $3,500 for merchandise purchased on account is received.
3. $250 of merchandise purchased on account is returned.
4. A new delivery truck is purchased for $300 in cash and a $7,000 note.
5. $50,000 is borrowed from the bank for 60 days at 12%.
6. The old delivery truck, which is carried on the books at $6,000 and has depreciation recorded to date of $4,150, is sold for $1,275.
7. Rent is paid in the amount of $1,150.
8. Salesmen are paid $5,000.
9. A suit against us is won and we pay $1,500.
10. A customer pays his account in the amount of $3,800 by a note.
11. The note is discounted at the bank, the proceeds of $3,760 being credited to our account.
12. A customer returns $250 of merchandise sold to him on account.
13. Semi-annual interest in the amount of $10,000 on the bond is paid to the bond holders.
14. A customer pays a $250 balance, taking 2% discount.
15. Legal fees are paid to our attorneys in the amount of $500.
16. The board of directors orders the annual contribution of $7,500 set up in the sinking fund reserve.
17. An error is discovered in a previous posting, in that $500 of supplies for the delivery department was incorrectly charged to the selling department.
18. A person paid us $200 rent for the use of our windows.
19. One account owing us $830 is found to be worthless.

20. Accrued wages on December 31 are as follows: selling department $500 and delivery department $400.

21. Bad debts for this year are estimated to be 2% of the $750,000 sales on account.

22. Close out the purchase returns and discounts to purchases.

23. Close out sales returns and discounts to sales.

24. Close out all of the income accounts.

25. Close out the profit and loss account, assuming there is a gross profit.

26. A dividend of $7,500 is declared.

27. The dividend is paid in cash.

ANSWER KEY

1. 1; 35
2. 20; 23
3. 23; 21
4. 9; 1; 24
5. 1; 24
6. 1; 10; 34; 9
7. 16; 1
8. 19; 1
9. 31; 1
10. 4; 2
11. 1; 14; 5
12. 36; 2
13. 14; 1
14. 1; 37; 2
15. 13; 1
16. 33; 30
17. 15; 19
18. 1; 39
19. 3; 2
20. 15; 19; 25
21. 18; 3
22. 21; 22; 20
23. 35; 36; 37
24. 35; 38; 39; 34
25. 34; 33
26. 33; 26
27. 26; 1

BALANCE SHEET

Balance sheet sections:

A. **Current Assets Section**
Consists of those assets that the firm intends to turn into cash in the normal course of business.
Example: Accounts Receivable; Merchandise Inventory. Also valuation accounts of those assets.
Example: Reserve for Bad Debts.

B. **Fixed Assets Section**
Consists of the properties and other values of a permanent nature to be continually retained as the fixed investment of the business but which is not the intention of the firm to turn into cash in the normal course of business.
Example: Machinery; Land. Also valuation accounts of those assets.
Example: Depreciation of Machinery.

C. **Deferred Charges Section**
Consists of those payments for materials or services that should not be charged to the current expenses, but that will eventually be such a charge.
Example: Prepaid Expenses: Organization Expenses.

D. **Intangible Assets**
Consists of those payments for intangible values such as goodwill, etc.

E. **Current Liabilities Section**
Consists of those liabilities that will have to be paid within a fixed period of time—usually one year.

F. **Deferred Credits Section**
Consists of that part of income that has not been earned by the balance sheet date.
Example: Deferred Rent Income.

G. **Fixed Liabilities Section**
Consists of those liabilities that will have to be paid after a period of time that is more than a year.
Example: Mortgage Payable; Bonds Payable.

H. **Net Worth Section**
Consists of Capital Accounts in the case of single proprietorship or partnerships or, in case of Corporations, of Capital Stock Accounts, Surplus, and divisions of Surplus.

Directions: The following listed accounts were taken from the balance sheets of the Middletown Corporation as of December 31, 2001. The sections used in setting up the balance sheet are lettered from A to H. Indicate by letters A to H in which section of the balance sheet each item appeared.

A. Current Asset Section
B. Fixed Asset Section
C. Deferred Charge Section
D. Intangible Assets Section
E. Current Liability Section
F. Deferred Credits Section
G. Fixed Liabilities Section
H. Net Worth Section

1. Accounts Receivable
2. Unissued Common Stock
3. Reserve for Federal Income Tax
4. Accrued Payables
5. Bonds Payable
6. Cash in Bank
7. Reserve for Depreciation
8. Reserve for Plant Extension
9. Insurance Unexpired
10. Common Stock Authorized
11. Prepaid Advertising
12. Dividends Payable
13. Interest Accrued on Notes Receivable
14. Interest Accrued on Bonds Payable
15. Machinery & Equipment
16. Reserve for Doubtful Accounts
17. Reserve for Real Estate Taxes
18. Sinking Fund Reserve
19. Surplus
20. Rent Collected in Advance
21. Treasury Stock
22. Notes Receivable Discounted
23. Goodwill
24. Accrued Commission Receivable
25. Discount on Bonds
26. Due from Officers and Employees
27. Bonus Payable
28. Trade Acceptance Payable
29. Mortgage Payable
30. Three-Year Notes Payable
31. Customers' Deposits—Due on Demand
32. Deposit on Royalties
33. Deficit
34. Donated Surplus
35. Reserve for Redemption of Preferred Stock
36. Reserves for Contingencies
37. Work in Process Inventory
38. Finished Goods Inventory
39. Office Supplies Inventory
40. Investment in Subsidiary

ANSWER KEY

1. A
2. H
3. E
4. E
5. G
6. A
7. B
8. H
9. C
10. H
11. C
12. E
13. A
14. E
15. B
16. A
17. E
18. H
19. H
20. F
21. H
22. A
23. D
24. A
25. C
26. A
27. E
28. E
29. G
30. G
31. E
32. C
33. H
34. H
35. H
36. H
37. A
38. A
39. C
40. B

ACCOUNTING PRACTICES

DIRECTIONS: For each of the following questions, select the choice that best answers the question or completes the statement.

1. A reserve for real estate taxes is a

(A) surplus reserve.
(B) current asset.
(C) fixed liability.
(D) current liability.
(E) valuation account.

2. A reserve for bad debts is a

(A) secret reserve.
(B) valuation account.
(C) surplus reserve.
(D) current asset.
(E) current liability.

3. If there is no agreement as to the method of sharing profits and losses, partners share them

(A) equally.
(B) in proportion to their original investment.
(C) in proportion to their present capital accounts.
(D) in proportion to the work done by the partners.
(E) in some other way.

4. The one of the following that is not a net worth item is

(A) capital stock.
(B) surplus.
(C) reserve for Federal Income Tax.
(D) sinking fund.
(E) reserve for pensions.

5. "Sold 10 shares of common stock for cash" involved

(A) debit to common stock authorized.
(B) credit to surplus.
(C) credit to capital stock authorized.
(D) credit to capital stock unissued.
(E) credit to cash.

6. The journal entry "Debit Accounts Receivable; Credit Notes Receivable" implies that

(A) we received a note from a customer.
(B) we gave a note to a creditor.
(C) we received payment of a note.
(D) our customer dishonored his note to us.
(E) we paid off one of our notes.

7. The journal entry "Debit Cash, Debit Capital Surplus; Credit Treasury Stock" implies that we

(A) purchased stock.
(B) sold treasury stock at par.
(C) sold treasury stock at more than par.
(D) sold treasury stock at less than par.
(E) received treasury stock as a gift.

8. The one of the following that is not a valuation account is

(A) reserve for bad debts.
(B) reserve for pensions.
(C) reserve for inventory shrinkage.
(D) reserve for depreciation.

9. The Proprietorship Equation is

(A) Liabilities = Net Worth – Assets.
(B) Net Worth = Assets + Liabilities.
(C) Assets – Net Worth = Liabilities.
(D) Assets + Liabilities = Net Worth.

10. The one of the following that is not an item of prime cost is

(A) direct labor.
(B) indirect labor.
(C) raw material purchases.
(D) raw material purchase returns and allowances.

11. When a partnership is incorporated, the correct accounting interpretation is that

(A) no change has occurred.
(B) the partnership continues but a corporation is formed.
(C) the partnership is dissolved.
(D) the partnership sells its assets and liabilities to the corporation.

12. An item that appears on both the balance sheet at Dec. 31, 2001, and the profit and loss statement for the year ending Dec. 31, 2001, is

(A) inventory Dec. 2001.
(B) inventory Jan. 1, 2001.
(C) sales.
(D) wages.
(E) deferred rent income.

13. The one of the following that is not a revenue expenditure is

    (A) cost of repairing factory equipment.
    (B) purchase of supplies used in constructing garages.
    (C) insurance for a year.
    (D) labor used in processing material.

14. That item which cannot be found from a profit and loss statement is

    (A) rate of stock turnover.
    (B) percentage of net profit to sales.
    (C) current ratio.
    (D) ratio of gross profit to net sales.
    (E) cost of goods sold.

15. When a trading account and a profit and loss account are used in closing the books, that item which is not closed to the trading account is

    (A) sales.
    (B) purchases.
    (C) freight and cartage.
    (D) freight and cartage out.
    (E) purchase returns and allowances.

16. An incorrect completion of the statement "The journal is essential to every system of accounts because" is it

    (A) helps to reduce errors.
    (B) provides a complete record of every transaction.
    (C) offers a summary of the transactions affecting any one account.
    (D) aids in locating errors.

17. The one of the following that does not require a journal entry is

    (A) recording sales.
    (B) bringing down a balance in the cash account.
    (C) closing entries.
    (D) recording purchase discounts.

18. On April 1, 2001, we accept at its present value a $500 note bearing interest at 10%. The note is for 90 days and is dated March 25, 2001. We discount it at 12%. Of the following statements, the *least* accurate is

    (A) the maturity date of the note is June 23, 2001.
    (B) total days to run are 83.
    (C) maturity value is $501.14.
    (D) discount is $14.

19. Drafts differ from notes in that a draft is

    (A) for a fixed sum.
    (B) an order to pay.
    (C) either on time or on sight.

20. The *least* accurate of the following statements is

    (A) time drafts are not recorded until accepted.
    (B) the drawer's contingent liability should be set up on the books when the time draft has been accepted and transferred to the payee.
    (C) discounted drafts are not recorded like discounted notes.
    (D) sight drafts are not recorded on the books until they are paid.

21. The one of the following that is not a case of voluntary dissolution of a partnership is

    (A) withdrawal of a partner.
    (B) sale of a partnership.
    (C) incorporation of a partnership.
    (D) death of a partner.
    (E) admission of a new partner.

22. When there is a difference between the debit and credit sides of a trial balance, a difference of .01 suggests a(n)

    (A) transposition of figures.
    (B) error in posting to the wrong side of an account.
    (C) error in shifting a decimal point.
    (D) error in addition or subtraction.

23. When there is a difference between the debit and credit sides of a trial balance, a difference of 9 or a multiple of 9 suggests a(n)

    (A) transposition of figures.
    (B) error in posting to the wrong side of an account.
    (C) error in shifting a decimal point.
    (D) error in addition or subtraction.

24. When there is a difference between the debit and credit sides of a trial balance, a difference divisible by 2 suggests a(n)

    (A) transposition of figures.
    (B) error in posting to the wrong side of an account.
    (C) error in shifting a decimal point.
    (D) error in addition or subtraction.

25. When there is a difference between the debit and credit sides of a trial balance, a difference divisible by 99 suggests a(n)

    (A) transposition of figures.
    (B) error in posting to the wrong side of an account.
    (C) error in shifting a decimal point.
    (D) error in addition or subtraction.

26. The essential feature of a single entry system is that it

(A) just records cash received.
(B) only records cash transaction (received and paid).
(C) records only the transactions that affect personal accounts.
(D) just records the operating accounts.

27. Current Assets plus Deferred Charges minus Current Liabilities is called

(A) working capital.
(B) current ratio.
(C) reserve strength.
(D) liquid strength.

28. A machine costing $2,187 is estimated to have a scrap value of $128 at the end of seven years. It is decided that a constant rate of depreciation on a diminishing value will be used. Rate is given by the formula:

$$R = 1 - N/(S/C)$$

where N is the number of years, S is the scrap value and C is the cost. The rate will then be

(A) 50%
(B) 40%
(C) 66.7%
(D) 33.3%

29. Debiting an asset instead of an expense

(A) decreases the net income.
(B) increases the net income and decreases the asset total.
(C) increases the net income and increases the liabilities.
(D) increases the net income and increases the assets.

30. A working sheet is used by accountants to

(A) give information to the management.
(B) eliminate the necessity of formal adjustments in the journal.
(C) eliminate closing entries in the journal.
(D) guide the accountant when he makes formal adjustments in the journal.

31. When a new partner is admitted and goodwill is to be set up, the following is involved

(A) a debit to the old partners.
(B) a credit to the old partners in proportion to their capital investments.
(C) a credit to the old partners in proportion to their profit and loss ratio.
(D) an equal credit to the old partners.
(E) none of the above.

32. When the sale of treasury stock brings less than the value at which it is carried on the books, the difference is a charge against

(A) treasury stock.
(B) capital surplus.
(C) capital stock.
(D) surplus.
(E) profit and loss.

33. An internal check is

(A) a check mark placed in the folio column of the ledger.
(B) a check from one depositor to another of the same bank.
(C) audit of the internal affairs of the firm.
(D) a system of routine supposed to guard against fraud and mistakes.

34. Undervaluation of assets results in

(A) goodwill.
(B) secret reserve.
(C) valuation reserve.
(D) deferred charge.

35. Failure to adjust for depreciation results in

(A) overstatement of liabilities.
(B) understatement of net worth.
(C) overstatement of assets.
(D) overstatement of current assets.

36. Failure to set up a deferred charge for prepaid insurance does not

(A) decrease assets.
(B) decrease net worth.
(C) increase current assets.
(D) understate total expense.

37. A trial balance before closing proves that

(A) no errors of accounting principle have been made.
(B) all transactions have been recorded.
(C) all adjustments have been made.
(D) the debits and credits entered in the ledger are equal.

38. Adjusting entries are those entries used to adjust

(A) mistakes.
(B) income and expense accounts before the books are closed.
(C) differences between the firm and its customers.

39. Purchases on account are usually entered in

(A) the journal and posted to the cash book.
(B) the general journal and posted to the ledger.

(C) a purchase book and posted to the customer's ledger.
(D) a purchase book and posted to the creditor's ledger.

40. An imprest cash fund is the same as

(A) petty cash fund.
(B) a fund that has been attached by the sheriff.
(C) a fund that has been reserved for a certain purpose.
(D) a fund in a closed bank.

41. The book value of a share of stock is found by

(A) dividing the total of assets by the number of shares outstanding.
(B) dividing the difference between current assets and current liabilities by the number of shares outstanding.
(C) dividing the net worth by the number of shares outstanding.
(D) none of the above.

42. A corporation has outstanding 100 shares 6% preferred, participating stock (par value $100 per share) and 100 shares common. A dividend of $1,000 is declared. Each share of preferred received

(A) $6
(B) $7
(C) $8
(D) $9.20

43. Goodwill should

(A) never be shown on the Balance Sheet.
(B) should be shown on the Balance Sheet as a footnote.
(C) only appear in the Profit and Loss statement.
(D) appear on the Balance Sheet at a valuation of $1.
(E) be shown at cost if paid for.

44. The decreasing value of an asset such as coal, land, timber, and mineral deposits, is known as

(A) depreciation.
(B) obsolescence.
(C) depletion.
(D) waste.

45. Goods out on consignment are shown on the Balance Sheet as part of

(A) accounts receivable.
(B) notes receivable.
(C) inventory.
(D) deferred income.

46. The item not leading to a secret reserve is

(A) charging off excessive depreciation.
(B) inflating inventory valuation.
(C) charging plant additions to expense accounts.
(D) writing off intangible assets that were paid for in cash.

47. The one of the following that should not be used as a charge to Land Account is

(A) assessment to cover street improvements adjacent to land.
(B) taxes on the land.
(C) assessment for sewer construction.

48. When buildings have been erected on leased premises, it is

(A) necessary to write off the entire value of the buildings during the term of the lease.
(B) not necessary to use any but the normal method of depreciation.
(C) necessary to use the reducing balance method.

49. Proved earning power in excess over normal interest returns on an investment is called

(A) goodwill.
(B) capital surplus.
(C) earned surplus.
(D) intrinsic value.

50. A suspense account is a(n)

(A) deferred charge.
(B) deferred credit to income.
(C) item whose true nature is apt to be determined.
(D) expense account.

51. Merchandise inventory would most ordinarily be valued at

(A) sales price.
(B) market price.
(C) cost price.
(D) the lower of cost or market price.

52. Depreciation is most apt to be caused by

(A) increased cost of replacement.
(B) wear and tear in usage.
(C) carelessness.
(D) income tax regulations.

53. The failure to make an adjustment at the end of any given period for interest received in advance

(A) overstates current assets.
(B) understates income.
(C) overstates income.
(D) understates assets.

54. In bookkeeping practice, debiting is

    (A) subtracting.
    (B) adding.
    (C) posting on the left side.
    (D) incurring an expense.

55. The individual creditor's accounts in the creditor's ledger receive their debit postings mainly from the

    (A) voucher register.
    (B) sales book.
    (C) purchase book.
    (D) check register.

56. Title to the assets of a corporation is most generally held by the

    (A) corporation as a legal entity.
    (B) board of directors.
    (C) stockholders.
    (D) president of the corporation.

57. Reserve for depreciation is best considered a(n)

    (A) expense account.
    (B) asset valuation account.
    (C) liability.
    (D) surplus reserve.

58. Appreciation should not be recognized, principally because it

    (A) is unrealized profit.
    (B) would tend to lend to unwise dividend action.
    (C) is illegal.
    (D) must receive stockholders' approval.

59. The reserve for retirement of bonds is best considered as a

    (A) valuation reserve.
    (B) liability.
    (C) contingent reserve.
    (D) true surplus reserve.

60. A Trading Account is best considered as one which

    (A) records the transactions in stocks and bonds.
    (B) records the transactions involved in a trade-in of used fixtures.
    (C) is used for closing entries.
    (D) is used to segregate the main items of gross profit.

61. The principal reason for valuing inventory at any time at cost or market value, whichever is lower, is because it

    (A) is so required by most banks.
    (B) gives a higher figure for profit.
    (C) gives a lower figure for profit.
    (D) is theoretically the most accurate.

62. In charging an account, it would be best to

    (A) debit it.
    (B) carry down its balance.
    (C) post it.
    (D) add it.

63. The best of the following reasons for keeping a perpetual inventory is to

    (A) maintain a merchandise control.
    (B) facilitate monthly closings of books.
    (C) prevent embezzlement of funds.
    (D) avoid the expense of an annual physical inventory.

64. Notes receivable discounted would best be shown in the Balance Sheet

    (A) as a liability.
    (B) in a footnote.
    (C) as a subtraction from a liability.
    (D) as a subtraction from an asset.

65. The cost of goods sold should most properly be equal to

    (A) purchase plus inventory at the end less inventory at the beginning.
    (B) inventory at the beginning plus purchases less inventory at the end.
    (C) inventory at the beginning less purchases plus inventory at the end.
    (D) purchases plus inventory at the beginning and the end.

66. It is advantageous to sell goods on account chiefly because it

    (A) permits the charging of higher prices.
    (B) increases sales.
    (C) improves credit.
    (D) eases accounting records.

67. Current ratio means most nearly the

    (A) ratio of total sales to purchase.
    (B) ratio of total current assets to total current liabilities.
    (C) excess of current assets over fixed assets.
    (D) ratio of cash and accounts receivable to current liabilities.

68. The reserve for Federal Taxes should be considered

    (A) current liability.
    (B) valuation reserve.
    (C) true surplus reserve.
    (D) contingent reserve.

69. A sinking fund would most appropriately be considered a(n)

    (A) asset.
    (B) valuation against an asset.
    (C) valuation against a liability.
    (D) contingent liability.

70. A company accepting a time draft would most ordinarily

    (A) debit cash.
    (B) debit notes payable.
    (C) credit accounts payable.
    (D) credit notes payable.

71. When securities are received as collateral,

    (A) accounts receivable should be credited.
    (B) accounts payable should be credited.
    (C) a memorandum entry should be made.
    (D) investments should be debited.

72. Merchandise turnover means most nearly

    (A) sales over cost of goods sold.
    (B) cost of goods sold over current inventory.
    (C) net purchases divided by average inventory.
    (D) average inventory over cost of goods sold.

73. The reserve for bad debts would most ordinarily be shown in the balance sheet as a

    (A) deferred charge.
    (B) deduction from accounts receivable.
    (C) contingent liability.
    (D) net worth valuation.

74. A financial statement would most closely be associated with a

    (A) report on a company's credit position.
    (B) balance sheet.
    (C) profit and loss statement.
    (D) cash receipts and disbursements statement.

75. A purchase discount would most generally be considered as

    (A) granted for large purchases.
    (B) a reduction for prompt payment.
    (C) a deduction from the list price in arriving at the true purchase price.
    (D) the difference between the wholesale and retail prices.

76. Bonds payable upon maturity would most probably be paid out of

    (A) the surplus account.
    (B) the sinking fund.
    (C) cash derived from the sinking fund.
    (D) the sinking fund reserve.

77. Bankruptcy is most closely associated with

    (A) a state of dissolution.
    (B) insolvency.
    (C) failure to meet a note on due date.
    (D) suffering of deficits in operation.

78. As a bookkeeping operation, an intangible asset is best characterized as

    (A) difficult to value.
    (B) hard to convert into cash.
    (C) of insignificant value.
    (D) nonphysical asset.

79. The one of the following items with which an imprest cash fund is most closely associated is a

    (A) savings account.
    (B) petty cash fund.
    (C) checking account.
    (D) sinking fund.

80. Goodwill should most properly

    (A) be shown at only $1, if carried on the books.
    (B) never be shown.
    (C) be shown at cost.
    (D) be indicated in a footnote to the balance sheet.

81. Investments in stocks would most properly be valued at

    (A) cost.
    (B) market value.
    (C) last book closing date value.
    (D) none of the foregoing.

82. The item that should not be included in the net worth section of a balance sheet is

    (A) surplus.
    (B) bonds payable.
    (C) capital.
    (D) donated surplus.

83. A real account is best considered as

    (A) any fixed asset or liability.
    (B) any balance sheet account.
    (C) real estate or buildings.
    (D) any expense account.

84. A purchase book is one that performs the same functions as a(n)

(A) purchase ledger.
(B) requisition register.
(C) voucher register.
(D) inventory system.

85. The list price should best be considered as

(A) the advertised or catalog price.
(B) a special price.
(C) the total price of a list of items.
(D) the net price after discounts are deducted.

86. An invoice would best be considered as a

(A) bill of exchange.
(B) monthly statement of unpaid balances.
(C) bill.
(D) receipt.

87. The total of cash indicated in a balance sheet should not include

(A) postal money orders.
(B) express money orders.
(C) certified checks.
(D) postage stamps.

88. The one of the following items that should be credited if appreciation is to be set up on the books is

(A) stock dividends.
(B) realized depreciation.
(C) surplus from appreciation.
(D) reserve for depreciation.

89. The one of the following phrases that best defines a bank draft is a(n)

(A) check drawn by a depositor upon a bank.
(B) draft drawn by one bank on another bank.
(C) draft drawn by a commercial firm on a bank.
(D) overdraft.

90. When a current liability is paid,

(A) working capital is increased.
(B) working capital is decreased.
(C) working capital is not affected.
(D) it increases asset and liability ratio.

91. Unissued capital stock would best be carried on the books as a(n)

(A) current asset.
(B) contingent asset.
(C) valuation account against capital stock authorized.
(D) investment.

92. A suspense account should best be regarded as a(n)

(A) item whose true nature is not yet determined.
(B) contingent liability.
(C) expense or income.
(D) valuation account.

93. A sales discount should best be considered as a(n)

(A) reduction allowed for prompt settlement of a bill.
(B) inducement offered for a large order.
(C) reduction offered during a sales campaign.
(D) allowance granted for damaged goods.

94. When used, the expense control account would most properly be found in the

(A) expense ledger.
(B) debtor's ledger.
(C) creditor's ledger.
(D) general ledger.

95. Treasury stock would most properly be carried on the books as a(n)

(A) valuation against capital stock.
(B) current asset.
(C) investment.
(D) fixed asset.

96. At the end of a specified period when a balance sheet is being prepared, rent accrued would most properly be shown as a

(A) current asset.
(B) current liability.
(C) deferred charge.
(D) deferred income.

97. Corporations are most generally chartered under

(A) city ordinances.
(B) federal statute.
(C) state statute.
(D) county statute.

98. The phrase that is not characteristic of a partnership is

(A) limited duration.
(B) formed by either oral or written agreement.
(C) limited liability of each partner for the firm debts.
(D) mutual agency.

99. Accounts on which several unsuccessful attempts to collect their balance have failed are most appropriately characterized by the term

(A) poor.
(B) doubtful.
(C) insolvent.
(D) bad.

100. The act of transferring to the ledger the entries of debit and credit indicated in the journal is known as

(A) transferral.
(B) deferring.
(C) posting.
(D) folioing.

ANSWER KEY

1. D	21. D	41. C	61. D	81. A
2. B	22. D	42. C	62. A	82. B
3. A	23. A	43. E	63. A	83. B
4. C	24. B	44. C	64. D	84. C
5. D	25. C	45. C	65. B	85. A
6. D	26. D	46. B	66. B	86. C
7. D	27. A	47. B	67. B	87. D
8. B	28. D	48. A	68. A	88. C
9. C	29. D	49. A	69. A	89. B
10. B	30. D	50. C	70. C	90. C
11. D	31. C	51. D	71. C	91. C
12. A	32. B	52. B	72. C	92. A
13. B	33. D	53. C	73. B	93. A
14. C	34. B	54. C	74. B	94. D
15. D	35. C	55. D	75. B	95. A
16. C	36. C	56. A	76. C	96. B
17. B	37. D	57. B	77. B	97. C
18. C	38. B	58. A	78. D	98. C
19. B	39. D	59. D	79. B	99. D
20. C	40. A	60. D	80. C	100. C

ACCOUNTING PRACTICE QUIZZER

The following carefully selected, actual, previous examination questions cover key points of a topic likely to be brought up on your examination. They have appeared before. Therefore, we're certain that you'll benefit from the concise summary provided by this quizzer. Write your own answers and then check with the correct answers that appear after the last question in this series.

TRUE /FALSE QUESTIONS

DIRECTIONS: Each of the following statements is either True or False. Mark the corresponding number on your answer sheet T if the statement is True, and F if the statement is False.

1. Capital is increased by income.
2. Current ratio is the ratio of total current assets to total current liabilities.
3. Cumulative preferred dividends in arrears should be shown as a liability in a balance sheet.
4. Operating profits should be credited to retained earnings.
5. Loss and expense are synonymous.
6. Merchandise inventory should be valued at market price.
7. Discount in stock should be written off over the life of the stock.
8. Unrealized profits, which result from mere book entries writing up assets, should most properly be credited to capital surplus.
9. Inventory is considered a current asset.
10. Accumulated depreciation is a liability.
11. Preferred stock is usually nonparticipating.
12. A corporation does not have the right under the law to declare a dividend unless it has sufficient cash with which to pay it.
13. Bonds payable is considered a current liability.
14. Notes received discounted should be shown in the balance sheet as a subtraction from an asset.
15. Preferred stock cannot be issued in no-par form.
16. The balance sheet should most properly include among the liabilities all declared dividends, payable in cash, provided that notice of the declaration has been made to the stockholders.
17. Bonds payable is not treated as a fixed asset.
18. The excess received on a sale of a bond over its par value is known as premium on bonds.
19. Treasury stock should be shown in the balance sheet as a deduction from capital stock outstanding.
20. Extraneous profits should be credited to retained earnings.
21. Reserve for income taxes is a current liability.
22. Voting power is never granted to preferred stock.
23. In the event that a partnership is incorporated, the assets should be taken over by the corporation at the same values at which they have been carried on the partnership books.
24. It is best to show in a footnote on the balance sheet the amount of dividends in arrears on all classes of preferred stock.

25. Treasury stock is stock that has not been subscribed for.

26. The allowance for doubtful accounts should be set up by a study of past experience.

27. In such case where the asset values of a corporation are to be adjusted, the adjusting entries should be made on the books of the corporation.

28. Bond discount should be amortized over the life of the bonds.

29. Usury is any interest rate over 6%.

30. The resulting increase or decrease in net worth, which is realized when asset values are adjusted on partnership books, should be divided among the partners in the profit and loss ratio.

31. Depreciation is caused by income tax regulations.

32. Interest accrued on bonds owned should be shown as a current asset.

33. An entirely new set of books should be opened by a partnership business at the time of its incorporation.

34. A perpetual inventory is maintained to avoid the expense of an annual physical inventory.

35. A time draft is a loan that may be called at any time.

36. Stock that has not been issued may be sold at a discount without the imposition of any discount liability on the purchaser.

37. Prepaid expenses are always assets.

38. Excess provision for depreciation results in an understatement of net income.

39. No discount liability need be imposed on the purchaser when treasury stock is sold to him at a discount.

40. Prepaid insurance, prepaid rent, and prepaid taxes were once considered "deferred charges."

41. The valuation accounts at the end of a period should be closed against the accounts against which they are valued.

42. All the stock that is owned by a corporation may be shown in its balance sheet as treasury stock.

43. Land is an intangible asset.

44. The increase in value of fixed assets due to unpredictable events, such as shortage caused by economic conditions, is known as appreciation.

45. There is not a necessary relation between the par value and the real value of a stock share.

46. A patent is an intangible asset.

47. Obsolescence is the loss in value of fixed assets due to the invention of more modern devices.

48. An individual purchasing no-par value stock cannot be held liable for discount on stock.

49. A post-closing trial balance proves that the closing entries have been correctly made.

50. During construction, interest paid on money borrowed may be capitalized.

51. When no-par stock is recorded, no journal entry can be made to record the authorized issue.

52. Interest prepaid on notes payable is an accrued expense.

53. Special columns are often put into the books of original entry in order to save time in journalizing.

54. When no-par stock is issued, it may be recorded by crediting the capital stock account with the entire proceeds.

55. Merchandise turnover is the ratio of cost of goods sold to average inventory.

56. Accumulated depreciation is a valuation account.

57. Dividends should be paid only out of earnings.

58. The pledging of an asset as security for a loan should be indicated in the balance sheet by a footnote.

59. Interest prepaid on notes receivable is deferred income.

ANSWER KEY

1. T	13. F	25. F	37. T	49. F
2. T	14. T	26. T	38. T	50. T
3. F	15. F	27. F	39. T	51. T
4. T	16. T	28. T	40. T	52. F
5. F	17. T	29. F	41. F	53. F
6. F	18. T	30. T	42. F	54. T
7. F	19. T	31. F	43. F	55. T
8. F	20. F	32. T	44. T	56. T
9. T	21. T	33. F	45. T	57. T
10. F	22. F	34. F	46. T	58. T
11. F	23. F	35. F	47. T	59. T
12. F	24. F	36. F	48. T	

MULTIPLE-CHOICE QUIZ—ACCOUNTING PRACTICE

DIRECTIONS: For each of the following questions, select the choice that best answers the question or completes the statement.

1. Of the following taxes, the one that is levied most nearly according to ability to pay is a(n)

(A) excise tax.
(B) income tax.
(C) general property tax.
(D) sales tax.

2. When a check has been lost, the bank on which it is drawn should be notified and instructed to

(A) stop payment on the check.
(B) issue a duplicate of the check.
(C) charge the account of the drawer for the amount of the check.
(D) certify the check.

3. The amounts of transactions recorded in a journal are transferred to general ledger accounts by a process known as

(A) auditing.
(B) balancing.
(C) posting.
(D) verifying.

4. Sales minus cost of goods sold equals

(A) net profit.
(B) gross sales.
(C) gross profit.
(D) net sales.

5. The chief disadvantage of single-entry bookkeeping is that it

(A) is too difficult to operate.
(B) is illegal for income tax purposes.
(C) provides no possibility of determining net profits.
(D) furnishes an incomplete picture of the business.

6. The phrase "3%—10 days" on an invoice usually means that

(A) 3% of the amount must be paid each 10 days.
(B) the purchaser is entitled to only ten days credit.
(C) a discount of 3% will be allowed for payment in 10 days.
(D) the entire amount must be paid in 10 days or a penalty of 3% of the amount due will be added.

7. A firm that voluntarily terminates business by selling its assets and paying its liabilities is said to be in
   (A) receivership.
   (B) liquidation.
   (C) depletion.
   (D) amortization.

8. Many business firms provide a petty cash fund from which to pay for small items in order to avoid issuing many small checks. If this fund is replenished periodically to restore it to its original amount, the fund is called a(n)
   (A) imprest fund.
   (B) debenture fund.
   (C) adjustment fund.
   (D) expense reserve fund.

9. Many business firms maintain a book of original entry in which all bills to be paid is recorded. This book is known as a
   (A) purchase returns journal.
   (B) subsidiary ledger.
   (C) voucher register.
   (D) notes payable register.

10. A trial balance will *not* indicate that an error has been made in
    (A) computing the balance of an account.
    (B) entering an amount in the wrong account.
    (C) carrying forward the balance of an account.
    (D) entering an amount on the wrong side of an account.

11. When an asset is depreciated on the straight-line basis, the amount charged off for depreciation
    (A) is greater in the earlier years of the asset's life.
    (B) is greater in the later years of the asset's life.
    (C) varies each year according to the extent to which the asset is used during the year.
    (D) is equal each full year of the asset's life.

12. The essential nature of an asset is that
    (A) it must be tangible.
    (B) it must be easily converted into cash.
    (C) it must have value.
    (D) its cost must be included in the profit and loss statement.

13. A controlling account contains the totals of
    (A) the accounts used in preparing the balance sheet at the end of the fiscal period.
    (B) the individual amounts entered in the accounts of a subsidiary ledger during the fiscal period.
    (C) all entries in the general journal during the fiscal period.
    (D) the accounts used in preparing the profit and loss statement for the fiscal period.

14. A trial balance is a list of
    (A) the credit balances in all accounts in a general ledger.
    (B) all general ledger accounts and their balances.
    (C) the asset accounts in a general ledger and their balances.
    (D) the liability accounts in a general ledger and their balances.

15. An accounting system that records revenues as soon as they are earned and records liabilities as soon as they are incurred, regardless of the date of payment, is said to operate on a(n)
    (A) accrual basis.
    (B) budgetary basis.
    (C) encumbrance basis.
    (D) cash basis.

16. The term "current assets" usually includes such things as
    (A) notes payable.
    (B) machinery and equipment.
    (C) furniture and fixtures.
    (D) accounts receivable.

17. An item that is never properly considered a negotiable instrument is a(n)
    (A) invoice.
    (B) bond.
    (C) promissory note.
    (D) endorsed check.

18. A statement of the assets, liabilities, and net worth of a business is called a
    (A) trial balance.
    (B) budget.
    (C) profit and loss statement.
    (D) balance sheet.

19. A subsidiary ledger contains accounts that show
    (A) details of contingent liabilities of undetermined amount.
    (B) totals of all asset accounts in the general ledger.
    (C) totals of all liability accounts in the general ledger.
    (D) details of an account in the general ledger.

ANSWER KEY

1. B	5. D	9. C	13. B	17. A
2. A	6. C	10. B	14. B	18. D
3. C	7. B	11. D	15. A	19. D
4. C	8. A	12. C	16. D	

ACCOUNTING TERMS AND PRACTICES

The following are representative examination-type questions. They should be carefully studied and completely understood. The actual test questions will probably not be as difficult as these.

DIRECTIONS: Each of the completion questions in this series consists of an incomplete sentence or idea. Use the appropriate space to write in the correct missing word or words.

1. Everything a business owns is called ________.
2. Everything a business owes is called ________.
3. The Proprietorship Equation is ________.
4. The statement that shows the state of a business at a certain date is called a ________.
5. The statement that shows the result of the operations over a certain period is called a ________.
6. The principal book of records in which a summary of the accounts is found is called the ________.
7. A book in which daily entries are recorded is called ________.
8. The book in which cash received is recorded is called the ________ book.
9. The book in which cash paid is recorded is called the ________ book.
10. What kind of purchases are entered in the purchase book? ________
11. What kind of sales are entered in the sales book? ________
12. Where are closing entries first recorded? ________.
13. Gross Sales minus Sales Returns and Allowances equals ________.
14. Net Sales minus cost of goods sold equals ________.
15. Gross Profit minus Operating Expenses equals ________.
16. The list of account balances taken from the General Ledger is called a ________.
17. Which asset item on the Balance Sheet at Dec. 31, 2001, is also found in the Profit and Loss Statement for year ended Dec. 31, 2001? ________.
18. Dividends Account is closed to ________.
19. Office Salaries account is closed to ________.

20. The entering of the debit and credit for each transaction in the journal is called ________.

21. The transferring of the debits and credits from the journal to ledger accounts is called ________.

22. "An unconditional promise in writing made by one person to another, signed by the maker, engaging to pay, on demand or at a fixed or determinable future time, a certain sum in money to order or to bearer" is called a ________.

23. The party signing a note is called the ________.

24. The party to whom the note is made payable is called the ________.

25. "Pay to the order of 'A' Company, without recourse" is called a ________ endorsement.

26. A written order by one person to another person that requires him to pay a certain sum of money to a third party is called a ________.

27. A written acknowledgment of a debt by a buyer in favor of the seller for merchandise that the seller had placed in the hands of the buyer is called a ________.

28. When a check bears on its back the words "Accepted X Bank; John Jones, Cashier," it is called a ________.

29. A draft drawn by one bank on another bank in transferring money to parties in another city is called a ________.

30. A temporary partnership for the purpose of carrying out some specific project of a trading nature is known as a ________.

31. The face or nominal value placed on a share of stock, when the value is the same for all shares of a like class, is called the ________.

32. The corporation's net worth divided by the number of shares of outstanding common stock (if the only stock is common stock) is called the ________ of a share.

33. Stock that has once been issued by a corporation and later reacquired by purchase or gift is called ________.

34. Common stock issued as a bonus to investors who purchase preferred stock is called ________.

35. What is the accountant's view of the incorporation of a partnership? ________

36. In mergers, two conditions that may exist are ________ and ________.

37. Purchase Price of a business less Net Worth of the business is called ________.

38. A statement that certifies or verifies the correctness of a transaction is called a ________.

39. The book of original entry in which vouchers and their distribution are recorded is called a ________.

40. Anything that undergoes some process in the factory before becoming a part of the product is called ________.

41. Such items as buttons and thread in a clothing factory that are essential materials in manufacturing fall under the general classification of ________.

42. That labor that is employed directly in processing the raw materials or in assembling the parts into the finished product is called ________.

43. Labor, such as janitor's duties to keep the factory clean, is called ________.

44. That element of cost of production, which includes all expenses arising from the operation of the factory, that cannot, like material and direct labor, be definitely traced to the product is termed ________.

45. Direct material plus Direct labor equals ________.

46. Cost of production equals ________ plus ________.

47. A continuous record of all materials and supplies as they are received in the storeroom, of all materials and supplies as they are taken out of the storeroom and put into process, and of all manufactured goods taken out of the factory and put in the finishing-stock room is called a ________.

48. The three inventory items in a manufacturing plant are ________, ________, and ________.

49. The stores ledger is controlled by the ________ Account.

50. The cost ledger is controlled by the ________ Account.

51. The system of bookkeeping concerning itself with recording transactions affecting only personal accounts is called ________.

52. Those expenditures that affect the real or capital accounts, and thus increase the net amount of capital invested in the business, are called ____________ expenditures.

53. Those expenditures that affect the operating or revenue accounts, and are thus a charge against profits for the period instead of an investment of capital, are called ________ expenditures.

54. Renewals differ from Repairs in that the former ________.

55. Repairs should be charged to what account? ________

56. Renewals should be charged to ________.

57. The two general methods of inventory valuation are ________ and ________.

58. Suburban land bought by a real estate company for the purpose of subdivision falls under ________ assets.

59. Ordinarily, land (increases, decreases) in value. ________

60. As a general principle, buildings should be shown at (cost price, selling price). ________

61. In general, patents should be amortized over a period of ________ years.

62. In general, copyrights should be amortized over a period of ________ years.

63. Five causes of depreciation are ________, ________, ________, ________, and ________.

64. If the current assets are $40,000 and the current liabilities are $20,000, the current ratio is ________.

65. Bonds that have been repurchased by a corporation, but not cancelled, are known as ________.

66. An endorsement that represents the acceptance of a note or a bill by one party who receives no value therefor, for the use or benefit of some other party is called an ________.

67. The mortgage on property, which designates the trustee who represents the bondholders and states all the terms and conditions of the issue and the security for the bonds, is called the ________.

68. An amount accumulated through periodical installments and invested in interest bearing securities, which together with the interest earned will provide a fund sufficient to liquidate a debt at maturity, is called a ________.

69. When the capital of a going concern is increased simply by inflating the assets, without the justification of earning power, the term applied to the stock of the concern is ________.

70. ________ stock represents the right to issue stock when the full amount authorized has not been issued.

71. The number of times the average amount of stock is sold during the fiscal period is best referred to as ________.

ANSWER KEY

1. Assets
2. Liabilities
3. Assets – Liabilities = Net Worth
4. Balance Sheet
5. Income Statement
6. General Ledger
7. Journal
8. Cash receipts
9. Cash Disbursements
10. Purchases on Account
11. Sales on Account
12. General Journal
13. Net Sales
14. Gross Profit
15. Net Operating Profit
16. Trial Balance
17. Merchandise Inventory Dec. 31, 2001
18. Surplus
19. Profit and Loss
20. Journalizing
21. Posting
22. Negotiable Promissory Note
23. Maker
24. Payee
25. Qualified
26. Draft
27. Trade Acceptance
28. Certified Check
29. Bank Draft
30. Joint Venture
31. Par Value
32. Book Value
33. Treasury Stock
34. Bonus Stock
35. That the partnership sells its assets and liabilities to the newly formed corporation.
36. Merger by consolidation; merger by absorption
37. Goodwill
38. Voucher
39. Voucher register
40. Raw material
41. Manufacturing Supplies
42. Direct Labor
43. Indirect Labor
44. Factory Overhead
45. Prime Cost
46. Prime Cost; factory expense
47. Perpetual inventory
48. Raw Materials; Work-in-Process; Finished Goods
49. Raw materials
50. Work-in-Process
51. Single-Entry
52. Capital
53. Revenue
54. Tend to extend the serviceable life of the property.
55. To some expense account
56. Accumulated Depreciation
57. At cost; cost or market, whichever is lower
58. Current
59. Increases
60. Cost price
61. Seventeen
62. Twenty-eight
63. Expiration of time; deterioration from exposure to the elements; wear and tear due to use; inadequacy; obsolescence
64. 2 to 1
65. Treasury Bonds
66. Accommodation endorsement
67. Deed of trust
68. Sinking Fund
69. Watered Stock
70. Unissued
71. Turnover

FIRE LOSS

Our analysis of previous examinations indicates that you should possess a fairly good knowledge of this subject. Here are the key points . . . the information on which you are likely to be quizzed. Following the text, you'll find a quiz composed of actual previous test questions. The text should help you score high on the quiz. And our answers, which follow the quiz, should clear up any remaining doubts.

1. The X Company had a fire on June 17, and the sales records were completely destroyed. From other sources you ascertain the following facts:

Inventory Jan. 1st	$19,500
Purchases to June 17th	$48,000

The X Company received a check of $15,000 from the Insurance Company; $3,000 for the furniture and fixtures, and $12,000 that represented the full value of the merchandise destroyed by fire. The average gross profit on sales in this business is 40%. Determine the sales from January 1st to June 17th.

2. The A Company owns a building valued at $20,000. It is insured under the 80% coinsurance clause and carries insurance on the building for $14,500. Fire breaks out, causing a damage to the building estimated at $10,000. What is the amount recoverable from the insurance company?

3. The X Company had a fire on Dec. 31, 2000, that destroyed the merchandise. The average gross profits for the past four years have been 40% of sales. During 2000 the sales were $90,000. Purchases during the period were $70,000. Returned purchases amounted to $4,000. On January 1, 2001, the inventory was $30,000. Determine the value of the merchandise destroyed.

4. Find the cash balance from the following data:

Sales for 2000	$45,000
Accounts receivable	$13,000
Mdse. inventory Dec. 31, 2000	$15,600
Capital stock issued at par for cash	$40,000
Accounts payable	$12,300
Expenses paid in cash	$27,000

Cost of goods sold is 70% of the selling price.

Business was started Jan. 1, 2001

ANSWERS AND EXPLANATIONS

1.

Inventory January 1st	$19,500
Purchases to June 17th	+48,000
	$67,500
Inventory June 17th	– 12,000
Cost of sales	$55,500

Since gross profit is 40% of sales, cost of sales is 60% of sales. Thus:

$$60\% \text{ of sales} = \$55,500$$

Total Sales = $55,000 / 60% = $92,500

2. $$\text{Amount receivable} = \frac{\text{face of policy}}{80\% \text{ of property}} \times \text{loss}$$

$$= \frac{\$14,500}{\$16,00} \times \$10,000$$

$$= \$9,062.50$$

3. Gross profit is 40% of sales.

   Therefore cost of sales is 60% of sales, or 60% × $90,000 = $54,000.

   Cost of sales is determined thus:

Inventory Jan. 1, 2001	$30,000
Purchases	$70,000
Returned purchases	– $4,000
Inventory Dec. 31, 2001	$96,000
Cost of sales	$54,000
Value of Merchandise Destroyed	$42,000

   It is therefore obvious that inventory on Dec. 31, 2000, is equal to $96,000 minus cost of sales, $54,000, which equals $42,000.

4. Calculation of purchases:

   Cost of goods sold is 70% of $45,000 = $31,500

   Cost of goods sold is determined thus:

Inventory Jan. 1st	$0
Purchases	?
Inventory Dec. 31st	$15,600
Cost of sales	$31,500

   It is therefore obvious that purchases are equal to $31,500 + $15,600 = $47,100.

4. TRIAL BALANCE

	Dr.	Cr.
Sales		$45,000
Accounts receivable	$13,000	
Capital stock		40,000
Accounts payable		12,300
Expenses	27,000	
Purchases (calculated)	47,100	
Totals	$87,100	$97,300

Therefore the cash balance must be $97,300 minus $87,100, which equals $10,200.

ADJUSTMENTS

Directions: In closing a set of books, a bookkeeper omitted or disregarded the following facts. As a result he showed a net profit of $5,000. If he had made the proper adjustments, would this profit have been increased, decreased, or would it have been unaffected? If profit would have increased, write I in the space next to each question. If it would have decreased, write D. If it would have been unaffected, write N. *Note:* No perpetual inventory was kept.

1. Rent paid on December 25, by subtenant for January 2001 was closed to income.

2. No record was made of orders received from customers on December 31, 2000. These were filed since goods could not be shipped until January 5, 2001.

3. Salaries of purchasing department were added to purchases.

4. Delivery expense was added to purchases.

5. The merchandise inventory on December 31, 2000, was overstated $5,000.

6. No adjustment was made for prepaid advertising on December 31, 2000.

7. Merchandise received on December 30, 2000, was included in the inventory, although no bill had been received or entered.

8. Discount on purchases in July was erroneously posted to the Returned Purchases Account.

9. Cash received in payment of a note was credited to the customer's account.

10. No record was made for interest accrued on Bonds Payable. Payment is not due until January 7, 2001.

11. Salesmen's commissions for the month of August were charged to Office Salaries account.

12. No adjustment was made for $47 interest accrued on notes from customers.

13. Unexpired insurance of $200 was entered on the books as $300.

14. An unpaid rent bill for December 2000 of $500 was not yet entered.

15. During the year, uninsured merchandise worth $500 was stolen and no record made.

16. Cash received from customer A was erroneously credited to customer B.

17. Old Age Benefit deductions were closed to Income.

18. Interest paid on Notes Payable was charged to Accounts Payable.

19. Accumulated Depreciation of Furniture and Fixtures was credited to the Furniture and Fixtures Account.

20. The cost of overhauling a machine was charged to General Expense.

21. The cost of repairing factory equipment was charged to Machinery and Equipment Account.

22. A purchase discount taken on an expenditure for a machine was credited to Purchase Discounts Account.

23. The cost of materials used in constructing a factory was charged to the Supplies Account.

24. A special assessment for street paving was charged to the Taxes Account.

25. Indirect Labor was charged with labor used in constructing factory.

26. Factory overhead was charged with cost of labor used in installing new machinery.

27. Discount on Purchases in November was credited to Discount on Sales Account.

28. The cost of a new lathe was charged to Accumulated Depreciation of Machinery Account.

29. A dividend that was declared December 28, payable January 3, 2001, was closed to Income Summary.

30. Furniture that had originally cost $200, on which the accrued depreciation was $100, was sold for $50. The only entry made was a credit to miscellaneous income of $50.

ANSWER KEY

1. D	7. D	13. D	19. N	25. I
2. N	8. N	14. D	20. I	26. I
3. N	9. N	15. N	21. D	27. N
4. N	10. D	16. N	22. D	28. N
5. D	11. N	17. D	23. I	29. I
6. I	12. I	18. D	24. D	30. D

MUNICIPAL ACCOUNTING

Question I.

TRIAL BALANCE–CITY OF X

June 30, 2000

	DEBITS	*CREDITS*
Cash – Current Fund	$ 20,000	
Cash – Sinking Fund	20,000	
Cash – Capital Fund	1,000,000	
Cash – Library Endowment Fund	500	
Cash – Firemen's Pension Fund	400	
Accounts Receivable	5,000	
Taxes Receivable	100,000	
Delinquent Taxes	2,000	
Materials and Supplies Inventory	30,000	
Accrued Water Charges	40,000	
Assessments Receivable	500,000	
Construction in Progress	400,000	
Lands	2,000,000	
Buildings	1,500,000	
Equipment	1,000,000	
Streets, Sewers, and Bridges	5,000,000	
Securities – Library Endowment Fund	100,000	
Securities – Firemen's Pension Fund	160,000	
Securities – Sinking Fund	1,500,000	
Securities –Teachers' Benefit Fund	15,000	
Reserve for Abatement of Taxes		$ 10,000
Revenue Bonds Payable		80,000
Vouchers Payable (Current Fund)		8,000
Vouchers Payable (Capital Fund)		10,000
Current Fund Surplus		99,000
Capital Fund Surplus		5,590,000
Construction Bonds		5,000,000
Assessment Bonds		800,000
Reserve for Bond Coupon Redemption		15,000
Reserve for Sinking Fund		1,505,000
Library Endowment Account		100,000
Firemen's Pension Fund Account		160,400
Teachers' Benefit Account		15,000

Set up a balance sheet as of June 30, 2000, for the proprietary accounts under the following divisions:

1. Current Fund Account
2. Capital Fund Account
3. Sinking Fund Account
4. Trust Fund Account

Answer I.

BALANCE SHEET

City of X

June 30, 2000

I. CURRENT FUND				
Cash		$ 20,000	Revenue Bonds Payable	$ 80,000
Acct. Rec.		5,000	Vouchers Payable	8,000
Taxes Rec.	$100,000		Current Fund Surplus	99,000
Less: Res.				
For abatement	10,000	90,000		
Delinquent Taxes		2,000		
Materials & Supplies		30,000		
Accrued Water Charges		40,000		
		$187,000		$187,000
II. CAPITAL FUND				
Cash		$ 1,000,000	Vouchers Payable	$ 10,000
Assessments Rec.		500,000	Construction Bonds	5,000,000
Construction in Progress		400,000	Assessment Bonds	800,000
Lands		2,000,000	Capital Fund Surplus	5,590,000
Buildings		1,500,000		
Equipment		1,000,000		
Sewers, Streets, & Bridges		5,000,000		
		$11,400,000		$11,400,000
III. SINKING FUND				
Cash		$20,000	Reserve for Bond	
Securities		1,500,000	Coupon Redemption	$15,000
			Reserve for Sinking Fund	1,505,000
		$ 1,520,000		$ 1,520,000
IV. TRUST FUND				
Library Endowment Fund:			Library Endowment Acct.	$100,500
Cash	$500			
Securities	$100,000	$100,500		
Firemen's Pension Fund:			Firemen's Pension Fund	
Cash	$400		Account	$160,400
Securities	$160,000	$160,400		
Teachers' Benefit Fund:			Teachers' Benefit	
Securities		$15,000		$15,000
		$275,900		$275,900

Question II.

The data below refers to the city of X for the year ending June 30, 1999.

(a) Based on estimated revenues for the ensuing year of $850,000 from taxes and $250,000 from sundry sources, the city council approved the following budget:

Departments and Amounts: Executive – $40,000; Finance – $45,000; Courts – $30,000; Police – $115,000; Education – $150,000; Charities – $25,000; Fire – $100,000; Health – $70,000.

Maintenance: Streets – $100,000; Sewers – $50,000; Buildings – $75,000; Debt Service – $200,000. TOTAL – $1,000,000.

(b) The tax levy entered shortly after the budget was approved showed that taxes receivable would amount to $810,000, against which a reserve for abatement of $10,000 was provided.

(c) During the first six months, the amount of $545,000 in taxes was collected. Taxpayers' accounts amounting to $5,000 were classified as delinquent. The balance was not due until July 15.

(d) Sundry revenues for the six months amounted to $160,000.

(e) Purchase and payroll orders were issued for $415,000.

(f) Contracts were approved and executed for $135,000.

The above orders and contracts were chargeable as follows: Executive – $22,000; Finance – $29,500; Court – $14,000; Police – $52,000; Fire – $62,000; Education – $85,000; Charities – $10,500; Health – $30,000; Streets – $40,000; Sewers – $39,000; Buildings – $56,000; Debt Service – $100,000. The charges to the appropriation accounts should be indicated in the explanation of the entries in (e) and (f).

(g) Claims were audited and vouchered for $465,000, of which $375,000 applies on purchase and payroll roders and $90,000 on contracts. The amount was all for current expenses. The vouchers were not paid at June 30, 1999.

Considering that there is no inventory of materials on hand, submit: (a) Asset and Liability Balance Sheet (b) Revenue and Expense Statement (c) Current Fund (Funding) Balance Sheet.

Note: *Use the following list of account titles*:

Proprietary Accounts: Cash, Taxes Receivable, Delinquent Taxes, Current Expenses, Sundry Revenue, Revenue from Taxes, Vouchers (or Warrants) Payable, Reserve for Abatement of Taxes, Current Fund Surplus.

Fund Accounts: Budget Requirements, Budget Appropriations, Reserve for Orders Issued, Reserve for Contracts, Available Current Surplus, Unapplied Current Surplus.

Answer II.

(a) Asset and Liability Balance Sheet

Cash		$705,000	Vouchers Payable	$465,000
Taxes Rec.	$260,000		Surplus	495,000
Less Res. for				$960,000
Abatement	10,000	250,000		
Delinquent Taxes		5,000		
	$960,000			

(b) Revenue and Expense Statement Revenues

Taxes	$800,000	
Sundry	160,000	
Less Current Expenses		$960,000
Net Revenue Transferred		465,000
to Surplus		$495,000

(c) Current Fund Balance Sheet

Budget Requirements		$ 40,000	Budget Appropriations	$450,000
Surplus Available	$240,000		Reserve for Orders	
Unapplied	255,000	495,000	Issued	40,000
	$535,000		Reserve for Contracts	45,000
				$535,000

PRINCIPLES OF SUPERVISION

If you carefully study the following material, you will get a bird's-eye view of the essential elements of Personnel Supervision and Control. Most of the material is presented as an easily understood quizzer that teaches while it tests. The questions have all been culled from previous exams and are therefore a consensus of what's most important in this field.

Though supervisors of long experience will undoubtedly be familiar with the material that is given in this section, it has been included to enable them to score high on tests. It is unfortunately true that the usual test question on administrative and supervisory subjects is very often more easily answered by the person with book knowledge than by the one who has successfully handled, in practice, the question posed on paper.

A widespread belief, which modern research has done much to correct, has it that once an individual has developed fully there is little that can be done to change him. Consequently, according to this belief, if people have qualities that prevent them from being good supervisors, there is little they can do to improve. The fact of the matter is that while personality improvement in maturity is much more difficult than in childhood, particular habits with respect to particular situations can be modified considerably.

The effective supervisor possesses the personal qualities and attributes that enable one to function in a capacity designed to accomplish work through others.

There are two kinds of leaders, born leaders and developed leaders. Born leaders always find themselves in the forefront, even during their years of development. People naturally look up to them and are willing to follow them. Very often the "captain" of an athletic team is not the best athlete but rather an individual whom team members will follow in difficult situations and whose advice they tend to accept. The other kind of leader is not by nature a born leader, one who possesses natural qualities of leadership, but instead one whose ambitions are directed toward assuming responsibility and leading others in an effort to achieve desired objectives. This kind of leader must develop himself in such a way that ultimately he possesses the same qualities that the born leader is endowed with naturally.

No individual possesses all of the qualities necessary to become a completely successful supervisor, but the individual who recognizes what these qualities are and who comprehends what one has to do to function effectively as a supervisor is making progress toward achieving the desired goal.

1. There should be mutual respect between the supervisor and subordinate, and the burden of fostering this respect falls on the supervisor.
2. Subordinates should have a precise understanding of what is expected of them. There should be periodic individual conferences held in order to form this understanding, and during these meetings the supervisor can also advise the subordinate of opportunities for advancement. It is essential that these meetings terminate with a firm understanding about the supervisor's evaluation of the subordinate's job performance and about just what is expected of the subordinate in the future.
3. The effective supervisor is readily approachable to discuss problems concerning the work and may entertain the discussion of personal problems when they are having an adverse effect on productivity.
4. The effective supervisor maintains an attitude of open-mindedness in disagreements and is receptive to suggestions for improving methods of work performance. Subordinates must be made to feel that they can approach the supervisor and be received in a patient manner, without any indications of annoyance on the part of the supervisor.

5. The supervisor is fair and impartial insofar as it is possible, making no special arrangements and having no particular dealings with individuals that could not be explained satisfactorily to others. He or she attempts to keep personal likes or dislikes from influencing the treatment of subordinates.

6. A good supervisor never loses control of his emotions in regard to work situations and makes it a point never to indulge in arguments with subordinates.

7. He or she keeps all promises made to subordinates. No promise should be made unless the supervisor knows full well that it can be kept. An unfulfilled promise is very likely to result in a troubled relationship between supervisor and subordinate.

8. A supervisor is a patient teacher. If a subordinate does not absorb material at once, it should be repeated in an appropriate manner.

9. The supervisor praises good work publicly and in a timely fashion. Special appreciation should be shown to the worker who subordinates personal welfare to the good of the organization.

10. The supervisor is consistent in demeanor and temperament in relations with subordinates.

11. The supervisor's loyalty to the interests of subordinates should be unquestioned. When dealing with superiors, all blame for errors should be accepted by the supervisor; no responsibility for errors should be passed down to subordinates.

12. The supervisor should be reasonable in demands from subordinates. Work assignments must be made within their capabilities.

13. Constant observation on the part of the supervisor is a necessity. Complete information concerning problem areas within his or her responsibility must be at the disposal of the fully aware supervisor. A major portion of the time of a supervisor should be devoted to work simplification and improvement.

12. The effective supervisor works toward the achievement of definite goals within prescribed time periods, in an effort to produce definite quantities of work and at the same time maintain qualitative standards. Ultimately, the supervisor is uniquely responsible for the development of subordinates in such a way that they may reach their true potential. This should enable the organization to improve its productivity, and it will also prepare the subordinates to eventually assume positions with more complex duties. Effective supervision is the tool that makes organizations grow; a stagnant organization is a poor organization.

RELATION OF SUPERVISOR AND EMPLOYEE

In the foregoing, stress has been laid upon the personal qualities of the supervisor, as they relate to his/her work. We must now go forward and consider the workers in their relation to the supervisor.

The supervisor's function as a leader is to develop the individuals under him/her and to integrate them into a cooperative team. To accomplish this end, the supervisor must constantly have subordinates' motives and feelings in mind. Though no individual's motives can be reduced to a formula, the supervisor should have some insight into the reasons other people have for working.

WHY WORKERS WORK

1. The most important reason is the necessity for earning money. Though some people earn money for the common necessities of life, others want it to achieve a higher standard of life or independence. People with families want to achieve economic security and provide an education to their children.
2. There are some who feel obligated to take part in the world's work; to do something constructive. When working, their chief desire is to feel the usefulness of their work.
3. Some people work so that they may attain a position of authority. People are affected in various degrees by this reason. Some take pleasure in directing others, while some simply like to have a sense of personal prowess.
4. Part of the pleasure in working comes from the approval and recognition that it may yield. This is inseparably related to the motives given previously. In fact all the reasons for working given here are related to each other. No person is subservient to any single motive, though close observation may reveal the dominant drives. Approval and recognition are probably the most important motives that the supervisor can make use of in dealing with people.
5. Man is essentially social; we find joy in being an accepted member of a social group. This forms one of the bases of teamwork.
6. Judicious cultivation of the spirit of rivalry is a wise office policy. Most individuals wish to excel above those about them.
7. People will work through loyalty to their group and their leader even though they are not interested in the work they are doing.

People will also work through fear, but this is a poor incentive in the long run because it is inhibitory in its action. Just as an animal is paralyzed by extreme fear, so, in more subtle fashion, the will and interest of the human being is deadened by constant driving through fear of discharge or displeasure.

Appeal should always be made to the positive motives in building up interest and teamwork. Since the motives mentioned early in the list are satisfied by almost any job, once a job has been obtained they are not likely to have much effect in getting the employee to work harder than is necessary to avoid being dismissed. The motives in the latter part of the list must be called into play to secure real effectiveness.

DEVELOPING INTEREST AND COOPERATION

Interest and cooperation cannot be elicited from an employee if the work is not suited to the person's abilities. Thus a highly intelligent employee may be difficult to handle if forced to do a monotonous job. If possible, previous knowledge, experience, and expressed interests should be utilized in placement. While indiscriminate transfer is not advisable, the supervisor should take the initiative in shifting a worker to a more suitable job if that course seems calculated to arouse interest in the work.

Since interest can hardly be expected to exist where there is no understanding, the supervisor should explain to each worker exactly how the duties performed by the individual relate to the accomplishment of the overall objective of the organization. If the worker can envision both the entire picture and the worker's own part in it, this will promote in him or her a feeling of belonging. Another aid in holding interest is the shifting of emphasis from one part of the work to another. Thus, the supervisor may sometimes stress the volume of work and sometimes the accuracy with which it is done, the speed of completion, or the cost of doing it.

Individual records of production stimulate the spirit of rivalry and consequently arouse interest. It is well not to suggest that the records are being kept in order to punish the poorer workers. The introduction of such an idea is a potent force in breaking down office morale. When individual records can only be kept with difficulty, it is good procedure to stimulate the group spirit by keeping a record of group production and making each member of the group feel that he is doing an essential part of the group work. If team rivalries can be stimulated, they can often be more potent than individual competitions in the organization's interests. If a group goal is set (for instance, the production of a good set of figures for the examination of some high official at some stated time), interest in the work is heightened.

When each member of the organization is interested in his work, the foundation of teamwork has been laid. In order to achieve teamwork, cooperation must be obtained from each worker, and this is the result of broadening the interest of the individual to include the whole group. In reaching this goal, the energy and enthusiasm of the leader are all important. Achieved through many months or years of right actions, teamwork, interest, and cooperation can be easily destroyed by causes that are easily discernible.

RULES

When interest and cooperation have been raised to a really effective level, the question of rules is of minor importance. However, the manner in which orders are given and rules laid down are one important determinant of teamwork.

The guiding principle should be "as few rules as possible." The more efficient the supervisor, the smaller his quota of rules.

Direction and routine are certainly necessary, for there is a great demand upon energies when clerks must continually direct themselves to their labors, but this direction should be given only as new circumstances arise, not continuously, persistently, or critically.

When rules have been made, they should be followed. However, the supervisor should not expect blind obedience, but instead an intelligent, understanding respect for the rules that have been established. When rules are not adhered to, the supervisor should discover the reason and if the new procedure is better he/she should adopt it. At the same time he/she should make clear that teamwork demands coordination and that an apparently insignificant point may be of vital importance to someone else in completing the job.

FRIENDLY RELATIONS

It is difficult to lay down a general rule regarding personal relationships of supervisor and subordinate.

One should be friendly and take an interest in each member of the staff; but too much intimacy should be avoided because the conditions in different places vary so widely. Organizations in small towns would naturally have different standards than those that prevail in a very large metropolitan organization employing people with widely divergent backgrounds.

Toleration of a nickname or the use of the first name may be the custom or it may denote too great familiarity. Playing practical jokes on or with the staff and failure to maintain firm and fair discipline should be avoided by the supervisor. The difficulty of being intimate with members of the staff lies in the resentment it arouses and the possible charge of favoritism.

WASTING TIME

The supervisor can usually do much to control this common fault, for it is usually caused by poor supervision or general management.

When a department is overmanned, when the flow of work is uneven, when machines or other equipment are improperly installed, and where departments do not cooperate, there is almost certain to be a waste of time. All these causes serve as excuses for the time wasters; they are used to greatest advantage by those who dislike the work the most.

REPRIMAND AND PRAISE

If criticism is necessary, it should not be given in front of fellow employees, for such a procedure violates the sense of loyalty and mutual consideration.

Praise can be given in the presence of others. It should neither be lavish nor stinted. The tendency of most supervisors seems to be to overdo a good thing and to give so much of it that it no longer has any meaning to those who are praised.

Two general methods of speeding up production are:

1. Past "good work" may be praised (not the worker). The difficulty of the present task may be admitted.
2. Reprimand in a disguised form may be employed by challenging the worker's ability to do a task at all or to do it as well as others. Challenge should be applied to the more aggressive individual, while encouragement should be given to the submissive type of person.

SUPERVISING SKILLED WORKERS

1. A supervisor has received orders for a work assignment to be carried out by his unit. He has firmly decided on methods for carrying out this assignment that he believes will lead to its completion both properly and expeditiously. He has no intention whatsoever of changing his mind. After he has reached his decision, he calls a staff conference to discuss alternative methods of carrying out the assignments without making clear that he has already decided upon the method to be used. To hold a conference of this type would generally be a

   (A) good idea, because his subordinates are likely to carry the assignment through better if they believe that they devised the methods used.

   (B) good idea, because the staff will have the opportunity and be properly motivated to gain knowledge and experience in methodology without endangering staff performance.

   (C) poor idea, because it would be a failure on the part of the supervisor to show the firm leadership that his unit has a right to expect.

   (D) poor idea, because the discovery by the staff that they had not actually participated in deciding upon the methods to be used would have an adverse effect upon their morale.

The correct answer is (D). It is an accepted concept that where employees are consulted as to methods of work performance before they are instituted, a higher level of morale will exist. Higher morale must lead to increased and superior work production.

2. A supervisor is put in charge of a special unit. She is exceptionally well qualified for this assignment by her training and experience. One of her very close personal friends has been working for some time in this unit. Both the supervisor and her friend are certain that the rest of the people in the unit, many of whom have been in the bureau for a long time, know of this close relationship. Under these circumstances, the most advisable action for the supervisor to take is to

   (A) ask that either she be allowed to return to her old assignment, or, if that cannot be arranged, that her friend be transferred to another unit.

   (B) avoid any overt sign of favoritism by acting impartially and with greater reserve when dealing with her friend than with the rest of the staff.

(C) discontinue any socializing with her friend either inside or outside the office so as to eliminate any gossip or dissatisfaction.

(D) talk the situation over with her friend and arrive at a mutually acceptable plan of proper office decorum.

The correct answer is (D). The correct course of action for a supervisor to follow when a close personal friend is assigned to her unit is for the two of them to arrive at a decision as to just how they will conduct themselves during working hours on the job. This can be accomplished at a meeting called by the supervisor.

3. Experts in the field of personnel relations feel that it is generally a bad practice for subordinate employees to become aware of pending or contemplated changes in policy or organizational setup via the "grapevine" chiefly because

   (A) evidence that one or more responsible officials have proved untrustworthy will undermine confidence in the agency.

   (B) the information disseminated by this method is seldom entirely accurate and generally spreads needless unrest among the subordinate staff.

   (C) the subordinate staff may conclude that the administration feels the staff cannot be trusted with the true information.

   (D) the subordinate staff may conclude that the administration lacks the courage to make an unpopular announcement through official channels.

The correct answer is (B). Most rumors deal with bad news. As the rumor is spread from employee to employee, it is likely to be altered and exaggerated. When a supervisor learns about a rumor that is causing unrest among his employees, he should take immediate steps to inform his employees of the true situation.

4. One factor that might be given consideration in deciding upon the optimum span of control of a supervisor over his immediate subordinates is the position of the supervisor in the hierarchy of the organization. It is generally considered proper that the number of subordinates immediately supervised by an upper echelon supervisor

   (A) is unrelated to and tends to form no pattern with the number supervised by lower-level supervisors.

   (B) should be about the same as the number supervised by a lower-level supervisor.

   (C) should be larger than the number supervised by a lower-level supervisor.

   (D) should be smaller than the number supervised by a lower-level supervisor.

The correct answer is (D). As the work of the subordinates of a supervisor becomes more complex, his span of control decreases. The functions of workers increase in complexity as the ladder of hierarchy in an organization is ascended.

5. When an experienced subordinate who has the authority and information necessary to make a decision on a certain difficult matter brings the matter to his supervisor without having made the decision, it would generally be best for the supervisor to

   (A) agree to make the decision for the subordinate after the subordinate has explained why he finds it difficult to make the decision and after he has made a recommendation.

   (B) make the decision for the subordinate, explaining to him the reasons for arriving at the decision.

(C) refuse to make the decision, but discuss the various alternatives with the subordinate in order to clarify the issues involved.

(D) refuse to make the decision, explaining to the subordinate that he is deemed to be fully qualified and competent to make the decision.

The correct answer is (C). The key words are *experienced* and *authority*. If an employee has been given the authority to make a decision and has the experience to make it, the most the supervisor should do is to point out the alternative courses of action in an attempt to guide him.

6. The *least* important of the following reasons why a particular activity should be assigned to a unit that performs activities dissimilar to it is that

(A) close coordination is needed between the particular activity and other activities performed by the unit.

(B) it will enhance the reputation and prestige of the unit supervisor.

(C) the unit makes frequent use of the results of this particular activity.

(D) the unit supervisor has a sound knowledge and understanding of the particular activity.

The correct answer is (B). This question asks the *least* important reason for assigning a particular activity to a unit. Choices (A), (C), and (D) contain good reasons for the assignment of an activity to a unit. Very few things in personnel administration are done to enhance the reputation and prestige of an individual. The assignment of work is definitely not one of them.

7. In a psychological study of leadership, it was found that it is possible to predict the behavior of a new person in a leadership position more accurately on the basis of the behavior of his/her predecessor in the post than on the behavior of the man/woman himself/herself in his/her previous job. The best explanation of this observation is that there is a tendency

(A) to select similar types of personalities to fill the same type of position.

(B) for a newly appointed person to avoid instituting basic changes in operational procedures.

(C) for a given organizational structure and set of duties to produce similar patterns of behavior.

(D) for increased responsibility to impose more mature patterns of behavior on an incumbent.

The correct answer is (C). Most people will react similarly under set conditions. In other words, the idiosyncrasies of a job tend to determine the behavior of the incumbent.

8. One of your workers has relatives who raise chickens. One day, you mention in casual conversation that you bought some eggs of poor quality at the grocery store. The following Monday the worker places a box of fresh eggs on your desk. You thank him/her and offer to pay but he/she refuses. On several occasions thereafter he/she brings in additional eggs but still refuses to take payment. He/She is obviously proud of these products and seems to take great pleasure in sharing them with you. However, you begin to hear rumors that the other workers believe that you and the worker are very friendly and that he/she is receiving special privileges from you. You should

(A) explain the situation to the worker, pointing out that he is being hurt by the conditions because of the feelings of others.

(B) ignore the situation since the worker is merely being friendly and is actually receiving no favors in return.

(C) supervise this worker more carefully than the others to insure that he will not take advantage of the situation.

(D) refuse all gifts from the worker thereafter without further explanation.

The correct answer is (A). This choice presents the best of the four courses of action. There is nothing in the question that leads one to believe that the intent of the worker is anything but harmless. If his actions are creating a situation that could have repercussions, it would be best for the supervisor to have a talk with the worker where they could agree on another course of conduct.

9. Lax supervision has been blamed largely on the unwillingness of supervisors to supervise their rank-and-file. The chief reason for this unwillingness to supervise is based mainly on the supervisor's

   (A) failure to accept modern concepts of proper supervision and its methods.

   (B) doubt of his own ability to keep pace with modern techniques and developments.

   (C) own inability to adhere to the same high standards of performance that are required of his subordinates.

   (D) fear of complaints from his subordinates and his desire to avoid unpleasantness.

The correct answer is (D). Lax supervision is the result of supervisors deliberately avoiding the workers on the job. They are aware that their subordinates have cause for complaint, that they are operating under adverse conditions, and that if they encounter them while they are performing their duties they will be recipients of many complaints.

10. In making assignments, a supervisor attempts to fit his men to the jobs. This procedure is

   (A) good, chiefly because it is a definite policy that lends itself to analysis and conclusions.

   (B) poor, chiefly because a job should be fitted to the person.

   (C) good, chiefly because accomplishment of the mission is the primary goal.

   (D) poor, chiefly because no consideration is paid to human values and relationships.

The correct answer is (C). A person should be fitted to a job, not a job to a person. In other words, a job must exist before a person is assigned to it.

11. The effectiveness of the work of a unit depends in a large measure on that unit's will to work. The best of the following methods for the unit supervisor to employ in order to increase the will of the members of the unit to work is for the unit supervisor to

   (A) allow each worker to proceed at his/her own pace.

   (B) be constantly on guard for any laxity among his/her workers.

   (C) provide comfortable working facilities for his/her workers.

   (D) clearly discuss with his/her workers the functions and objectives of the agency.

The correct answer is (D). Of the four choices, this is the only one that would have a beneficial effect on employee morale and would therefore result in better work performance. When an employee is aware of the functions and objectives of the agency and he/she can see the part that his/her work plays in attaining these objectives, he/she is likely to do a better job.

12. While supervising a crew performing inspectional duties, you come across practices on an installation that are on the fringe of many law violations. For you to imply to the owner that your department will conduct frequent inspections of his premises until he eliminates some of the questionable conditions on his property is

    (A) proper mainly because the owner may be persuaded to maintain satisfactory conditions.

    (B) improper mainly because the owner may feel that he is being harassed.

    (C) proper mainly because any means that result in the elimination of hazardous conditions are permissible.

    (D) improper because threats that may not be carried out should not be made.

The correct answer is (A). This action may be evaluated as proper because it will most likely result in improvement of the conditions in question at the installation. Choice (C) is not true at all; the word *any* is much too positive.

13. A supervisor in charge during a hazardous operation made a great effort to give orders in his normal tone of voice and generally to conduct himself in his normal manner, as though the situation was routine and without danger. In this situation, the supervisor's behavior was

    (A) improper mainly because the people under his supervision are not alerted to their danger.

    (B) proper mainly because danger is part of the job and should be faced without flinching.

    (C) improper mainly because the supervisor is not behaving normally or honestly.

    (D) proper mainly because the people under his supervision also will tend to act calmly.

The correct answer is (D). The supervisor's action should first be evaluated as proper. Choice (D) is correct and logical. Choice (B) is not true at all because even though the workers are aware of the danger connected with their job, it is perfectly normal to be afraid during dangerous situations. At any rate, loss of composure is infectious. If the supervisor became excited, his conduct would surely be carried over to his men.

14. The main reason for a supervisor to delegate authority to a subordinate is to

    (A) develop the leadership potential of the subordinate.

    (B) make the authority equal to the responsibility of an assignment.

    (C) free the supervisor for more important tasks.

    (D) obtain new and better methods of performing the duties assigned.

The correct answer is (C). A supervisor who is bogged down with too much detail work will be unable to devote sufficient time to his/her supervisory duties. A supervisor is paid to supervise, and if he/she does not have sufficient time to devote to this, he/she is derelict in the performance of his duties.

15. A chief of an inspectional division encounters one of his subordinates in the course of an inspection. The inspector is in the process of issuing violations for five infractions. The chief of the division considers four of the violations clear violations of the law, but the fifth he considers a borderline case which he, himself, would not have handled by issuing a violation order. In this situation, the best of the following courses for the chief to take is to

    (A) direct the inspector to cancel the violation order for the borderline situation.

    (B) say nothing to the inspector at this time but later warn him against unduly strict interpretation of the law.

(C) accept the inspector's findings without any comment at this time or later.

(D) question the inspector closely about various sections of the law to determine whether he has a proper understanding of its requirements.

The correct answer is (C). This situation involves a sensitive area. The inspection of violations sometimes is a matter of individual interpretation. The inspector has been delegated the authority to perform the inspection and he should be permitted to perform it unimpeded, especially since the point in question is not definite one way or the other.

16. Although there is a normal distinction between the successive ranks of supervision in an agency, the greatest distinction and change in rank occurs when a worker becomes a supervisor. This is true chiefly because the supervisor

(A) must be better informed than his/her workers in all aspects of the work.

(B) must learn to assume new and more complex duties.

(C) becomes responsible for the first time for the job performance of members of the staff.

(D) has greater responsibility and authority than the subordinates under his supervision.

The correct answer is (C). For the first time, the worker will be responsible for the performance of others.

17. It has been said that the success or failure of the work of the unit rests on the unit supervisor. If the supervisor wants to stimulate growth among his/her workers, it would generally be best for him/her to

(A) set an easy pace for his/her workers so that they will not become confused because of having to learn too much too rapidly.

(B) set the pace for his/her workers so that the job is never too easy but is a constant challenge calling for more and better work.

(C) spot-check the workers' case records at irregular intervals in order to determine whether they are performing their duties properly.

(D) see to it that the broad objectives and goals of the department are periodically communicated and interpreted to his/her workers.

The correct answer is (B). When work standards are set at a level where they may be attained with little effort, they will tend to create boredom among the organization's employees. Work standards should be set so that a considerable effort must be made to attain them, although they should not be set so high that they are out of reach and discourage the workers.

18. For a supervisor to encourage his/her workers to think about the reasons for a policy is

(A) advisable, mainly because the workers are then more likely to apply the policy appropriately.

(B) inadvisable, mainly because the workers may then apply the policy too flexibly.

(C) advisable, mainly because the workers may then feel that they have participated in policy making.

(D) inadvisable, mainly because the workers may interpret the policy incorrectly if they misunderstand its meaning.

The correct answer is (A). If a worker understands the reasons behind the setting of a policy and just why it has been put into effect, he will support it with much more enthusiasm than if he believes it to be an arbitrary decision on the part of management.

19. "A good supervisor should know when to refer a matter to his/her superior and when to handle it himself/herself." Of the following, the situation that a supervisor would most appropriately refer to his/her superior is

    (A) poor cooperation by a subordinate in his/her section.
    (B) a complaint about poor service.
    (C) a disagreement between two of his/her subordinates.
    (D) a breakdown of recently purchased equipment.

The correct answer is (D). A supervisor should be able to handle most aspects of his/her job by himself/herself. The first three choices involve a complaint of poor work within his/her jurisdiction or everyday personnel problems. These are within the province of the supervisor and should be handled by him/her alone. However, he/she is usually not responsible for the purchase of equipment, and if equipment breaks down he/she should seek the aid of the individual responsible for its purchase or maintenance.

20. A supervisor who plans his/her work properly and who has no difficulty in meeting deadlines insists that his/her new workers pattern their activities after his/her in every detail. This method is

    (A) undesirable, chiefly because such compliance can cause antagonism and hamper the workers' growth.
    (B) undesirable, chiefly because this method cannot work as successfully for the new workers.
    (C) desirable, chiefly because the supervisor's methods have proved successful and will eliminate waste.
    (D) desirable, chiefly because the untrained worker needs guidelines to follow.

The correct answer is (A). In the first place, this supervisor is not allowing for differences in people. Secondly, he/she is stifling initiative by insisting that everyone performs as is best for the supervisor. No two people are exactly alike. What is good for one person may not be good for another.

21. For a supervisor to encourage competitive feelings among his/her staff is

    (A) advisable, chiefly because the workers will perform more efficiently when they have proper motivation.
    (B) inadvisable, chiefly because the workers will not perform well under the pressure of competition.
    (C) advisable, chiefly because the workers will have a greater incentive to perform their jobs properly.
    (D) inadvisable, chiefly because the workers may focus their attention on areas where they excel and neglect other essential aspects of the job.

The correct answer is (D). This situation should first be appraised as an inadvisable one. A supervisor should not encourage competitiveness among his/her employees; he/she should encourage harmony, coordination, and team spirit. The reason given in choice (D) is much better then the one in choice (B) because the condition in choice (B) may not turn out to be true.

22. In selecting tasks to be assigned to a new worker, the supervisor should assign those tasks that

    (A) give the worker the greatest variety of experience.
    (B) offer the worker the greatest opportunity to achieve concrete results.

(C) present the worker with the greatest stimulation because of their interesting nature.

(D) require the least amount of contact with outside agencies.

The correct answer is (B). Success is known to follow other successes. If the new employee is assigned a task he/she is reasonably sure to be successful in, it will give him/her the confidence to tackle the other tasks assigned to him/her.

23. An essential element of administrative control over the operations for which a superior is responsible is that the superior

    (A) should perform an important task himself/herself instead of assigning a competent subordinate to perform it.

    (B) should personally check every ordered action taken by his/her subordinates to insure that they have been properly performed.

    (C) who has issued an order to a subordinate should ascertain that it has been carried out properly.

    (D) who has assigned an important task to a subordinate should inform him/her that he/she, the subordinate, will be held fully accountable for its proper execution.

The correct answer is (C). It is the ultimate responsibility of a superior officer to see that the work he/she has assigned to subordinates is carried out in a proper manner.

24. Of the following, the factor that is least important in determining the number of subordinates a superior can effectively supervise is the

    (A) type of work being done.

    (B) abilities of superior and subordinates.

    (C) level of command in the organization.

    (D) overall size of the department.

The correct answer is (D). The concept in question here deals with *span of control*. The type of work being performed, the abilities of the supervisor and his/her subordinates, and the level of command in the organization all are pertinent to the number of subordinates the supervisor is able to supervise effectively. The overall size of the department is not a factor at all.

25. The one of the following activities that is generally the *least* proper function of a centralized procedure section is

    (A) issuing new and revised procedural instructions.

    (B) coordinating forms revision and procedural changes.

    (C) accepting or rejecting authorized procedural changes.

    (D) controlling standard numbering systems for procedural releases.

The correct answer is (C). The other three choices depict proper functions of a centralized procedure section. This section, however, is a coordinating unit and it would not have the authority to rule on the validity of authorized procedural changes.

26. A proposal is made to allow a large measure of planning responsibility to each departmental division rather than to place sole responsibility in a central planning division. Adoption of such decentralized planning would lead to

    (A) more effective planning; plans will be conceived in terms of the existing situations and will be more likely to be carried out willingly.

    (B) less effective planning; a central planning division will have a more objective overall view than any operating division can possibly achieve.

(C) more effective planning; operating divisions are usually better equipped technically than the central planning divisions and thus better able to make valid plans.

(D) less effective planning; personnel in an operating division do not have the time to plan efficiently and painstakingly.

The correct answer is (A). In many instances the function of planning will be carried out most effectively if the individual units are permitted to do it on their own. This is true because they are nearer the work and are in a better position to construct effective plans. In addition, they would be more willing to carry out plans that emanated from within their own unit than if the plans were formulated elsewhere.

27. In some jurisdictions, work performance above the call of duty is rewarded by special assignments and consideration for promotion to higher ranks. A basic weakness of this system is that it

(A) tends to inspire ambitious young employees to deliberately seek situations in which they can excel and will enhance their standing in the eyes of their superiors.

(B) tends to weaken respect for the senior members of the agency since the system described favors younger employees.

(C) overlooks the fact that the rapid growth of organizations tends to give all employees the opportunity to encounter situations that will win them attention.

(D) tends to penalize to an unfair extent those employees who are most productive.

The correct answer is (D). In such a setup described, promotion and special assignments would go to those who happen to be in situations that are likely to be rewarded. Those employees who simply performed their routine work well would not have the opportunity for promotion or special assignments.

28. For a supervisor to permit his subordinates to participate in the decision-making process is generally desirable, when practicable, primarily because

(A) it leads to the elimination of grievances.

(B) better solutions may be obtained.

(C) individual development requires an ever-expanding view of operations.

(D) the supervisor is forced to "keep on his toes" under the stimulation of the interchange of ideas.

The correct answer is (B). This is strictly a case of many heads being better then one. Valid suggestions may come from the most unlikely sources.

29. A crew is faced with a troublesome problem. The supervisor calls all his/her subordinates to a meeting, outlines the problem, and asks them to suggest any ideas that occur to them as possible ways of handling it. Each idea is written down and later discussed carefully. The chief advantage of this procedure is that

(A) time is not wasted on needless talk.

(B) ideas are obtained that otherwise might not be developed.

(C) there is less tendency for the meeting to stray from the subject under discussion.

(D) subordinates receive training in analysis of problems and evaluation of solutions.

The correct answer is (B). This is an excellent manner of obtaining various outlooks that may then be developed until they satisfactorily meet a given situation. Choices (A) and (C) are fallacious statements. Although the statement in choice (D) may be true to an extent, it is not the main purpose of the meeting at all. The meeting was called by the supervisor to get help from his subordinates in solving a problem.

30. A new procedure is about to be instituted in your division. Before presenting it to your workers, you try to think of what objections they may raise and how to deal with these objections. Of the following, the best reason for this practice is that the

    (A) workers will respect your competence when you can handle their objections on the spot.

    (B) analysis involved will help you better understand the new procedure.

    (C) objections can be channeled upward and the procedure revised before it is implemented.

    (D) knowledge you have of your workers' ways of thinking and behaving will be increased.

The correct answer is (A). The supervisor will enhance the chances of a new procedure being accepted willingly by his workers if he/she is prepared to answer any objections they may raise while he/she is presenting it to them. Any indecisiveness on his/her part will be looked upon as a sign that he/she does not really understand the procedure and that the order for a change was arbitrary and not well thought out.

31. A recently assigned supervisor is concerned about the fact that he has taken an instantaneous liking to some of his workers whereas one seems to antagonize him. Of the following, the most useful first step he could take with respect to this person is to

    (A) determine the chances of transferring him/her.

    (B) tactfully ascertain from his workers their reactions to this person and his/her reputation as a worker.

    (C) recognize that this is the well-known "halo" effect and make a conscious effort to be fair to this person.

    (D) explain his feelings to his superior and ask for his/her advice.

The correct answer is (B). Perhaps the supervisor's initial impression was faulty. He should attempt to ascertain whether others who had close contact with the person in question reacted in the same way.

32. A senior supervisor institutes a policy of minimizing the amount of information he passes on to his subordinates since he feels they are overburdened with details. This practice is

    (A) proper; it is part of the job to act as a buffer for his workers.

    (B) improper; the senior supervisor is trying to carry too many responsibilities on his own shoulders.

    (C) proper; his leadership strength is increased by the degree to which his subordinates turn to him for guidance.

    (D) improper; the subordinates lack information that may be necessary to proper performance of their duties.

The correct answer is (D). This procedure should definitely be evaluated as improper. Subordinates must be well informed if they are to function effectively. Although choice (B) is correct to some degree, choice (D) is much better.

33. When unexpected obstacles arise during the course of operations, the supervisor must find means of overcoming them. Of the following, the most important factor in this endeavor is the supervisor's

    (A) attitude.
    (B) advance planning.
    (C) training.
    (D) knowledge of procedures.

The correct answer is (A). All formulated plans leave some room for the unexpected to happen, because it usually does. A supervisor, when he/she encounters the unexpected, should not permit himself/herself to be rattled. Only in this way will he/she be able to modify his/her plans to take care of the new situations.

34. Of the following duties to be performed, a supervisor would be least justified in delegating to a member, rather than performing personally, the

    (A) inspection of committee work.
    (B) preparation of a report of an investigation of a complaint.
    (C) follow-up training of a recently transferred employee.
    (D) making out of inspection cards.

The correct answer is (A). The functions in choices (B), (C), and (D) are all suitable for delegation to a qualified subordinate by a supervisor. Inspection of committee work is not, because the supervisor would be directly responsible for the results of a committee performing under his/her jurisdiction.

35. The outcome that is most likely to result from setting work standards slightly higher than subordinates can achieve with ease is that they will have

    (A) clearly defined and perceivable objectives.
    (B) a desire to avoid potential failure.
    (C) the opportunity to enjoy gratifying success.
    (D) an area about which they can safely complain.

The correct answer is (C). The best work standards are those that are set just slightly above what the average employee can easily attain. A worker must be made to extend himself just a bit if he/she is to feel a sense of accomplishment.

36. You have a group of people working under you on a special assignment. One of them is not competent. If you show him his errors, he resents it and says you are discriminating against him. He needs close supervision to accomplish his work and yet he resents being supervised. The best solution to this problem is to

    (A) prepare a written reprimand that will be made part of the man's record and will be an official warning to him that his conduct must improve.
    (B) permit the group to correct the situation since group action is usually more effective than corrective action imposed by the supervisor.
    (C) recommend a change in assignment in an attempt to remove him from a work situation that is affecting him adversely.
    (D) identify the real cause of the behavior problem and determine how the employee can be helped to find greater personal satisfaction from his work.

The correct answer is (C). This man is working on a special assignment and is not doing a good job at it. A recommendation for a change in assignment in this instance is not really considered a transfer. This man is showing that he is not suited for this special work. It should be kept in mind, however, that under ordinary circumstances a transfer of an incompetent worker is not considered good personnel practice, because actually what is being done is to shift one supervisor's problem to another.

37. When a supervisor gives a valid command to one of his/her subordinates, he/she at the same time tacitly confers upon him/her the legal power to perform it. This is based on the principle that

    (A) the person to whom authority is granted becomes as accountable for its use as the superior who delegated the authority.

    (B) responsibility for proper performance of an order cannot be placed without the delegation of the authority needed to execute it.

    (C) only through the establishment of effective controls can a supervisor insure the proper execution of his/her orders.

    (D) superiors who give orders are responsible for seeing to it later that the orders have been carried out as assigned.

The correct answer is (B). Sufficient authority must be delegated with the responsibility to carry out a function.

38. Much has been said in recent years about the advisability of instituting suggestion programs or of inviting subordinates to participate in attempting to find solutions to company problems. In general, the most likely result of instituting either or both of these ideas would be

    (A) an increased motivation of the subordinates to do a better job

    (B) an increased need for disciplinary action against subordinates as a result of their feeling more free to introduce new ideas

    (C) a loss of efficiency resulting from the introduction of new ideas

    (D) a stifling of initiative among the subordinates

The correct answer is (A). A well-run suggestion program will not only produce good ideas from some of the most unexpected sources, it will also tend to make all members of the organization feel that they belong. Their ideas are not only wanted, they are appreciated.

39. A supervisor must frequently delegate authority to subordinates, and the success of the delegation depends in a large degree upon the ability of the subordinate to accept the delegated authority. Of the following, the most important factor in encouraging positive and wholehearted acceptance on the part of a subordinate is that

    (A) the delegation be on a permanent basis.

    (B) the assignment does not require greater effort than customarily exerted by the subordinate.

    (C) appropriate members of the organization be duly notified and instructed to accept the delegation.

    (D) the delegation does not involve assumption of authority over coworkers.

The correct answer is (C). Due notice must be given to affected parties when authority is delegated by the supervisor to one of his/her subordinates. In the absence of this notification, the subordinate assuming the authority will not command the respect and cooperation of the workers necessary to fulfill the function.

40. An important principle of the science of supervision is that the span of control should be narrow enough to permit effective control. Of the following, the principle that is most *contradictory* to this is that

    (A) organizational levels should be kept to a minimum.

    (B) employees should be grouped according to geographic area.

    (C) the units composing an organization have a tendency to grow away from each other and become independent.

    (D) control should be placed in people in key positions.

The correct answer is (A). It is an accepted concept that the levels of an organization should be kept down to as few as possible. However, if this would result in too broad a span of control, the levels in the organization would have to be adjusted. The span of control and the organizational levels are inversely related.

41. A chief of an inspectional division charged with seeing that safety regulations are enforced encounters one of his subordinates making an inspection of a factory. The subordinate is not sure just which safety regulations are being violated and he seeks the aid of his chief. The chief and his subordinate discuss the possible violations in the presence of the factory manager, and then the chief directs the subordinate to issue summonses for specific violations. Discussing the problem in the presence of the factory manager was

    (A) proper mainly because he probably would realize the chief and his subordinate were not acting arbitrarily or unreasonably.

    (B) improper mainly because he might prefer one of the approaches that was suggested and rejected.

    (C) proper mainly because the activities of the department should, whenever possible, be open to the public.

    (D) improper mainly because inaccurate statements may have been made during the preliminary discussion.

The correct answer is (D). The factory manager would most likely lose respect for the chief and his subordinate if any indecision about the correct course of action was exhibited by the two officials in their preliminary discussion.

42. A good leader encourages subordinates to use their initiative, but realizes that such a practice has a price. Of the following, the main drawback is that subordinates will occasionally

    (A) overstep the bounds of their authority.

    (B) make errors in judgment.

    (C) duplicate work of others.

    (D) engage in fruitless experimentation.

The correct answer is (B). The main danger involved when subordinates are permitted and encouraged to make their own decisions is that they probably do not have as much experience as their supervisors. However, a practice of encouraging subordinates to use their *initiative* will result in their development.

43. The one of the following results that would be the most likely consequence of decentralization of authority and responsibility in an organization is

    (A) improved discipline.

    (B) increased specialization of functions.

    (C) greater diversity in procedures.

    (D) greater interchangeability of personnel.

The correct answer is (C). When authority is decentralized, more people will be making decisions concerning courses of action. Therefore it is probable that the same type of work may be performed differently from unit to unit in the same organization. When authority is centralized, decisions emit from one source in an organization, and work procedures of a like nature will be handled similarly.

44. A special unit of a department is rife with rumors concerning plans for its future and the possibility of its abolition. As a result, morale and production of members assigned to it have suffered. To handle this situation, the supervisor in command adopts a policy of promptly corroborating factual rumors and denying false ones. This method of dealing with the problem will achieve some good results, but its chief weakness is that

    (A) it gives status to the rumors by the attention paid to them.

    (B) the supervisor may not have the necessary information at hand to dispose promptly of all rumors.

    (C) it "chases" the rumors rather than forestalling them by giving information concerning the unit's future.

    (D) the supervisor may have confidential information that he should not divulge.

The correct answer is (C). This action is doing nothing to prevent these many rumors. The supervisor is just disposing of them as fast as he/she can after they occur.

TRAINING AND EVALUATING SUBORDINATES

The questions that follow touch on all the essentials of training and evaluating subordinates. The explanations provided bring out the basic concept behind each question so that you will be able to apply these concepts in similar situations.

1. You find that one of the workers in your crew constantly consults with fellow workers on how to do the work that has been assigned. As the supervisor, it would be best for you to

    (A) commend the worker for securing the cooperation of fellow workers.

    (B) tell the crew to let this individual to learn by his/her mistakes.

    (C) give this worker a job that is easy to do.

    (D) see to it that the worker learns the job.

The correct answer is (D). This employee is either insufficiently trained or unsure of himself/herself. Training will not only prepare the individual to carry out duties with greater efficiency, but it will also serve to give him/her the confidence that seems to be lacking.

2. Of the following, the one that can most easily be increased or improved in an employee by the supervisor is
   (A) ability to learn.
   (B) aptitude.
   (C) common sense.
   (D) knowledge.

The correct answer is (D). Knowledge may be acquired through education. Ability to learn, common sense, and aptitude are all to some extent inborn.

3. After you have given a newly-appointed subordinate complete instructions on how to use a piece of equipment, you should usually
   (A) assign this person to work with another subordinate.
   (B) go over the instructions once more.
   (C) let the individual use the equipment while you observe.
   (D) explain the importance of the work.

The correct answer is (C). One of the best methods for training people is to let them perform a job under close supervision until they have mastered it. Then let them proceed on their own.

4. You assign an employee to take inventory of a certain item. The employee gives you a figure that seems too high. Of the following, the best course of action for you to take is to
   (A) accept the figure given to you if the employee is willing to initial it.
   (B) accompany the employee while the inventory is taken again.
   (C) ask the employee to take the inventory again and explain why it is necessary.
   (D) take inventory yourself.

The correct answer is (C). This choice will not only give you a double-checked figure but will also give the employee valuable training.

5. Upon being assigned to an important job that is to be done alone, a worker insists that he or she knows exactly how to proceed and that no instructions or explanations by the supervisor are necessary. The best way for the supervisor to handle the situation is to
   (A) let the worker proceed without instructions.
   (B) report the worker to your superior for not listening to instructions.
   (C) remain present while the worker does the job.
   (D) question the worker briefly regarding the intended procedure.

The correct answer is (D). This situation is not uncommon. The worker could have had previous experience at this job or a similar job. However, the supervisor, who has the ultimate responsibility for seeing that the job is performed correctly, should question the worker briefly on the assignment before it is begun, and should check from time to time to see how the work is progressing.

6. When conducting training, a supervisor made an effort to devote approximately the same amount of time to each member of the group. This procedure generally is
   (A) good, because the members will realize that they are receiving equal treatment.
   (B) bad, because some members require more training than others.
   (C) good, because the supervisor is less likely to neglect any member.
   (D) bad, because the supervisor has to devote too much effort to keeping track of the time spent with each member.

The correct answer is (B). It is unusual for any two people to be able to absorb training material in exactly the same length of time. For that reason it would be wise for the supervisor to compensate for the differences in learning capacities of employees by giving more time to those in need of it.

7. The most logical reason for a supervisor to rotate job assignments among the workers in the crew would be to

    (A) improve maintenance procedures.

    (B) make sure that absences do not slow up the work too much.

    (C) determine which of the workers are not readily adaptable.

    (D) reduce absenteeism.

The correct answer is (B). Note that there was no mention of the type of job assignments that were to be rotated. Assuming that there is a variety of different jobs, rotation will give the workers a degree of skill in handling any of them. If one worker were to be absent on any given day, there would be another available to fill in without the need for training. Therefore you would have a flexible unit in which one worker could fill in for another whenever necessary.

8. Assume that one of your subordinates made an error. It was found and corrected, but your subordinate seems rather depressed about the matter. Of the following, the most advisable course of action for you to take is to

    (A) ignore the entire situation unless it happens again.

    (B) praise the subordinate.

    (C) reprimand the subordinate mildly.

    (D) show the subordinate how such a mistake can be avoided in the future.

The correct answer is (D). Everybody is likely to make errors at one time or another. Of the four courses of action depicted in the choices, the only sensible one would be to show the subordinate how to avoid similar errors in the future.

9. A training program for workers assigned to the information section should include actual practice in simulated interviews under simulated conditions. The one of the following educational principles that is the chief justification for this statement is that

    (A) the workers will remember what they see better and longer than what they read or hear.

    (B) the workers will learn more effectively by actually doing the act themselves than they would learn from watching others do it.

    (C) conducting one or two simulated interviews will enable them to cope with the real situation with little difficulty.

    (D) a training program must employ methods of a practical nature if the workers are to find anything of lasting value in it.

The correct answer is (B). The best way of teaching a new task is to permit the trainee to perform it under close supervision, correct any errors, and when it is mastered, permit the trainee to work without supervision.

10. A newly appointed worker has been assigned to your crew. Of the following, the best practice to follow with this worker is to

    (A) immediately put the worker with the crew, since laboring requires no special skill.

    (B) allow the worker to do only the type of work he or she claims to be capable of doing until the other jobs can be learned.

    (C) instruct the worker as to how the job should be done before actually starting.

    (D) give the worker the most difficult job, since the best method of learning is by doing.

The correct answer is (C). An effective way to train new workers is to have them do the work under close supervision until they are ready to perform it on their own. This is usually preceded by a demonstration on the correct method of performance and is followed by a checkup of the finished product.

11. At a training session involving the use of a new piece of equipment, the supervisor, after demonstrating one of the uses of the equipment, calls upon a subordinate to operate it. The subordinate makes several mistakes, but the supervisor says nothing until the operation is completed. Then the supervisor points out the mistakes and once again demonstrates the correct method of operation. The supervisor's method of teaching was

    (A) good, mainly because the subordinate was permitted to complete the operation without frequent interruptions.

    (B) bad, mainly because the subordinate's errors were not corrected immediately.

    (C) good, mainly because the supervisor demonstrated thorough knowledge of the equipment.

    (D) bad, mainly because the supervisor did not call upon other subordinates to correct the errors and demonstrate the correct method of operation.

The correct answer is (B). For best and most lasting results, all errors made by workers should be corrected immediately, especially during the training process. The actions of the supervisor in this training session were indeed faulty.

12. To carry out an order most effectively, it is important that a worker

    (A) be aware of the reasons for the order and understand his or her exact role in the department's organizational structure.

    (B) know what the order is about and be convinced of the necessity for the order.

    (C) respect the superior's authority and have confidence in the superior's ability.

    (D) understand the order thoroughly and have the necessary skills to carry it out.

The correct answer is (D). Every worker must thoroughly understand all orders. Otherwise, the worker cannot perform the job effectively.

13. In conducting a meeting to pass along information to subordinates, a supervisor may talk without giving subordinates the opportunity to interrupt. This method is called one-way communication. On the other hand, the supervisor may talk to subordinates and give them the opportunity to ask questions or make comments during the talk. This method is called two-way communication. It would be more desirable for the supervisor to use two-way communication rather than one-way communication at a meeting when the primary purpose is to

    (A) avoid open criticism of any mistake made during the meeting.

    (B) conduct the meeting in an orderly fashion.

(C) pass along information quickly.

(D) transmit information that must be clearly understood.

The correct answer is (D). A supervisor must permit subordinates to ask questions on material in order for it to be thoroughly understood. In the absence of this opportunity, subordinates could not be held responsible for work performance because they were not afforded the opportunity to clear up any questionable matter. This could be used as an excuse for poor work performance.

14. A worker tries hard, but his work is still not up to that of the other employees. This worker most probably needs

(A) a sharp reprimand.

(B) a medical examination.

(C) transfer to another section where standards aren't as high.

(D) more training.

The correct answer is (D). The worker is willing enough. Therefore the poor work must be due to insufficient training.

15. A supervisor should acquaint a new worker about all of the following matters EXCEPT the

(A) correct use of tools and equipment.

(B) dangers of the job.

(C) departmental rules and regulations as they affect the worker.

(D) peculiarities of coworkers.

The correct answer is (D). A new employee, while undergoing orientation, should not be told of the peculiarities of the people in the organization. These things will be found out soon enough. This information is certainly not essential to getting the employee started.

16. A four-step method of training is widely used to train unskilled people on new jobs quickly. The proper order in which to use the four steps for training unskilled workers is

(A) (1) Tell the worker how, (2) Show the worker how, (3) Let the worker try the job, and (4) Check the worker's work.

(B) (1) Check the worker's work, (2) Tell the worker how, (3) Show the worker how, and (4) Let the worker try the job.

(C) (1) Let the worker try the job, (2) Tell the worker how, (3) Show the worker how, and (4) Check the worker's work.

(D) (1) Show the worker how, (2) Tell the worker how, (3) Let the worker try the job, and (4) Check the worker's work.

The correct answer is (A). These four steps constitute the ideal method for training workers in job performance. Previous experience is not taken into consideration here.

17. The one of the following methods of instructing workers in the discharge of their duties that a supervisor would find *least* valuable is to

(A) construct a hypothetical case that might possibly occur and then discuss the solution with the workers.

(B) discuss the weaknesses of each worker at unit meetings.

(C) observe the errors each worker makes in handling the work and then discuss these errors with each worker individually.

(D) refer workers to the proper procedure or section of the manual when it appears that its application might be required.

The correct answer is (B). It is never a good training process to have an individual's mistakes pointed out and corrected before a group. This should be done on an individual basis and in private. This question requires the *least* valuable method; choices (C) and (D) illustrate very good training procedures, and choice (A) contains an acceptable but inadequate training procedure.

18. After having given a subordinate an assignment, a supervisor returns and notices that the subordinate has not done the work according to instructions. The *first* thing that the supervisor should try to discover is whether the subordinate

    (A) dislikes this type of assignment.
    (B) had ever done anything similar before.
    (C) had understood the instructions given.
    (D) is a willing worker, but often incompetent.

The correct answer is (C). Perhaps the reason for the subordinate using a different method than the one ordered by the supervisor was that the subordinate had misunderstood instructions. This in itself would require no action other than a session of retraining. If the reason for the choice of work performance was other than a misunderstanding, more stringent disciplinary action might be called for.

19. A member of your crew was absent on a day when you instructed the crew in the use of a new piece of motorized equipment that can be dangerous if improperly operated. To acquaint this worker with the use of the machine, it would be most desirable for you as a supervisor to

    (A) give the worker the manufacturer's instruction booklet to study, after which the equipment could be used.
    (B) have the worker observe the other crew members using this equipment before operating it.
    (C) advise the worker to observe special caution in using the machine.
    (D) teach the worker about the machine the next time it is used.

The correct answer is (D). The key to the answer to this question is that a dangerous situation may be created if the equipment is not properly used. Therefore this employee must be instructed in the proper use of the equipment as soon as possible, which will probably be the next time it is put into operation.

20. As a supervisor, you realize that a certain member of the crew is very quick in understanding instructions and in learning how to perform different jobs. Concerning this crew member, you as a supervisor, should

    (A) devote as much time in instructing this individual as the other crew members.
    (B) spend only as much time as required to teach the employee the various jobs.
    (C) make it a practice to give the employee a much greater number of jobs.
    (D) be especially pleasant to this employee who is such a valuable member of the crew.

The correct answer is (B). Unnecessary training is costly. It is rare that any two people would take exactly the same time to grasp something. Only devote enough time to a trainee to permit the proper learning of the job.

21. A supervisor, while instructing workers on a new procedure, asked at frequent intervals whether any member of the crew had any questions. Asking for questions in such a situation is

    (A) bad, mainly because quite often silly or inappropriate questions are asked.

    (B) good, mainly because it secures the fullest participation of the crew in the learning process.

    (C) bad, mainly because the supervisor shows a lack of certainty about the procedure being taught.

    (D) good, mainly because it may reveal matters that are not fully understood by the crew.

The correct answer is (D). A supervisor has no way of knowing whether or not instructions are being understood by subordinates unless questions are asked at frequent intervals. The supervisor should display a manner that encourages questions, no matter how elementary they may seem.

22. Suppose you are going to train your staff on a new piece of equipment. In planning your course of instruction, to which of the following questions should you give *first* consideration?

    (A) Exactly what do I want the staff to learn in this course?

    (B) How much time should I devote to this instruction?

    (C) What assistance can I get in running this training course?

    (D) What is the background of the employees whom I will instruct?

The correct answer is (A). The first step in the formation of a training procedure is the determination of just what the training is intended to teach. All other considerations will result from the first—such as what method should be used, how long should the course take, when should it be given, who should give it, etc.

23. If a subordinate complained to you, a supervisor, that your evaluation of his or her work is too low, the most appropriate action for you to take *first* is to

    (A) explain how you arrived at your evaluation.

    (B) point out how some coworkers are able to achieve satisfactory evaluations of their work.

    (C) remind the subordinate of the right of appeal.

    (D) show the subordinate specifically how both the quality and quantity of work can be improved.

The correct answer is (A). When a subordinate has a complaint about a low evaluation of his or her work by the supervisor, the supervisor should arrange for a meeting to explain the basis for the rating and just where the worker's performance is in need of improvement.

24. Suppose that work by your employees in the field is sometimes delayed because they wait for you to arrive to make certain decisions before continuing with their work. As a supervisor, this should indicate to you the need for

    (A) breaking up job assignments into smaller units.

    (B) developing more initiative in your workers.

    (C) having the employees select someone to be in charge if you are not there.

    (D) issuing complete instructions if you know you are going to be away.

The correct answer is (B). Workers who wait around doing nothing because they have not been told what to do next are lacking initiative. When one aspect of a total job is completed, workers would have at least an idea of what they are to do next and should make an attempt to do it.

25. Suppose that you are instructing a worker about a new procedure. The worker appears to be puzzled, but does not ask you any questions. Of the following, the best way to make sure that the worker understands the procedure is to

    (A) ask the worker to explain the new procedure to you.

    (B) carefully check on the way your instructions are carried out.

    (C) repeat the procedure slowly and carefully, emphasizing the most important points.

    (D) rephrase the instructions using different words.

The correct answer is (A). If you are not sure that a worker you are training is absorbing the material, the most effective means of finding out is to question the worker frequently during the instruction period.

26. Several times during a training lecture, a supervisor repeats the main points of the lecture using different words. This training technique is most advisable when

    (A) one trainee in the group is slower to learn than the others.

    (B) the amount of material to be covered in the session would not ordinarily use up the time available for the lecture.

    (C) the average trainee in the group appears to find the material being presented difficult to grasp.

    (D) the supervisor is not too sure about the subject matter.

The correct answer is (C). The lecture method of training does not present a suitable situation for questioning the participants. Consequently, if there is any doubt about being understood, it would be wise for the supervisor to repeat the material as often as is necessary and in language as simple as possible for complete understanding.

27. Some supervisors encourage their workers to submit a list of their questions about specific cases or their comments about problems they wish to discuss in advance of the worker-supervisor conference. This practice is

    (A) desirable, chiefly because it helps to stimulate and focus the worker's thinking about the caseload.

    (B) undesirable, chiefly because it will stifle the worker's free expression of problems and attitudes.

    (C) desirable, chiefly because it will allow the conference to move along more smoothly and quickly.

    (D) undesirable, chiefly because it will restrict the scope of the conference and the variety of cases discussed.

The correct answer is (A). This should first be evaluated as a desirable practice. Therefore the answer is narrowed to choices (A) or (C). Although choice (C) is true to a certain extent, the reason stated in choice (A) is better. The requirement of submitting a list prior to the conference will stimulate workers to search their records for problems they believe worthy of discussion.

28. Assume that you are the leader of a training conference on supervisory techniques and problems. One of the participants in the conference proposes what you consider to be an unsatisfactory technique for handling the problem under discussion. The one of the following courses of action that you should take in this situation is to

    (A) explain to the participants why the proposed technique is unsatisfactory.

    (B) stimulate the other participants to discuss the appropriateness of the proposed technique.

    (C) proceed immediately to another problem without discussing the proposed technique.

    (D) end further discussion of the problem but explain to the participant in private, after the conference is over, why the proposed technique is unsatisfactory.

The correct answer is (B). The function of a conference leader is to stimulate the participants to contribute ideas along certain predetermined lines. If one of the participants proposes what you, as a conference leader, consider an unsatisfactory performance technique, you should encourage the other participants into a discussion of it and in that way bring out what you think is wrong with the proposal.

29. Supervisors are frequently faced with the necessity of training old employees in new tasks. An employee inexperienced in a task is much more likely to make a mistake than an employee who is experienced in it. In delegating authority to an old employee to perform a new task, a supervisor should generally

    (A) delegate the authority as soon as the subordinate gains minimum competence, allowing him or her to make mistakes that will not do major damage to the client or to the company.

    (B) delegate the authority as soon as the subordinate gains minimum competence, but supervise closely enough so that the subordinate will not have the opportunity to make even minor mistakes.

    (C) make the delegation of authority dependent upon the importance that the client places upon the problems involved.

    (D) withhold the authority until the employee has become experienced in performing the task.

The correct answer is (A) and (D). Actually a worker, whether old or new, should not be delegated the authority and responsibility to perform a task until he or she has gained the competence to do it effectively. Choice (A) contains an alternate solution to a widely accepted concept, which can do little or no harm if it is followed.

30. In order to be best able to teach a newly appointed employee who must learn to do a type of unfamiliar work, the supervisor should realize that during this first stage in the learning process the subordinate is generally characterized by

    (A) acute consciousness of self.

    (B) acute consciousness of subject matter, with little interest in people or personalities.

    (C) inertness or passive acceptance of assigned role.

    (D) understanding of problems without understanding of the means of solving them.

The correct answer is (A). Most new employees have a difficult time overcoming self-consciousness while learning a new job. The supervisor who is responsible for the training should attempt to put a worker at ease during the teaching period.

31. A supervisor has been transferred from supervision of one group of units to another group of units in the same center. She spends the first three weeks in her new assignment in getting acquainted with her new subordinates, their problems, and their work. In this process, she notices that some of the records and forms that are submitted to her by two of the subordinates are carelessly or improperly prepared. The best of the following actions for the supervisor to take in this situation is to

    (A) carefully check the work submitted by these subordinates during an additional three weeks before taking any more positive action.

    (B) confer with the offending workers and show each one where her work needs improvement and how to go about achieving it.

    (C) institute an in-service training program specifically designed to solve such a problem and instruct the entire subordinate staff in proper work methods.

    (D) make a note of these errors for documentary use in preparing the annual service rating reports and advise the workers involved to prepare their work more carefully.

The correct answer is (B). The careless and improperly filled out reports that are being submitted to her indicate a need for more training in that area.

32. A choice has to be made between two employees in the selection of a training officer. Employee A, the older of the two, is even-tempered, patient, methodical in work habits, never appears to be in a hurry, and finds time to talk shop with fellow workers. This person did not have the advantage of formal education and progressed to the present high post through hard work and diligent study. Employee B is very intelligent and a fast worker, has had considerable formal education, and is quick to learn anything new. No one has to tell Employee B how to do anything more than once. This employee does good work but seldom talks with fellow workers. Employee B has advanced rapidly in the department, but has spoken of leaving the company for a better paying job. In this situation

    (A) Employee A should be chosen as the training officer because of a greater sense of patience and tact in dealing with the newcomer.

    (B) Employee B should be chosen as the training officer because of the formal education, which will facilitate speaking in a manner that inspires willingness to learn.

    (C) insufficient information is given to make a choice between the two employees as to which one should act as training officer.

    (D) the employee who is most available should be chosen as training officer since both are equally capable of fulfilling the assignment.

The correct answer is (C). A training officer (teacher) must possess certain qualities. The most important of these is the ability to teach, to disseminate knowledge to others. There is no mention of this quality in either employee's description.

33. The one of the following that is *not* an accepted principle governing the effectiveness of learning is that

    (A) trial and error are a part of learning and one should expect that mistakes may be made.

    (B) physical condition definitely affects one's ability to learn.

    (C) learning a task in parts is more lasting than learning a task as a whole.

    (D) intelligence will control, in part only, the rate and permanency of learning.

The correct answer is (C). The concepts in choices (A), (B), and (D) are true and generally accepted in the field of education. The concept in choice (C) is not true. When a task is learned as a whole it will more likely be retained for a longer period of time.

34. One of the tools of the administrator in the performance of the varied functions involving planning and direction is the conference. Of the following, the criterion that is of least importance in determining the effectiveness of a conference after it has been held is the

    (A) amount of disagreement with the decisions reached at the conference.
    (B) positive results achieved at the conference.
    (C) ability to arrive at a full solution to the problem at hand.
    (D) satisfaction of participating members with the conference.

The correct answer is (C). The success of a conference cannot be measured solely on the basis of whether or not a full solution to the problem at hand was reached. Conferences can be deemed successful if some progress was made toward the solution of a problem or if it served to bring to light misunderstandings or misinterpretations. Many conferences can be considered successful solely because they got employees of equal rank together to discuss mutual problems.

35. From an administrative standpoint, an important result that is achieved by training supervisors in their administrative responsibilities is that such training

    (A) lessens the desirability of establishing specialized units.
    (B) permits a higher degree of centralization of the decision-making process.
    (C) permits a higher degree of decentralization of the decision-making process.
    (D) increases the difficulty of delegating authority commensurate with responsibility.

The correct answer is (C). Effective training programs prepare the trainees to be better informed regarding their work and so enable them to make effective decisions on their own.

36. Employees' recommendations as to their training needs are sometimes gathered. The best of the following statements is that this practice

    (A) can generally provide the main, if not the sole, basis for deciding what training should be given.
    (B) is the best way of obtaining completely sound information.
    (C) is worthless, since most information thus obtained is slanted by the individual's personal bias.
    (D) is worthwhile, since it gives employees a sense of participation and self-direction even though all information obtained is not always sound.

The correct answer is (D). This information will probably prove beneficial if it is accepted in the right way. At the least, some good can come out of suggestions from the workers themselves regarding their training needs.

37. In an agency with a high turnover rate and constant new appointments, opportunities for orientation are limited to once every three months due to a shortage of funds for this purpose. Interim instruction on the agency program could be given most economically and uniformly by

    (A) holding unit supervisors responsible for individual instruction of new employees.
    (B) providing new employees with a list of reference texts on the program.
    (C) scheduling voluntary after-hours training classes.
    (D) furnishing new appointees with handbooks explaining the program and aims of the organization.

The correct answer is (D). Although employee handbooks are useful in orienting new employees and are in wide use where formal orientation programs are not practical, they have their limitations and should be used only when absolutely necessary.

38. Although one desirable by-product of an in-service training program is an increase in the morale of the staff, such a program may be so conceived or conducted as to lower morale unintentionally. For example, lowered morale is a most likely result if the training

    (A) failed to be directly related to the promotional plan.
    (B) were conducted during working hours, with the consequent disruption of routine.
    (C) inexplicably excluded certain employees who have responsibilities similar to those of employees included in the program.
    (D) included the use of reports from trainees to measure results.

The correct answer is (C). The situations described in choices (A), (B), and (D) are not likely to affect employee morale. However, if all of the workers in a like classification were not included in a training program and no explanation was offered, the morale of the excluded employees would probably suffer.

39. A training program for workers on work performance should include actual practice in simulated situations under simulated conditions. The one of the following educational principles that is the chief justification for this statement is that

    (A) the workers will remember what they see better and longer than what they read or hear.
    (B) the workers will learn more effectively by actually doing the act themselves than they would learn from watching others do it.
    (C) if the workers to perform the simulated act once or twice, it will enable them to cope with the real situation with little difficulty.
    (D) for the workers to find anything of lasting value in a training program, it must employ materials and methods of a practical nature.

The correct answer is (B). Workers are able to learn to perform a job better if they are permitted to do it themselves, instead of observing others, and then doing it on their own later on.

40. The degree to which first-line subordinate officers will apply the principles they learn at centralized training sessions is principally determined by the degree to which

    (A) the principles are reinforced by follow-up training and evaluation.
    (B) the top echelons support these courses.
    (C) their immediate supervisors apply these principles.
    (D) the principles are useful in solving day-to-day problems.

The correct answer is (C). No matter how much the first-line subordinates are convinced of the validity of the principles they are taught in a training session, they will not be able to utilize them if they are not supported by their superiors when they attempt to implement them.

41. A supervisor is to hold a training session on a new operation that is long and complicated. The one of the following measures that is most important in planning for this training session is to

    (A) reserve sufficient time for the training session so that it can be presented completely and unhurriedly.

    (B) schedule daily repetition of the training session until it is mastered by the group.

    (C) obtain the assistance of experienced members in demonstrating the operation and correcting the performance of members of the group.

    (D) break up the operation into small instructional units and cover one unit at a time.

The correct answer is (D). The most effective method for teaching a complicated procedure is to break it down into its component parts. It is usually best to have one part of the program thoroughly understood by all of the trainees before going on to the next.

42. Several days before conducting a training session on a new tool, a supervisor prepared a detailed job breakdown and distributed copies to members of the crew so that they could become familiar with it beforehand. The main error in the supervisor's procedure was in

    (A) distributing the job breakdown without approval of the superior.

    (B) distributing the job breakdown before, rather than after, conducting the session.

    (C) preparing the job breakdown before conducting the session and ascertaining the points that cause difficulty.

    (D) using the job breakdown as an instruction sheet for the learners rather than a teaching tool for the instructor.

The correct answer is (D). A job breakdown is a tool of a teacher, and it is not wise to let the students examine it before the actual training begins. If they do, they may form wrong impressions before any instruction begins.

43. While giving job instructions on a new tool, a supervisor was asked why the operation was not performed in a different manner. The method suggested included some actions that could cause injury. The supervisor answered that the method being demonstrated was the correct one, that the suggested method was unsafe, and that there was no point in discussing wrong methods. The supervisor's approach to the question was

    (A) proper, mainly because the members will not have the chance to pick up bad habits.

    (B) improper, mainly because the supervisor did not consider the possibility of modifying the suggestion to make it safer.

    (C) proper, mainly because speed of learning is most rapid when only one method is followed.

    (D) improper, mainly because hazards of incorrect methods can be avoided if they are known.

The correct answer is (D). The supervisor's approach was definitely improper. Choice (D) is better than choice (B) mainly because choice (B) contains a fallacious statement that cannot be assumed on the basis of the evidence given. The statement in choice (D) is proper on its own.

44. A supervisor, in an effort to improve training results, made a training progress table on which were listed the employees in the group and the various skills the supervisor expected to teach in each lesson. As a member performed each task, the supervisor placed a check or cross on the chart that indicated satisfactory or unsatisfactory performance. The use of a training table in this manner is

    (A) desirable, mainly because it enables the supervisor to keep track of the members' progress and the tasks that require additional training.

    (B) undesirable, mainly because it reduces the amount of time available for teaching and observing.

    (C) desirable, mainly because it helps the supervisor to rate subordinates.

    (D) undesirable, mainly because the emphasis is placed on the performance of the parts of the operation rather than on the operation as a whole.

The correct answer is (A). A training progress table as depicted in this question represents an accepted training technique and is widely used in training circles.

45. "An experienced supervisor teaching new employees often overlooks so-called minor points because of his great familiarity with the job. When an instructor takes such points for granted, gaps are left in instruction." Of the following, the best way of preventing this type of oversight is to

    (A) ask the new employees if they have any questions during the explanation and demonstration.

    (B) observe the new employees closely for errors and misconceptions as they perform the operation.

    (C) utilize visual aids in demonstrating the operation.

    (D) break down the operation into simple parts when planning the lesson.

The correct answer is (D). The situation described in this question presents a considerable weakness in the training process. Minor points should not be overlooked in the training of personnel. Nothing should be taken for granted. When an operation is broken down into simple parts, there is little likelihood that an important aspect will be overlooked.

46. The most accurate of the following principles of education and learning for a supervisor to keep in mind when planning a training program for assistant supervisors is that

    (A) assistant supervisors, like all other individuals, vary in the rate at which they learn new material and in the degree to which they can retain what they do learn.

    (B) experienced assistant supervisors who have the same basic college education and work experience will be able to learn new material at approximately the same rate of speed.

    (C) the speed with which assistant supervisors can learn new material after the age of 40 is half as rapid as at ages 20–30.

    (D) with regard to any specific task, it is easier and takes less time to break an experienced assistant supervisor of old, unsatisfactory work habits than it is to teach new, acceptable ones.

The correct answer is (A). The ability to absorb education and training varies from person to person. An effective training program will make provision for this and will provide more time for training those in need of it.

47. Assume that you are a supervisor and that you are planning to train a group of experienced subordinates in certain specific skills that they need in their daily work. The one of the following methods that may generally be expected to be most valuable in ascertaining the effectiveness of the training program is to

    (A) administer an objective examination to these subordinates prior to conducting the training program and an equivalent form of the examination after the program and compare the results.

    (B) evaluate and compare the work records of these subordinates with regard to these skills prior to, and after completion of, the training program.

    (C) hold a staff meeting with the subordinates after the training program is completed and allow them to discuss frankly their opinions of the values they derived from the various parts of the training.

    (D) prepare an objective and detailed questionnaire covering the program, have the subordinates answer without identifying themselves, and analyze the answers given.

The correct answer is (B). The most effective method for the evaluation of a training program is the comparison of the trainees' work before and after they have undergone the training.

48. One of your employees requests an above-standard service rating. This person's work has been good, but it has not been above standard. Your answer should be that

    (A) while the employee has done good work, the work has not been above standard in your judgment.

    (B) if you put in a recommendation for an above-standard service rating for one employee, you will have to do the same thing for most of the others in your crew.

    (C) you cannot discuss the matter with the employee but that you will discuss it with your superior.

    (D) you will speak to the others in the crew and you will recommend a higher service rating if there are no objections.

The correct answer is (A). If a subordinate believes he is entitled to an above-standard service rating and the supervisor does not, the supervisor should tell the subordinate the specific reason for not believing the subordinate is entitled to the higher rating.

49. A supervisor must consider many factors in evaluating a worker whom he or she has supervised for a considerable time. In evaluating the capacity of such a worker to use independent judgment, the one of the following to which the supervisor should generally give most consideration is the worker's

    (A) capacity to establish good relationships with people.

    (B) educational background.

    (C) emotional stability.

    (D) quality and judgment as shown by the subordinate in previous work situations known to the supervisor.

The correct answer is (D). The only effective way for a supervisor to evaluate the judgment of a subordinate is by reviewing previous occasions when the subordinate exercised independent judgment.

50. The supervisor's main objective in holding an evaluation conference with a subordinate whose performance must be rated is to

    (A) give the subordinate an opportunity to voice objections to the evaluation.
    (B) provide the superior with a basis for evaluating the subordinate's knowledge of the job.
    (C) provide an opportunity for the superior to discuss the subordinate's strengths and weaknesses.
    (D) enable the supervisor to train the subordinate in areas in which deficiency has been demonstrated.

The correct answer is (C). This meeting can provide the basis of an understanding between the supervisor and the worker as to just what areas of work can be improved and just how the worker can go about improving them. It should always begin with the supervisor praising the employee for any deserved superior work performance. This praise will serve to "lower the barriers" between the two.

51. The employee who performs all or the greater portion of job responsibilities in a satisfactory manner is considered standard in performance. Of the following, the factor that is not significant in choosing between a standard evaluation or a below-standard evaluation for a particular employee is

    (A) the employee's growth potential in terms of the ability to handle duties that pertain to a higher level position.
    (B) potential for improvement in areas where the employee is deficient.
    (C) the extent of supervision necessary for satisfactory performance.
    (D) the employee's work habits and adherence to the rules of the agency.

The correct answer is (A). Employees are rated on what they actually do rather than on what they should be doing according to the title held. Growth potential is not supposed to be taken into consideration.

PART FOUR

Sample Practice Examinations

ANSWER SHEET
FOR
SAMPLE PRACTICE EXAMINATION I

1 Ⓐ Ⓑ Ⓒ Ⓓ	11 Ⓐ Ⓑ Ⓒ Ⓓ	21 Ⓐ Ⓑ Ⓒ Ⓓ	31 Ⓐ Ⓑ Ⓒ Ⓓ
2 Ⓐ Ⓑ Ⓒ Ⓓ	12 Ⓐ Ⓑ Ⓒ Ⓓ	22 Ⓐ Ⓑ Ⓒ Ⓓ	32 Ⓐ Ⓑ Ⓒ Ⓓ
3 Ⓐ Ⓑ Ⓒ Ⓓ	13 Ⓐ Ⓑ Ⓒ Ⓓ	23 Ⓐ Ⓑ Ⓒ Ⓓ	33 Ⓐ Ⓑ Ⓒ Ⓓ
4 Ⓐ Ⓑ Ⓒ Ⓓ	14 Ⓐ Ⓑ Ⓒ Ⓓ	24 Ⓐ Ⓑ Ⓒ Ⓓ	34 Ⓐ Ⓑ Ⓒ Ⓓ
5 Ⓐ Ⓑ Ⓒ Ⓓ	15 Ⓐ Ⓑ Ⓒ Ⓓ	25 Ⓐ Ⓑ Ⓒ Ⓓ	35 Ⓐ Ⓑ Ⓒ Ⓓ
6 Ⓐ Ⓑ Ⓒ Ⓓ	16 Ⓐ Ⓑ Ⓒ Ⓓ	26 Ⓐ Ⓑ Ⓒ Ⓓ	36 Ⓐ Ⓑ Ⓒ Ⓓ
7 Ⓐ Ⓑ Ⓒ Ⓓ	17 Ⓐ Ⓑ Ⓒ Ⓓ	27 Ⓐ Ⓑ Ⓒ Ⓓ	37 Ⓐ Ⓑ Ⓒ Ⓓ
8 Ⓐ Ⓑ Ⓒ Ⓓ	18 Ⓐ Ⓑ Ⓒ Ⓓ	28 Ⓐ Ⓑ Ⓒ Ⓓ	38 Ⓐ Ⓑ Ⓒ Ⓓ
9 Ⓐ Ⓑ Ⓒ Ⓓ	19 Ⓐ Ⓑ Ⓒ Ⓓ	29 Ⓐ Ⓑ Ⓒ Ⓓ	39 Ⓐ Ⓑ Ⓒ Ⓓ
10 Ⓐ Ⓑ Ⓒ Ⓓ	20 Ⓐ Ⓑ Ⓒ Ⓓ	30 Ⓐ Ⓑ Ⓒ Ⓓ	40 Ⓐ Ⓑ Ⓒ Ⓓ

SAMPLE PRACTICE EXAMINATION I

Directions: Each question has four suggested answers, (A), (B), (C), and (D). Decide which one is the best answer, and on the answer sheet find the question number that corresponds to the answer that you have selected and darken the area with a soft pencil.

The time allowed for the entire examination is 4 hours.

1. For the measurement of net income to be as realistic as possible, it is desirable that revenue be recognized at the point that

   (A) cash is collected from customers.
   (B) an order for merchandise or services is received from a customer.
   (C) a deposit or advance payment is received from a customer.
   (D) goods are delivered or services are rendered to customers.

2. An accounting principle must receive substantial authoritative support to qualify as "generally accepted." Many organizations and agencies have been influential in the development of generally accepted accounting principles, but the most influential leadership has come from the

   (A) New York Stock Exchange.
   (B) American Institute of Certified Public Accountants.
   (C) Securities and Exchange Commission.
   (D) American Accounting Association.

3. In which one of the following ways does the declaration and payment of a cash dividend affect corporate net income?

   (A) It does not affect net income.
   (B) It reduces net income.
   (C) It increases net income.
   (D) It capitalizes net income.

4. Under which one of the following headings of the corporate balance sheet should the liability for a dividend payable in stock appear?

   (A) Current Liabilities
   (B) Long Term Liabilities
   (C) Stockholders' Equity
   (D) Current Assets

5. In which one of the following is "Working Capital" most likely to be found?

   (A) In "Income Statement"
   (B) In "Analysis of Retained Earnings"
   (C) In "Computation of Cost of Capital"
   (D) In "Statement of Funds Provided and Applied"

6. Which of the following procedures is not generally mandatory in auditing a merchandising corporation?

   (A) Physical observation of inventory count
   (B) Written circularization of accounts receivable
   (C) Confirmation of bank balance
   (D) Circularization of the stockholders

7. A company purchased office supplies during 2001 in the total amount of $1,400 and charged the entire amount to the asset account. An inventory of supplies taken on December 31, 2001, shows the cost of unused supplies to be $250. The entry to record this fact, assuming the books have not been closed, involves

   (A) credit to capital.
   (B) debit to supplies expense.
   (C) credit to supplies expense.
   (D) debit to supplies on hand.

8. A corporation's records show $600,000 (credit) in net sales; $200,000 (debit) in year-end accounts receivable; and a $2,000 (debit) in Allowance for Bad Debts. The company's aged schedule of accounts receivable indicates a probable future loss from failure to collect year-end receivables in the amount of $6,000. Of the following, the most correct entry to adjust the Allowance for Bad Debts at year-end is

   (A) $1,000 credit.
   (B) $4,000 credit.
   (C) $8,000 debit.
   (D) $8,000 credit.

Answer questions 9 and 10 on the basis of the information given below.

A company commenced business in 2001and purchased inventory as follows:

March	100 units	@	$5	$	500
June	300 units	@	6		1,800
October	200 units	@	7		1,400
November	500 units	@	7		3,500
December	100 units	@	6		600
Total	1,200 units		Total	$	7,800

Units sold in 2001 amounted to 900.

9. Under the LIFO inventory principle, the value of the remaining inventory is

(A) $1,700
(B) $1,950
(C) $2,000
(D) $2,050

10. Under the FIFO inventory principle, the value of the remaining inventory is

(A) $1,700
(B) $1,950
(C) $2,000
(D) $2,050

11. When doing a trial balance, assume that as a result of a single error, the total of the credit balances is greater than the total of the debit balances. Which one of the following single errors could be the cause of this discrepancy?

(A) Failure to post a debit
(B) Posting a debit as a credit
(C) Failure to post a credit
(D) Posting a credit twice

Answer questions 12 and 13 on the basis of the information given below.

A and B are partners with capital balances of $20,000 and $30,000 respectively at June 30, 2001, who share profits and losses 40% and 60% respectively. On July 1, 2001, C is to be admitted into the partnership under the following conditions:

Partnership assets are to be revalued and increased by $10,000.

C is to invest $40,000 but be credited for $30,000, while the remaining $10,000 is to be credited to A and B to compensate them for their preexisting goodwill.

12. After C is admitted and the proper entries are made, A's capital account will have a credit balance of

(A) $20,000
(B) $28,000
(C) $32,000
(D) $42,000

13. After the admission of C to the partnership, C's share of profits and losses is agreed upon at 20%. Assuming no other adjustments, the new percentage for profit and loss distribution to A will be

(A) 20%
(B) 32%
(C) 33.3%
(D) 40%

14. A company reports as income for tax purposes $70,000 and its book income before the provision for income taxes is $100,000. Assuming a 50% tax rate, the proper tax expense to be recorded following tax allocation procedures is

(A) $30,000
(B) $35,000
(C) $50,000
(D) none of the above.

15. The relationship between the total of cash and current receivables to total current liabilities is commonly referred to by accountants as the

(A) acid-test ratio.
(B) cross-statement ratio.
(C) current ratio.
(D) R.O.I. ratio.

16. On a statement of sources and application of funds, the depreciation expense is normally shown as a(n)

(A) addition to operating income.
(B) subtraction from funds provided.
(C) addition to funds applied.
(D) reduction from operating income.

17. The one of the following is *not* advisable for a supervisor to do when dealing with individual employees is to

(A) recognize a person's outstanding service as well as his/her mistakes.
(B) help an employee satisfy his/her need to excel.
(C) encourage an efficient employee to seek better opportunities even if this action may cause the supervisor to lose a good worker.
(D) take public notice of an employee's mistakes so that fewer errors will be made in the future.

18. Suppose that you are an Accountant in a department where you are given the responsibility for teaching seven new Assistant Accountants a number of routine procedures that all Assistant Accountants should know. Of the following, the best method for you to follow in teaching these procedures is to

 (A) separate the slower learners from the faster learners, and adapt your presentation to their level of ability.
 (B) instruct all the new employees in a group without attempting to assess differences in learning rates.
 (C) restrict your approach to giving them detailed written instructions in order to save time.
 (D) avoid giving the employees written instructions in order to force them to memorize job procedures quickly.

19. Suppose that you are an Accountant to whom several Assistant Accountants must hand in work for review. You notice that one of the Assistant Accountants gets very upset whenever you discover an error in his work, although all of the Assistants make mistakes from time to time. Of the following, it would be best for you to

 (A) arrange discreetly for the employee's work to be reviewed by another Accountant.
 (B) ignore his reaction since giving attention to such behavior increases its intensity.
 (C) suggest that the employee seek medical help since he has such great difficulty in accepting normal criticism.
 (D) try to build the employee's self-confidence by emphasizing those parts of his work that are done well.

20. Suppose you are an Accountant responsible for supervising a number of Assistant Accountants in a city agency where each Assistant Accountant receives a manual of policies and procedures when he first reports for work. You have been asked to teach your subordinates a new procedure that requires knowledge of several items of policy and procedure found in the manual. The one of the following techniques that it would be best for you to employ is to

 (A) give verbal instructions, which include a review of the appropriate standard procedures as well as an explanation of new tasks.
 (B) give individual instruction restricted to the new procedure to each Assistant Accountant as the need arises.
 (C) provide written instructions for new procedural elements and refer employees to their manuals for explanation of standard procedures.
 (D) ask employees to review appropriate sections of their manual and then explain those aspects of the new procedure that the manual did not cover.

21. Suppose that you are an Accountant in charge of a unit in which changes in work procedures are about to be instituted. The one of the following that you, as the supervisor, should anticipate as being most likely to occur during the changeover is

 (A) a temporary rise in production because of interest in the new procedures.
 (B) uniform acceptance of these procedures on the part of your staff.
 (C) varying interpretations of the new procedures by your staff.
 (D) general agreement among staff members that the new procedures are advantageous.

22. Company A owns 100% of the capital stock of Company B and reports on a consolidated basis. During the year, Company A sold inventory to Company B at a profit of $100,000. Company B has sold one half of this inventory at year-end to the public. Which one of the following would be the most correct adjustment, if any, to make the consolidated retained earnings conform to generally accepted accounting principles?

 (A) Decrease by $50,000
 (B) Increase by $50,000
 (C) Increase by $100,000
 (D) No adjustment

23. X, Y, and Z are partners with capital of $11,000, $12,000, and $4,500. X has a loan due from the partnership to him of $2,000. Profits and losses are shared in the ratio of 4:5:1 respectively. The partnership has paid off all outside liabilities, and its remaining assets consist of $9,000 in cash and $20,500 of accounts receivable. The partners agree to disburse the $9,000 to themselves in such a way that, even if none of the receivables is realized, no partner will have been overpaid. Under these conditions, which of the following most nearly represents the amount to be paid to partner X?

 (A) $1,800
 (B) $3,600
 (C) $4,800
 (D) $5,600

24. R Company needs $2,000,000 to finance an expansion of plant facilities. The company expects to earn a return of 15% on this investment before considering the cost of capital or income taxes. The average income tax rate for the R Company is 40%. If the company raises the funds by issuing 6% bonds at face value, the earnings available to common stockholders after the new plant facilities are in operation may be expected to increase by

(A) $60,000
(B) $72,000
(C) $108,000
(D) $180,000

25. The budget for a given factory overhead cost was $150,000 for the year. The actual cost for the year was $125,000. Based on these facts, it can be said that the plant manager has done a better job than expected in controlling this cost if the cost is a

(A) semi-variable cost.
(B) variable cost and actual production was 83 ⅓ % of budgeted production.
(C) semi-variable cost, which includes a fixed element of $25,000 per period.
(D) variable cost and actual production was equal to budgeted production.

26. The Home Office account on the books of the City Branch shows a credit balance of $15,000 at the end of a year and the City Branch account on the books of the Home Office shows a debit balance of $12,000. Of the following, the most likely reason for the discrepancy in the two accounts is that the

(A) branch has not recorded merchandise shipped by the Home Office to the branch.
(B) Home Office has not recorded a branch loss for the first quarter of the year.
(C) branch has just mailed a check for $3,000 to the Home Office that has not yet been received by the Home Office.
(D) Home Office has not yet recorded the branch profit for the first quarter of the year.

27. The concept of matching costs and revenues means that

(A) the expenses offset against revenues should be related to the same time period.
(B) revenues are at least as great as expenses on the average.
(C) revenues and expenses are equal.
(D) net income equals revenues minus expenses for the same earning period.

28. If the inventory at the end of the current year is understated, and the error is not caught during the following year, the effect is to

(A) overstate the income for the two-year period.
(B) overstate income this year and understate income next year.
(C) understate income this year and overstate income next year.
(D) understate income this year, with no effect on the income of the next year.

Answer questions 29 and 30 on the basis of the information given below.

INVESTMENT ACCOUNT

Date	Explanation	Shares	Amount	Date	Explanation	Shares	Amount
1/7/99	Cash purchase	250	$27,000	2000	Cash Dividends		$ 5,000
12/1/01	2-for-1 Split	250	$27,000*	4/15/01	Proceeds of Sale	125	26,000
				12/31/01	Balance	375	$23,000
		Total	$54,000			Total	$54,000
1/1/02	Balance	375	$23,000				

*This amount is a result of the following entry:

Debit - Investment Account	$27,000	
Credit - Investment Income		$27,000

In addition to the above information, you are informed that a stock dividend of 125 shares was received on January 1, 2001, but had not been recorded. All of these transactions are related to the investment in stock of the same corporation.

29. The correct dollar balance of the investment account on December 31, 2001, should be

    (A) $13,000
    (B) $18,000
    (C) $28,000
    (D) none of the above.

30. The correct number of shares owned on December 31, 2001 was

    (A) 375
    (B) 500
    (C) 625
    (D) 750

31. During a period of rising prices, the inventory pricing method that might be expected to give the lowest net income on the income statement is

    (A) FIFO.
    (B) LIFO.
    (C) Weighted-Average cost.
    (D) Lower of Cost or Market (cost on a FIFO basis).

32. Drew Corporation bought land for $100,000. The land was subject to delinquent property taxes of $6,900. The Drew Corporation immediately paid these delinquent taxes and also paid interest charges and penalties in the amount of $625 related to the delinquent taxes. The land was immediately placed in use as a parking lot. During the first year of use, the property taxes amounted to $1,800. The cost of the land should be recorded on the books as

    (A) $100,000
    (B) $106,900
    (C) $107,525
    (D) $109,325

33. Which of the following series of accounts are among those that will appear on a statement of Cost of Goods Manufactured?

    (A) Freight-in on raw materials, ending inventory of goods in process, indirect labor, purchase discounts on raw materials
    (B) Goods in process inventory, factory supplies used, sales of manufactured goods, property tax expense
    (C) Raw materials purchased, finished goods inventory, depreciation on factory machinery
    (D) Direct labor, sales commission on manufactured products, factory building occupancy costs

34. Standard costing will produce the same cost of goods sold as actual costing when the cost variances are

    (A) treated as income or expense items.
    (B) allocated to the Cost of Goods Sold and ending inventories.
    (C) reported in the Balance Sheet as a deferred charge or deferred credit.
    (D) closed to Cost of Goods Sold account.

35. A job-order cost system would be appropriate in the manufacture of

    (A) paints.
    (B) custom-made furniture.
    (C) breakfast cereals.
    (D) standard grade of plywood.

36. Suppose that an Accountant and one of the Assistant Accountants under his supervision are known to be friends who play golf together on weekends. The maintenance of such a friendship on the part of the supervisor is generally

    (A) acceptable as long as this Assistant Accountant continues to perform his duties satisfactorily.
    (B) unacceptable since the supervisor will find it difficult to treat the Assistant Accountant as a subordinate.
    (C) acceptable if the supervisor does not favor this Assistant Accountant above other employees.
    (D) unacceptable because the other Assistant Accountants will resent the friendship regardless of the supervisor's behavior on the job.

37. Suppose that you are an Accountant assigned to review the financial records of a City agency that has recently undergone a major reorganization. Which of the following would be best for you to do *first*?

    (A) Interview the individual in charge of agency financial operations to determine whether the organizational changes affect the system of financial review.
    (B) Discuss the nature of the reorganization with your own supervisor to anticipate and plan a new financial review procedure.
    (C) Carry out the financial review as usual, and adjust your methods to any problems arising from the reorganization.
    (D) Request a written report from the agency head explaining the nature of the reorganization and recommending changes in the system of financial review.

38. Suppose that a newly assigned Accountant finds that he must delegate some of his duties to subordinates in order to get the work done. Which one of the following would *not* be a block to his delegating these duties effectively?

    (A) Inability to give proper directions as to what he wants done
    (B) Reluctance to take calculated risks
    (C) Lack of trust in his subordinates
    (D) Retaining ultimate responsibility for the delegated work

39. An Accountant sometimes performs the staff function of preparing and circulating reports among Bureau Chiefs. Which of the following is *least* important as an objective in designing and writing such reports?

    (A) Providing relevant information on past, present, and future actions
    (B) Modifying his language in order to insure goodwill among the Bureau Chiefs
    (C) Helping the readers of the report to make appropriate decisions
    (D) Summarizing important information to help readers see trends or outstanding points

40. Suppose you are an Accountant assigned to prepare a report to be read by all Bureau Chiefs in your agency. The most important reason for avoiding highly technical accounting terminology in writing this report is to

    (A) ensure the accuracy and relevancy of the text.
    (B) insure winning the readers' cooperation.
    (C) make the report more interesting to the readers.
    (D) make it easier for the readers to understand.

ANSWER KEY

1. D	9. A	17. D	25. D	33. A
2. B	10. C	18. B	26. D	34. B
3. A	11. C	19. D	27. A	35. B
4. C	12. B	20. A	28. C	36. C
5. D	13. B	21. C	29. B	37. A
6. D	14. C	22. A	30. B	38. D
7. B	15. A	23. C	31. B	39. B
8. D	16. A	24. C	32. C	40. D

ANSWER SHEET
FOR
SAMPLE PRACTICE EXAMINATION II

1 Ⓐ Ⓑ Ⓒ Ⓓ	11 Ⓐ Ⓑ Ⓒ Ⓓ	21 Ⓐ Ⓑ Ⓒ Ⓓ	31 Ⓐ Ⓑ Ⓒ Ⓓ
2 Ⓐ Ⓑ Ⓒ Ⓓ	12 Ⓐ Ⓑ Ⓒ Ⓓ	22 Ⓐ Ⓑ Ⓒ Ⓓ	32 Ⓐ Ⓑ Ⓒ Ⓓ
3 Ⓐ Ⓑ Ⓒ Ⓓ	13 Ⓐ Ⓑ Ⓒ Ⓓ	23 Ⓐ Ⓑ Ⓒ Ⓓ	33 Ⓐ Ⓑ Ⓒ Ⓓ
4 Ⓐ Ⓑ Ⓒ Ⓓ	14 Ⓐ Ⓑ Ⓒ Ⓓ	24 Ⓐ Ⓑ Ⓒ Ⓓ	34 Ⓐ Ⓑ Ⓒ Ⓓ
5 Ⓐ Ⓑ Ⓒ Ⓓ	15 Ⓐ Ⓑ Ⓒ Ⓓ	25 Ⓐ Ⓑ Ⓒ Ⓓ	35 Ⓐ Ⓑ Ⓒ Ⓓ
6 Ⓐ Ⓑ Ⓒ Ⓓ	16 Ⓐ Ⓑ Ⓒ Ⓓ	26 Ⓐ Ⓑ Ⓒ Ⓓ	36 Ⓐ Ⓑ Ⓒ Ⓓ
7 Ⓐ Ⓑ Ⓒ Ⓓ	17 Ⓐ Ⓑ Ⓒ Ⓓ	27 Ⓐ Ⓑ Ⓒ Ⓓ	37 Ⓐ Ⓑ Ⓒ Ⓓ
8 Ⓐ Ⓑ Ⓒ Ⓓ	18 Ⓐ Ⓑ Ⓒ Ⓓ	28 Ⓐ Ⓑ Ⓒ Ⓓ	38 Ⓐ Ⓑ Ⓒ Ⓓ
9 Ⓐ Ⓑ Ⓒ Ⓓ	19 Ⓐ Ⓑ Ⓒ Ⓓ	29 Ⓐ Ⓑ Ⓒ Ⓓ	39 Ⓐ Ⓑ Ⓒ Ⓓ
10 Ⓐ Ⓑ Ⓒ Ⓓ	20 Ⓐ Ⓑ Ⓒ Ⓓ	30 Ⓐ Ⓑ Ⓒ Ⓓ	40 Ⓐ Ⓑ Ⓒ Ⓓ

SAMPLE PRACTICE EXAMINATION II

Directions: Each question has four suggested answers, (A), (B), (C), and (D). Decide which one is the best answer, and on the answer sheet find the question number that corresponds to the answer that you have selected and darken the area with a soft pencil.

The time allowed for the entire examination is 4 hours.

1. With regard to the requirement of the auditing standard that sufficient and competent evidential matter be obtained, the term competent primarily refers to the

   (A) consistency of the evidence.
   (B) relevance of the evidence.
   (C) measurability of evidence.
   (D) dependability of evidence.

2. Audit working papers should *not*

   (A) include any client-prepared papers or documents other than those prepared by the auditor.
   (B) be kept by the auditor after review and completion of the audit, except for items required for the income tax return.
   (C) be submitted to the client to support the financial statements and to provide evidence of the audit work performed.
   (D) by themselves be expected to provide sufficient support for the auditor's operation.

3. Mr. John Shea operates a small drug store in New York City as an individual proprietor. During the past year his books were not kept properly. He asks you, as a CPA, to give him some advice concerning the earnings of his business during the calendar year 2000. A review of his bank accounts and a diary of financial data reveal the information presented below:

   Deposits made during 2000 per bank statements totaled $226,000. Deposits include investments made by Mr. Shea as well as a loan he obtained from the bank for $25,000.

   Disbursements during 2000 per bank statement totaled $185,000. Included are personal withdrawals of $15,000 and payments on debt of $10,000.

   Net Equity of John Shea at January 1, 2000, was determined to be $45,000.

   Net Equity of John Shea at December 31, 2000, was determined to be $75,000.

   During 2000, funds invested by John Shea in the business amounted to $6,500.

   Based upon the "Net Worth" method, net income for the year ended December 31, 2000 was

   (A) $30,000
   (B) $38,500
   (C) $41,000
   (D) $45,000

4. Because of past association, a Senior Accountant is convinced of the competence and honesty of those who prepared the financial information that he is auditing. He consequently concludes that certain verification procedures are unnecessary. This conclusion by the Senior Accountant is ill-advised for the proper performance of his present audit mainly because the

   (A) members of the staff often lack specialized skills and training; without verification, an audit cannot proceed.
   (B) verification procedures depend upon the materiality of the subject matter under examination and not upon the personal characteristics of the individuals involved.
   (C) nature of opinion expressed in the report issued by the Senior Accountant at the end of his audit is grounded on personal considerations.
   (D) quality of the Senior Accountant's independence and his objective examination of the information under review is impaired.

5. Of the following statement ratios, the one that represents a growth ratio is

   (A) working capital ratio.
   (B) acid-test ratio.
   (C) long-term debt to total capitalization.
   (D) dollar earnings per share.

Answer questions 6–8 on the basis of the information given below.

During the course of an examination of the financial statements of a wholesale establishment, the following facts were revealed for the year ended December 31, 2000:

a. Although merchandise inventory costing $3,000 was on hand and was included in the inventory count on December 31, 2000, title had passed and it was billed to the customer on December 31, 2000, at a sale price of $4,500.

b. Merchandise had been billed to the customer on December 31, 2000, in the amount of $5,200 but had not been shipped to him. This merchandise, which cost $3,500, was not included in the inventory at the end of the year. The goods were shipped and title passed on January 15, 2001.

c. Merchandise costing $6,000 was recorded as a purchase on December 31, 2000, but was not included in the inventory at that date.

d. Merchandise costing $5,000 was received on January 3, 2001, but was recorded on the books as of December 31, 2000, and included in inventory as of December 31, 2000. The goods were shipped on December 30, 2000, by the vendor f.o.b. shipping point.

e. An examination of receiving records indicated that merchandise costing $7,000 was received on December 31, 2000. It was included in inventory as of that date but not recorded as a purchase.

6. Adjustments to correct the inventory figure will reflect a net adjustment so as to

(A) reduce it by $5,000.
(B) increase it by $6,500.
(C) reduce it by $8,000.
(D) increase it by $10,000.

7. Adjustments to correct the sales figure will result in a net adjustment to sales of a(n)

(A) increase by $3,000.
(B) decrease by $5,200.
(C) increase by $6,300.
(D) decrease by $4,510.

8. The net adjustment to purchases for the period ending December 31, 2000, will result in a(n)

(A) increase of $2,000.
(B) decrease of $5,000.
(C) increase of $7,000.
(D) increase of $12,000.

Answer questions 9 and 10 on the basis of the information given below.

A company worth $500,000 of common capital stock, par value $100 per share, with retained earnings of $100,000, decides to change its capitalization from a par to a no-par basis. Therefore, it called in its 5,000 shares of par value stock and issued in place thereof 10,000 shares of no-par value stock.

9. The balance in the capital stock account after the change is

(A) $600,000
(B) $500,000
(C) $100,000
(D) $50,000

10. The balance in the retained earnings account after the change is

(A) $50,000
(B) $100,000
(C) $600,000
(D) $5,000,000

11. Among the assets on the December 31, 2000, balance sheet of the Ragof Corporation was the following:

Investment in Lamb Company – 1,000 shares @ $90 bought January 1, 2000	$90,000

The net worth section of the balance sheet of the Lamb Company on the same date was as follows:

Net Worth		
Capital stock, 1,000 shares		$100,000
Deficit January 1, 2000	$ 20,000	
Less Operating Profit 2000	15,000	
Deficit December 31, 2000		–5,000
Total Net Worth		$ 95,000

The net debit or credit to "Consolidated Surplus" arising from consolidation of the Lamb Company with the parent Ragof Corporation is

(A) $2,000 credit.
(B) $8,000 credit.
(C) $9,000 debit.
(D) $10,000 debit.

Answer questions 12–15 on the basis of the information given below.

The following Trial Balances and Notes relate to the books and records of the Apex Corporation:

TRIAL BALANCES (000 Omitted)

	December 31, 2000		December 31, 1999	
	Debit	Credit	Debit	Credit
Cash	$ 178		$ 84	
Accounts Receivable	300		240	
Allowance for Bad Debts		$ 13		$ 10
Merchandise Inventory	370		400	
Building & Equipment	420		360	
Allowance for Depreciation		180		190
Accounts Payable		220		210
Mortgage Bonds		300		300
Unamortized Bond Discount	18		21	
Capital Stock		357		270
Retained Earnings		125		90
Net Sales		$4,200		$4,000
Cost of goods sold	$2,300		$2,100	
Salaries & Wages	1,500		1,400	
Heat & Utilities	110		100	
Depreciation	20		20	
Taxes & Insurance	10		10	
Interest	16		15	
Bad Debts	20		20	
Loss on equipment Sales (Note 1)	6		—	
Dividends paid (Note 2)	127		300	
	$5,395	$5,395	$5,070	$5,070

Notes:

(1) In 2000, equipment costing $40,000 and having a net book value of $10,000 was sold for $4,000.
(2) Dividends paid in 2000 include a stock dividend of $27,000.

12. The net change in working capital from 1999 to 2000 is

(A) $111,000
(B) $140,000
(C) $330,000
(D) $615,000

13. The amount of funds provided from net income for the year ended 12/31/2000 is

(A) $224,000
(B) $244,000
(C) $264,000
(D) $265,000

14. The amount of funds applied to dividends during the year 2000 is

(A) $100,000
(B) $127,000
(C) $165,000
(D) $180,000

15. The amount of funds applied to building and equipment during the year 2000 is

    (A) $100,000
    (B) $60,000
    (C) $40,000
    (D) $20,000

Answer questions 16 and 17 on the basis of the information given below.

The Novelty Sales Company issues gift certificates in denominations of $5, $10, and $25. They are redeemable in merchandise having a markup of 30% of Selling Price.

During December, $35,000 of gift certificates were sold and $20,000 were redeemed. It is estimated that 5% of the certificates issued will never be redeemed.

16. The proper entry to reflect the current liability with respect to these certificates is

    (A) $13,250
    (B) $15,000
    (C) $18,000
    (D) $20,000

17. The cost of the merchandise issued to meet the redeemed certificates is

    (A) $10,000
    (B) $12,000
    (C) $14,000
    (D) $15,000

Answer questions 18 and 19 on the basis of the information given below.

George Smith commenced business in 1999 but did not maintain a complete set of proper records. He relied on the bank statements in order to compute his income. All his receipts are deposited and all his expenditures are made by check.

His bank statements and other records reflected the following:

Bank balance per bank 12/31/1999	$ 14,735
Bank balance per bank 12/31/2000	18,380
Deposits for 2000 per bank statement	209,450
Deposits in transit 12/31/1999	3,590
Deposits in transit 12/31/2000	4,150

Checks returned with the January 2000 bank statement showed a total of $4,770 of checks issued in 1999.

2000 checks not returned by the bank at December 31, 2000, amounted to $5,150.

$6,430 of checks were issued in 2000 in payment of purchases made in 1999.

Mr. Smith made $9,425 of deposits in 1999 representing 1999 sales.

Unpaid bills for 2000 amounted to $2,150 on December 31, 2000.

Accounts Receivable for 2000 on December 31, 2000, were $10,930.

Merchandise inventory figures on the following dates were:

December 31, 1999	$13,000
December 31, 2000	17,580

On July 1, 2000, machinery costing $8,000 was purchased. The estimated life was five years with a salvage value of $500.

18. The balance of the cash in the bank according to the books on December 31, 2000, was

    (A) $19,310
    (B) $17,380
    (C) $16,200
    (D) $15,330

19. The Sales Revenue for 2000 was

    (A) $211,515
    (B) $210,010
    (C) $209,450
    (D) $200,585

Answer questions 20 and 21 on the basis of the information given below.

In the examination of an imprest petty cash fund of $600, you were presented with the following fund composition shown below. The date of examining the petty cash fund was the balance sheet date.

Currency - bills	$310.00
Cash - coins	3.15
Postage stamps	50.00
Sales returns memos for cash refunded to customers	15.50
Check of one employee dated one month in advance	75.00
Vouchers for miscellaneous office expenses	100.85
Sales slips of an employee who purchased company merchandise; the money in payment was taken from the fund, entered as cash sale, and the sales slip inserted in the fund	45.50

20. The corrected balance of petty cash for balance sheet purposes is

    (A) $313.15
    (B) $322
    (C) $310.61
    (D) $485

21. A correcting journal entry to establish the correct fund balance would increase expenses by

    (A) $100.85
    (B) $175.85
    (C) $19.35
    (D) $45.50

22. The primary objective of an "audit," as generally understood in accounting practice, is to

    (A) assert a series of claims for management as to the financial condition of the company.
    (B) establish the reliability or unreliability of the financial statements and supporting accounting records of the company.
    (C) install special procedures involved in the periodic closing of the accounts prior to the preparation of financial statements of the company.
    (D) summarize accounts and financial transactions to determine the costs of processes or units of production for the company.

Answer questions 23–25 on the basis of the information given below.

The following data are related to the business operations for the calendar years 1999, 2000, and 2001 of the Wholesale Corporation:

	1999	2000	2001
Net Income per books	$170,000	$190,000	$140,000
Dividends	15,000	20,000	10,000
Purchases made in year 2000 recorded as purchased in 2001 but recorded in inventory in 2000		25,000	
Inventory value December 31, 2001, underestimated			5,000
Depreciation omitted			
applicable to 1999	3,000		
applicable to 2000		4,500	
applicable to 2001			6,000
Overstatement of prepaid advertising as of January 1, 2000		1,500	
Salaries			
earned during 1999 paid during 2000 no accruals	18,000		
Payroll Taxes on Salaries	1,440		

23. The net profit for 1999 after adjusting for the facts given above is

(A) $146,060
(B) $147,560
(C) $165,500
(D) $167,000

24. The net profit for 2000 after adjusting for facts given above is

(A) $160,500
(B) $162,000
(C) $165,000
(D) $181,440

25. If the balance of the retained earnings account was $265,000 on January 1, 1999, the balance of the retained earnings account on December 31, 2001, after corrections is

(A) $711,500
(B) $573,060
(C) $308,060
(D) $201,060

Each question numbered 26–30 consists of a description of a transaction that indicates a two-fold change on the balance sheet. Each of these transactions may be classified under one of the following categories:

(A) Current Assets are *overstated* and Retained Earnings are *overstated.*
(B) Current Assets are *understated* and Retained Earnings are *understated.*
(C) Current Liabilities are *overstated* and Retained Earnings are *overstated.*
(D) Current Liabilities are *understated* and Retained Earnings are *overstated.*

Examine each question carefully. In the correspondingly numbered row on your answer sheet, mark the appropriate space for the letter preceding the category above that best represents the change that should be made on the balance sheet as of December 31, 2000.

26. Goods shipped on consignment-out were not included in the final inventory, although the entries were properly made for such consignments.

27. A number of cash sales made subsequent to the balance sheet date were recorded as sales in the prior period before the balance sheet date. The merchandise was included in inventories.

28. A cash dividend declared December 21, 2000, payable on January 15, 2001, to stockholders of record as of December 28, 2000, had not been recorded as of December 31, 2000.

29. The provision for the allowance for doubtful accounts receivable for the current period that should have been made had not been recorded.

30. Merchandise received by December 31, 2000, and properly included in inventory on that date, was not entered as a purchase until January 2001.

Answer questions 31–33 on the basis of the information given below.

Ten men work as a group on a particular manufacturing operation. When the weekly production of the group exceeds a standard number of pieces per hour, each man in the group is paid a bonus for the excess production; the bonus is in addition to his wages at the hourly rate. The amount of the bonus is computed by first determining the percentage by which the group's production exceeds the standard. One half of this percentage is then applied to a wage rate of $1.25 to determine an hourly bonus rate. Each man in the group is paid, as a bonus, the bonus rate applied to his total hours worked during the week. The standard rate of production before a bonus can be earned is two hundred pieces per hour.

The production record for a given week was:

	Hours Worked	Production
Monday	72	17,680
Tuesday	72	17,348
Wednesday	72	18,000
Thursday	72	18,560
Friday	71.5	17,888
Saturday	40	9,600
	399.5	99,076

31. The rate of the bonus for the week is

(A) 30%
(B) 24%
(C) 16%
(D) 12%

32. The bonus paid to the 10-man group for the week is

(A) $59.93
(B) $60

(C) $100
(D) $599.25

33. The total wages of one employee who worked 40 hours at a base rate of $1 per hour are

(A) $46
(B) $52
(C) $85
(D) $90

34. A junior accountant reported to his senior that he had performed the operations listed below. Which one of the following statements about these operations correctly describes the operation?

(A) Vouchered the amount of petty cash.
(B) Vouchered the receivables ledger accounts with the Sales Register.
(C) Analyzed the fixed asset account.
(D) Checked all entries in the General Journal to original evidence.

35. Sales during July 2001, for the Lesser Company operating in New York City were $267,500, of which $170,000 was on account. The sales figure presented to you includes the total sales tax charged to retail customers (assume a sales tax rate of 7%). The sales tax liability that should be shown at the end of July 2001, is

(A) $7,500
(B) $10,500
(C) $17,500
(D) $20,000

Answer questions 36 and 37 on the basis of the information given below.

During the audit of records of the Long Corporation for the year ended December 31, 2000, the auditor was presented with the following information:

The finished goods inventory consisted of 22,000 units carried at a cost of $17,600 at December 31, 2000.

The finished goods inventory at the beginning of the year (January 1, 2000) consisted of 24,000 units, priced at a cost of $16,800. During the year, 4,000 units were manufactured at a cost of $3,600, and 6,000 units were sold.

36. To properly reflect the cost of the finished goods inventory at December 31, 2000, if the FIFO method was used, assuming there was no Work-in-Process Inventory, would require an adjustment of

(A) $1,400 credit.
(B) $1,400 debit.
(C) $1,600 credit.
(D) $1,600 debit.

37. To properly reflect the cost of the finished goods inventory at December 31, 2000, if the LIFO method was used, assuming there was no Work-in-Process Inventory, would require an adjustment of

(A) $2,200 debit.
(B) $2,200 credit.
(C) $4,200 credit.
(D) $4,200 debit.

38. Within the general field of auditing, there are internal auditors and independent auditors who differ significantly from one another in that the latter group

(A) is responsible for a more complete, detailed examination of accounting data.
(B) conduct "standard" audits established by custom end usage for a particular trade or industry.
(C) direct their investigations primarily to matters of fraud and criminal misrepresentation.
(D) issue reports for the benefit of other interests, such as shareholders and creditors.

39. Austing Corporation sells merchandise at a gross profit of 25% of sales. Fire on the premises of this Corporation on July 16, 2000, resulted in the destruction of the merchandise. The Corporation's merchandise is insured against fire by a $150,000 insurance policy with an 80% coinsurance clause. The Corporation's records show the following:

Sales—January 1, 2000, to July 16, 2000	$400,000
Inventory—January 1, 2000	$ 65,000
Purchases—January 1, 2000, to July 16, 2000	$460,000
Merchandise salvaged	$ 25,000

The amount of inventory destroyed by fire is

(A) $150,000
(B) $200,000
(C) $225,000
(D) $300,000

40. Below are the totals of the Cash Receipts and Disbursement Books of the Grand Corporation for the calendar year 2000:

Receipts—$392,369.72
Disbursements—$331,477.87

The bank balance on January 1, 2000, was $38,610,21. The bank balance on December 31, 2000, was $101,918.34. No checks were outstanding on January 1, 2000. Checks outstanding on December 31, 2000, amounted to $5,416.28. Undeposited checks on hand December 31, 2000, were $3,000, which are included in the December cash receipts. Bank deposits for the year total $387,643.72.

The total shortage in cash is

(A) $1,726
(B) $2,416.28
(C) $3,000
(D) $3,452

ANSWER KEY

1. D	9. B	17. C	25. A	33. A
2. C	10. B	18. B	26. B	34. C
3. B	11. D	19. A	27. A	35. C
4. D	12. A	20. A	28. D	36. A
5. D	13. B	21. A	29. A	37. B
6. B	14. A	22. B	30. D	38. D
7. B	15. A	23. A	31. D	39. B
8. C	16. A	24. D	32. A	40. A

SAMPLE PRACTICE EXAMINATION III

The time allowed for the entire examination is 4 hours.

Explanatory Answers are given at the end of this Practice Exam

These six questions contain the entire written test for Accountant and Promotion to Accountant.

1. The Westside Restaurant, Inc., keeps its books on a cash basis during the year. At the end of the year, the depreciation charges for the year and the accruals at the end of the year are entered on the books, thus placing the books on an accrual basis.

   At the end of each month, the depreciation charges and the accruals are set up on a work sheet only and the report of the month's operations are obtained on an accrual basis.

   The following is the post-closing trial balance as of December 31, 2000: Cash $4,900; Inventory $2,200; Equipment, $30,000; Allowance for Depreciation $18,000; Capital Stock (Outstanding) $8,500; Surplus $2,800; Accounts Payable $5,200; Accrued Expenses $2,600.

   The Cash Book shows the following for the months of January and February 2001:

January:	Cash Sales (all deposited) $23,500
February:	Cash Sales (all deposited) $23,900
January:	Cash Payments for Merchandise $13,050; for Expenses $10,180
February:	Cash Payments for Merchandise $12,460; for Expenses $10,620

   The following additional information is obtained as of the dates indicated:

   January 31, 2001: Inventory $1,950; unpaid merchandise bills $4,300; unpaid expense items $1,860.

   February 28, 2001: Inventory $1,600; unpaid merchandise bills $4,800; unpaid expense items $2,120

   Depreciation is charged off at the rate of $250 per month.

   From the above information, set up the ledger accounts as they would appear on the books of this firm for January and February 2001, and prepare

   (A) a statement of Profit and Loss for the two months ending February 28, 2001, and
   (B) a statement of Profit and Loss for the month of February 2001.

2. On March 1, 2001, the Balance Sheet of the Wimple Mfg. Co., Inc., consisted of the following:

Cash	$ 75,000
Buildings and Equipment	800,000
Prepaid Items	30,000
Other Assets	1,323,000
	$2,228,000
Liabilities	$1,056,000
Capital Stock	1,000,000
Surplus	172,000
	$2,228,000

   On June 1, 2001, the company sold $300,000 of 10-year First Mortgage 12% Bonds, dated March 1, 2001, at 103.9 and accrued interest. Interest is payable semi-annually on March 1 and September 1.

   (A) Prepare journal entries for the sale of the bonds.
   (B) Prepare journal entries for the payments of interest on the bonds on September 1, 2001, and March 1, 2002, and the amortization of the premium on these dates. (Use straight-line amortization.)
   (B) Assuming there were no other transactions, show the Balance sheet of March 2, 2002, after giving effect to all of the above transactions. Assume the books were closed as of March 2, 2002. (Disregard depreciation of fixed assets.)

3. Mr. X is the sole owner of the stock of a corporation. The Surplus account at the end of December 2001, appeared in his ledger as follows:

   Surplus

3/1/99 Dividend	5,000	12/31/98 Balance	9,000
12/31/99 P & L	6,000	12/31/2001 P & L	1,900
12/31/2000 P & L	4,200		

   An examination of the books and records reveals the following errors:

   (1) Mr. X has twice understated his inventory. On December 31, 1999, the physical inventory to-

taled $12,600, but an inventory of $8,100 was recorded on the books. On December 31, 2001, the actual inventory was $15,400, but only $10,200 was recorded on the books.

(2) All furniture and equipment has been depreciated at the rate of 10% per annum. An office safe originally costing $2,400, bought on April 1, 1990, has been fully depreciated by April 1, 2000, but depreciation had been taken on this item for all of 2000 and 2001.

(3) On July 1, 2000, Mr. X had purchased, with corporate funds, an automobile costing $4,400, for his personal use. This purchase had been charged to the Motor Equipment account and had been depreciated with all other motor equipment at a 20% rate from July 1, 2000, to December 31, 2001.

(4) A sale of $4,900 completed in December 2000 was charged to Accounts Receivable and credited to the account Advances from Customers in December 2000. In January 2001, the bookkeeper closed out the account Advances from Customers to the Sales account for 2001.

(5) Cash advances given on December 31, 2000, to a salesman for 2001 traveling expenses, amounting to $580, were charged to Traveling Expenses for 2000. These expenses are borne by the company.

(A) Prepare proper journal entries to correct all of the above and show the true condition of the books as of December 31, 2001.

(B) Prepare a worksheet showing the corrected profit and loss for each of the 3 years, 1999, 2000, and 2001, and show the true balance in the Surplus account as of December 31, 2001.

4. The Fairfax Gas and Electric Co. is engaged in selling gas and electricity to residents in a certain county. You are given the following facts for the six months ending June 30, 2001:

Gas sales $491,500, of which $82,300 has not been collected; received from customers for electric service $328,300, of which $24,900 represents the collection of all billings made for previous periods. Bills for electricity amounting to $7,910 for the six months ended June 30, 2001, have not yet been collected. Operating expenses and salaries, paid $432,800, and accrued $30,200; repairs and maintenance amounted to $280,400, of which $40,800 is unpaid. New equipment was purchased for $90,000, of which one half was paid. Cash balance on January 1, 2001, was $162,800.

(A) Prepare a Statement of Cash Receipts and Disbursements showing the cash balance at June 30, 2001.

(B) Prepare a Statement of Revenue and Expenses on an accrual basis (disregard depreciation).

(C) Assuming there are no other assets or liabilities (and no balance in the Surplus account at the beginning of the year), prepare a Balance Sheet as of June 30, 2001 (disregard depreciation).

5. The Kaycee Lingerie Shops has its home office in New York and a branch in Connecticut. At the end of 2000, the accountant for the firm had adjusted the accounts of the home office and the branch so that they were in balance. On January 1, 2001, the balances on the branch books, corrected, were as follows: Cash $2,175; Merchandise Inventory (at the shipped price) $18,450; Accrued Salaries $240.

The branch sells the merchandise it receives from the home office at 25% above the shipped price.

(1) During the year 2001, the home office sent the branch $62,800 worth of merchandise (at the shipped price). Of this amount, one shipment of $4,740 had been entered on the branch books as $4,470.

(2) A return by the branch of $229 of defective merchandise (shipped price) was recorded on the branch books but had never been entered on the home office books

(3) Freight charges amounting to $65 on a shipment by the home office to the branch were paid by the home office, charged to the freight account in the home office, and never charged to the branch.

(4) An employee of the branch came to the home office one day and resigned his position. The home office bookkeeper paid his branch salary of $57 (no deductions) and charged the proper branch account. This was never recorded on the branch books.

During the year 2001, sales of merchandise at the branch, all for cash, amounted to $80,900. During the year the branch paid in cash for salaries $9,080 and for expenses $4,410. There were unpaid salaries of $375 at the end of the year at the branch. Cash remittances to the home office during the year amounted to $65,750. The inventory of merchandise at the branch at the end of the year was $15,500 at the shipped price.

(A) Prepare journal entries to adjust the books of the home office and the branch.

(B) Prepare journal entries to close the books of the branch after the above adjustments are made.

6. You are given the following information taken from the records of Joseph Holt:

	Jan 1, 2001	Dec 31, 2001
Accounts Receivable	$14,450	$16,770
Merchandise Inventory	6,500	8,200
Equipment (less Allowance for Depreciation)	2,500	2,000
Accounts Payable (for merchandise)	12,500	15,050

From the Cash Book you are able to obtain these facts for the year 2001:

Bank Balance:	
January 1, 2001	$ 2,580
Receipts:	
From Customers	78,490
From Bank Loan	3,000
Disbursements:	
Accounts Payable (for merchandise)	59,850
General Expenses	17,360
J. Holt, Drawings	4,000

There is accrued and unpaid interest on the bank loan amounting to $60.

Prepare a complete Statement of Profit and Loss for the year and a Balance Sheet at the end of the year. There were no purchases or sales of equipment during the year.

END OF EXAMINATION

EXPLANATORY ANSWERS

1. Since this problem calls for accounts as they would appear at the end of two consecutive months, as well as for a single month and cumulative profit and loss statement, the simplest method is to set up a worksheet (see the 10-column one on the following page) showing beginning and ending trial balances for each month (the ending one following a pair of columns in which the month's operations are summarized). The profit and loss statement that follows is then drawn off as a comparative statement, picking up the monthly figures from the worksheet operations columns for the single month and the cumulative from the ending trial balance for the second month.

2. (A)

Date	Account	Debit	Credit
June 1, 2001	Cash		$320,700
	Bond Interest Expense		9,000
	Bonds Payable		300,000
	Premium on Bonds Payable		11,700

(B)

Date	Account	Debit	Credit
Sept. 1, 2001	Bond Interest Expense	$18,000	
	Cash		18,000
Sept. 1, 2001	Premium on Bonds Payable	585	
	Bond Interest Expense		585
Mar. 1, 2002	entries would be the same as those for September 1, 2001		

(C)

WIMPLE MFG. CO. INC.
Balance Sheet
March 2, 2002

Cash	$ 359,700	Liabilities:		
Buildings & Equipment	800,000	Bonds Payable	$ 300,000	
		Other Liabil.	1,056,000	$ 1,356,000
Prepaid Items	30,000	Deferred Income—		
Other Assets	1,323,000	Premium on Bonds Payable		10,530
		Capital Stock		1,000,000
		Surplus		146,170
	$ 2,512,700			$ 2,512,700

Note that since no other transactions were assumed, the net reduction in the surplus account between June 1, 2001, and March 2, 2002, was equal to the net debit in the one operating account (Bond Interest Expense) used in the problem. The Deferred Income account has been shown here separate from liability and capital accounts. Some accountants prefer to classify all deferred income accounts as liabilities. Bonds payable premiums, however, are not true liabilities (like, for example, deferred subscription income, which is returnable if a subscription is cancelled). They simply represent income, which received at time of bond sale should be taken up gradually as reduction of the bond interest expense over the life of the bonds.

1. (A) Since the books have been closed for 2001, all correction entries must be adjustments of the Surplus account (rather than of operating accounts).

WESTSIDE RESTAURANT, INC.
Work Sheet
December 31, 2000 – February 28, 2001

	12/41/00 Trial Balance		Jan. 2001 Operations		Jan 31, 2001 Trial Balance		Feb. 2001 Operations		Feb. 28, 2001 Trial Balance	
	Dr.	Cr.	Dr.	Cr.	Dr.	Cr.	Dr.	Cr.	Dr.	Cr.
Cash	$ 4,900		(a) $23,500	(b) $23,230	$ 5,170		(a) $23,900	(b) $23,080	$ 5,990	
Inventory	2,200			(d) 250	1,950			(d) 350	1,600	
Equipment	30,000				30,000				30,000	
Accumulated Depreciation		18,000		(e) 250		18,250		(e) 250		18,500
Accounts Payable		5,200	(b) 13,050	(c) 12,150		4,300	(b) 12,460	(c) 12,960		4,800
Accrued Expenses		2,600	(b) 10,180	(f) 9,440		1,860	(b) 10,620	(f) 10,880		2,120
Capital Stock		8,500				8,500				8,500
Surplus		2,800		(g) 1,410		4,210	(g) 540			3,670
Sales				(a) 23,500		23,500		(a) 23,900		47,400
Purchases			(c) 12,150				(c) 12,960			
			(d) 250		12,400		(d) 350		25,710	
Depreciation			(e) 250		250		(e) 250		500	
Other Expenses			(f) 9,440		9,440		(f) 10,880		20,320	
	37,100	37,100	68,820	70,230	59,210	60,620	71,960	71,420	84,120	84,990
Profit or Loss			(g) 1,410		1,410			(g) 540	870	
			$70,230	$70,230	$60,620	$60,620	$71,960	$71,960	$84,990	$84,990

Explanation of Entries:

(a) Cash receipts from sales

(b) Cash payments of liabilities

(c) To set up merchandise purchases for month by adjusting accounts payable balance to amount of unpaid bills

(d) To adjust merchandise inventory account to month-end inventory value and adjust purchases to show merchandise used for month

(e) To record depreciation for month

(f) To adjust accrued expenses to amount of unpaid bills and set up expenses for month

(g) To reflect difference between income and expense as month's profit or loss and adjust surplus account

WESTSIDE RESTAURANT, INC.

Profit and Loss Statements for

	Month of February 2001		Two Months Ended February 28, 2001	
Sales		$23,900		$47,400
Deduct: Cost of Merchandise Used:				
Beginning Inventory	1,950		2,200	
Add: Purchases	12,960		25,110	
Available for use	14,910		27,310	
Deduct: Ending Inventory	1,600	13,310	1,600	25,710
Gross Profit		10,590		21,690
Expenses:				
Depreciation	250		500	
Other Expenses	10,880	11,130	20,320	20,820
Profit of (Loss)		($540)		$870

	Debit	Credit
3. (A) (1) Merchandise Inventory	$5,200	
Surplus		$5,200
To correct for 12/31/01 understatement of inventory. (The 12/31/99 understatement was offset by its reappearance as an understatement of 2000 opening inventory.)		
(2) Accumulated Depreciation, Furniture, & Equipment-ment	$ 420	
Surplus		$ 420
To remove 21 months (4/1/00–12/31/01) depreciation recorded after the asset, costing $2,400 with a 10-year life, had already been fully depreciated.		
(3) Accumulated Depreciation, Motor Equipment	$1,320	
Surplus	3,080	
Motor equipment		$4,400
To remove 18 months' depreciation erroneously recorded on Mr. X's personal car (not a company asset) at 20%/year of $4,400.		

No adjustments of surplus are required for Items 4 and 5 since these were 2000 errors, which, uncorrected, produced errors of the same amount in the opposite direction in 2001. See worksheet, however, for effect on individual years' profits.

Note: When information is as incompletely presented as it is for Item 3, the answer should point out the incompleteness and show what assumption has been made in the answer to fill the information gap. It is not clear from Item 3 whether Mr. X or the corporation is the owner of the car. If Mr. X is the owner, the *correction entry* is correct since the corporation cannot carry someone else's asset as its own. If the corporation is owner, the *original entries* are correct and no correction is required.

(B) Uncorrected profit or (loss) for	1999	2000	2001	Total
	($6,000)	($4,200)	$1,900	($8,300)
(1) Correction of 12/31/99 inventory understatement	4,500	(4,500)		
(2) Correction of 12/31/01 inventory understatement			5,200	5,200
(3) Correction of overdepreciation, 9 months 2000, 12 months 2001		180	240	420
(4) Removal of depreciation of personal automobile		440	880	1,320
(5) Correction for 2000 sale shown as 2001 income		4,900	(4,900)	
(6) Correction for 2001 expenses charged in 2000			580	(580)
Corrected profit or (loss)	($1,500)	($2,600)	$2,740	($1,360)

Additional note: The net of the three entries correcting surplus is a credit of $2,540, which would simply reduce the incorrect deficit of 12/31/01 from $4,300 to $1,760. But if only corrections of profits are considered, the worksheet above shows a net credit of $6,940, which would shift the $4,300 deficit to $2,640 surplus. Here again the incomplete statement of the facts as to Mr. X's car prevents a final answer. Is Mr. X to pay for the car? If so, then entry (A) (3) should show a special account receivable debit for $4,400 and a credit to Surplus for $1,320, the amount of depreciation expense reversed. Is it a gift to Mr. X? If so, the corporation may consider it a direct charge to Surplus, as the correction is made here, or as expense for 2000, which would change the 2000 worksheet Item 4 to a bracketed ($3,960) and the "total" Item 4 to a bracketed ($3,080). In either event, Mr. X is likely to have to pay Federal income tax on an additional $4,400 for 2000 (and the corporation will pay reduced income tax on reduced profits if it is a charge to expense rather than directly to Surplus) if the corporation pays for the car.

4. (A)

FAIRFAX GAS AND ELECTRIC CO.
Cash Receipts and Disbursements
Six Months Ended June 30, 2001

Cash balance, January 1, 2001			$162,800
Receipts:	Current billings, electricity	$303,400	
	Prior billings, electricity	24,900	328,300
	Current billings, gas		409,200
	Total cash available		$900,300
Disbursements:			
	Equipment	$ 45,000	
	Operating expenses and salaries	432,800	
	Repairs and maintenance	239,600	717,400
Cash balance, June 30, 2001			$182,900

(B)

FAIRFAX GAS AND ELECTRIC CO.
Statement of Revenues and Expenses
Six Months Ended June 30, 2001

Revenues:	Gas sales	$491,500	
	Electricity sales	311,310	$802,810
Expenses:	Operating expenses and salaries	$463,000	
	Repair and maintenance	280,400	743,400
Net income before depreciation and taxes			$ 59,410

(C) According to the figures given in the problem, the January 1, 2001, balance sheet must have shown:

Cash	$162,800	Liabilities - none	
Receivables, electric	24,900	Capital Stock	$187,700
	$187,700		$187,700

Based on (A) and (B), these would be revised to the following as of June 30, 2001:

FAIRFAX GAS AND ELECTRIC CO.
Balance Sheet
June 30, 2001

Assets			Liabilities		
Cash		$182,900	Accounts Payable		$116,000*
Accounts Receivable:					
Electricity	7,910		Capital		
Gas	82,300	90,210			
			Capital Stock	$187,700	
Fixed Assets		90,000	Surplus	59,410	247,110
Total Assets		$363,110	Total Liabilities & Capital		$363,110

*Consists of accrued operation expenses and salaries,	$30,200
unpaid repair and maintenance items	40,800
unpaid balance on equipment purchase	45,000

5. (A) Correction entries, on branch and/or home office books as required:

	Debit	Credit
(1) On branch books only:		
Shipments from Home Office	270	
Home Office Ledger		270
To correct entry of \$4,740 as \$4,470		
(2) On Home office books only:		
Shipments to Branch	229	
Branch Ledger		229
To pick up unrecorded return of merchandise from branch		
(3) On home office books:		
Branch Ledger	65	
Freight		65
To charge branch for freight erroneously charged to home office freight account		
On branch books:		
Expenses (Freight)	65	
Home Office Ledger		65
To pick up charge previously not recorded by home office or vouchered to branch		
(4) On branch books only:		
Salaries	57	
Home Office Ledger		57
To pick up unrecorded payment of a branch salary by home office, appearing on home office books		

(B) Closing entries on branch books:

	Debit	Credit
(1) Profit and Loss	18,450	
Merchandise Inventory		18,450
To transfer opening inventory to profit and loss		
(2) Merchandise Inventory	15,500	
Profit and Loss		15,500
To enter the closing inventory		
(3) Profit and Loss	62,571	
Shipments from Home Office		62,571
To close the Shipments from Home Office Account		
(4) Profit and Loss	13,747	
Salaries		9,272
Expenses		4,475
To close operating expense accounts		
(5) Sales	80,900	
Profit and Loss		80,900
To close the Sales account		
(6) Profit and Loss	1,632	
Home Office Ledger		1,632
To close the Profit and Loss Account		

Note: (1) With six problems to be done in 4 hours, time hardly permits setting up a worksheet for this problem to prove correctness of the closing entries. It is strongly suggested, however, that an opening (here January 1, 2001) balance sheet be noted on the answer paper in pencil, as described in the examination instructions, as scratch work. Using these figures as a beginning, add and subtract the totals of branch office entries for the year that they appear in balance sheet accounts, and arrive at an ending balance sheet. If it does not balance, inclusive of the closing entries, check to see whether you have missed, transposed, or entered incorrectly any of the figures given in the problem. Suggested scratch work for this problem is shown below:

1/1/01		
Cash	$ 2,175	
Merchandise	18,450	
Accrued Salaries		$ 240
Home Office Ledger		20,385
	$20,625	$20,625

1/1/02		
Cash: 2,175 + 80,900 – 13,490 – 65,750	$ 3,835	
Merchandise	15,500	
Accrued Salaries		$ 375
H.O. Ledger Dr: 229 + 65,750		
Cr: 20,385 + 62,800 + 65 + 57 + 1,632		18,960
	$19,335	$19,335

(2) It is probably desirable practice for the candidate to show his understanding of significance of figures given in a problem when they have important meaning but are not usable in the formal figurework required. For example, the candidate might note the following *in ink* at the end of his solution to this problem: "The first three closing entries place the cost of goods sold, at shipped price, at $65,521. Since the branch is supposed to sell at 25% above this price, it appears that $80,900 in sales requires a cost of goods sold of $64,720. This suggests one or more of the following: Understatement of branch inventory; shortage in branch inventory; unreported or underreported branch sales; underpricing in branch sales."

6.

JOSEPH HOLT
Profit and Loss Statement
For Year Ending December 31, 2001

Sales Income:			
Cash receipts from customers	$ 78,490		
Receivables, December 31, 2001	16,770	$95,260	
Deduct: Receivables, January 1, 2001		14,450	$80,810
Deduct: Cost of Goods Sold			
Merchandise purchases paid for	$ 59,850		
Purchased 2001, but unpaid Dec. 31	15,050	$74,900	
Deduct: Unpaid, January 1, 2001		12,500	
Total merchandise purchases, 2001		$62,400	
Add: Merchandise Inventory, January 1, 2001		6,500	
Available for sale in 2001		$68,900	
Deduct: Merchandise Inventory, Dec. 31, 2001		8,200	60,700
Gross Profit			20,110
Deduct Expenses: General		$17,360	
Depreciation		500	
Interest		60	17,920
Net Profit for Year			$ 2,190
Deduct: Drawings			4,000
Increase or (decrease) in Net Worth, 2001			$(1,810)

Note: To make the solution of the problem both quicker and more complete, it is suggested that a comparative balance sheet be prepared as answer for the second part of this problem. In the illustration below, note that the Net Worth at beginning and end of year has been picked up as a balancing figure. Since the December 31 net worth is $1,810 less than that of January 1, and agrees with the decrease shown above as an addendum to the profit and loss statement, you can be fairly confident that both parts of the solution are correct.

JOSEPH HOLT – COMPARATIVE BALANCE SHEET

	1/1/01	12/31/01
Assets:		
Cash	$ 2,580	$ 2,860
Accounts Receivable	14,450	16,770
Merchandise Inventory	6,500	8,200
Equipment—at cost minus accumulated depreciation	2,500	2,000
Total Assets	$26,030	$29,830
Liabilities		
Accounts Payable	$12,500	$15,050
Loan Payable	–	3,000
Accrued Interest Payable	–	60
Total Liabilities	$12,500	$18,110
Net Worth	13,530	11,720
Total Liabilities and Net Worth	$26,030	$29,830

SAMPLE PRACTICE EXAMINATION IV

The time allowed for the entire examination is 4 hours.

Explanatory Answers are given at the end of this Practice Exam

These six questions contain the entire written test for Accountant and Promotion Accountant.

1. As an accountant for the City of New York, you are sent to make a field audit to determine the liability of S. Marron for the General Business Tax for the year 2001. Mr. Marron began business on January 1, 2001. He has reported sales for 2001 in the amount of $121,600, an amount you suspect is understated. His books of account are incomplete. A thorough examination of his checkbook and bank statements reveals the following:

   Mr. Marron began business with $15,000 cash in bank. He bought fixtures for $9,000 cash. During 2001 he drew $125 per week for himself; paid $350 per month for rent; paid salaries totaling $400 per week to his employees; paid other expenses of $100 per month. You accept as true Mr. Marron's statement that he deposited all receipts and that all purchases and sales were for cash. In the checkbook, you also find a special deposit of $3,000 on May 3, 2001, and a record of a check payable to the Bronx Auto Sales Company for $2,380. Mr. Marron tells you he had cashed bonds for $3,000 and had bought an auto for his wife for $2,380. Mr. Marron's profit and loss statement for 2001 shows a closing inventory of $3,400, valued at cost, and depreciation of fixtures amounting to $900 (which are to be accepted). The cash balance, as of December 31, 2001, also correct, was $3,020. In this business, merchandise is sold at one-third above the cost price.

   (A) Prepare a correct balance sheet as of December 31, 2001, and a correct and complete statement of profit and loss for the year.
   (B) Prepare a correct detailed cash account for the year.

2. The following is the balance sheet of the Empire Manufacturing Company as of December 31, 2001. (The books are closed semiannually):

EMPIRE MANUFACTURING COMPANY

Balance Sheet, December 31, 2001

Assets		Liabilities and Capital	
Cash	$ 56,200	Accounts Payable	$ 460,000
Accounts Receivable	350,000	Accrued Interest Payable	
Merchandise Inventory	290,000	on Mortgage	4,000
Land and Buildings (net)	400,000	Mortgage Payable	80,000
Machinery and Equipment (net)	200,000	Common Stock, authorized and	
Deficit	47,800	outstanding (8,000 shares)	800,000
	$1,344,000		$1,344,000

The operations during the first 6 months of 2001 were very profitable. Since the company had every reason to believe the last 6 months of 2001 would also be profitable, a reserve for federal income taxes for 2001 amounting to $12,000 was set up on June 30, 2001. (Federal income tax reports were made on a calendar year basis). Due to a decline in business during the last quarter of 2001, the company suffered an operating loss of $97,400 for the second half of 2001 and wound up with a final operating loss for the entire year of $55,300. Dividends of $1 a share were declared on April 10, July 10, and October 10 and paid on those days.

Set up the surplus account of the corporation, showing in detail all changes in the account and the balances in the account on January 1, 2001 and July 1, 2001.

3. A fire destroyed the total inventory of goods in process stored in a warehouse adjoining the main factory building of the Simmons Manufacturing Company on March 19, 2001. You are given the following additional information:

Inventories—January 1, 2001	
Raw Materials	$ 900,000
Finished Goods	540,000
Inventories—March 19, 2001	
Raw Materials	$ 660,000
Finished Goods	280,000
Sales from 1-1-01 to date of fire	$1,040,000
Direct Labor	200,000
Manufacturing Expenses	140,000
Purchases of Raw Materials	240,000
Administrative Expenses	120,000
Selling Expenses	60,000
Gross Profit on Sales	320,000

You are informed that the inventory of goods in process at the time of the fire was 50 percent greater than at the beginning of the year.

Prepare the Statement of Cost of Goods Manufactured of this company for the period from January 1, 2001–March 19, 2001, in detail, supplying the missing items and showing how much should be claimed for goods-in-process destroyed by the fire. Show all computations.

4. Kantor and Samuels form a partnership to buy and sell war surplus materials. Kantor is to operate in Philadelphia and Samuels in New York. Kantor invests $20,000 and Samuels $30,000. They agree to share profits, after expenses and salaries of $1,000 per month for each, in proportion to their original investments. Samuels is to keep the partnership books and make an accounting to Kantor whenever demanded. They operate for four months when Kantor, having sold all he had bought, decides to withdraw from the partnership. He demands an accounting and Samuels sends him a check for $12,500 in full settlement. Kantor is dissatisfied and retains you to examine the books.

You have access to all the records of both partners and find the following: A partnership bank account was opened in New York with the $50,000 original investment. Kantor's purchases were $28,000, for which he paid $18,000 with a partnership check and the balance, after deducting purchase discounts of $400, he paid with personal funds. His sales totaled $57,000. He received from customers $49,000 in cash (deposited in his personal account), allowed discounts of $860, and sent the remaining accounts receivable (all good) to Samuels for future collection (with no allowances for discounts). From his receipts, Kantor took 4 months salary for himself and paid $4,600 for other salaries and expenses.

Samuels made purchases of $34,000 and sales of $72,000 and had inventory at cost, at the end of the four months, of $3,700. He had deposited all receipts and made all expenditures from the partnership bank account. He had paid in full for goods purchased. He received from customers $59,000 in cash and allowed discounts of $1,040. He had drawn four months salary for himself and paid $3,200 for other salaries and expenses.

Set up all the accounts that should have been kept by Samuels, labelling the entries clearly, and showing how much, if anything, is still due Kantor.

5. Below you will find the Accounts Payable account (balance not shown) taken from the general ledger of G. Bauerman, the owner of a small dress factory. You will also find the schedule of his creditors' ledger on December 31, 2001. The former accountant for Mr. Bauerman had closed the books early in January 2002. He was taken ill and you are hired to replace him on January 20, 2002. You find that the former accountant had failed to correct the errors and omissions of the bookkeeper.

Accounts Payable

2001

Dec. 31 Balance

Schedule of Creditors Ledger
as of December 31, 2001

Abbott	$ 345
Berman	910
Englander (debit balance)	10
Fried	46
Walter	210
White	350
All other creditors (balances correct)	5,080

Your audit of the bookkeeper's work reveals the following:

(1) The footings of the Accounts Payable column in the Cash Disbursements Journal for December 2001 totaled $4,169, not the $4,096 that the bookkeeper had posted. To make the journal balance across the page, the bookkeeper had increased the total of Miscellaneous Expense column by $73.

(2) On October 29, an entry for the purchase of $120 worth of materials from Fried had been made in the Purchase Journal and posted. On December 4, Fried had bought two dresses for $50 from Mr. Bauerman. A sales invoice had been made out and an account opened for Fried in the customers' ledger. On December 6, Mr. Bauerman, desiring to pay Fried, figured that Fried was entitled to a discount of 8 percent on the sale made to him. Mr. Bauerman accordingly drew a check for $74, which was entered as such in the Accounts Payable column of the Cash Disbursements Journal. No other entries had been made by the bookkeeper.

(3) The $10 debit balance in Englander's account resulted from the fact that Mr. Bauerman had paid the creditor $157, directly from the bill, which had been entered incorrectly in the Purchase Journal in November as $147.

(4) A refund of $82 from Berman, the result of an overpayment, had been entered in the Accounts Receivable column of the Cash Receipts Journal and had been posted from there to Berman's account.

(5) On December 27, Mr. Bauerman paid a note due to Abbott for $350, plus interest $5, by drawing a check for $355. The bookkeeper entered the payment of $355 in the Cash Disbursements Journal and treated the entire sum as a payment on account to Abbott. She made no other entry for this transaction.

(6) In December 2001, returned goods to Walter were invoiced at $120. The journal entry was made correctly but the bookkeeper posted in error to the account of White.

Make necessary journal entries with explanations to correct the books and prepare the Accounts Payable controlling account in detail showing clearly the December 31, 2001, balance you found before making any adjustments and the corrected balance after adjustments.

6. On February 15, 2000, Frank and Shafer became equal partners in a business, investing $12,000 and $9,500 respectively. Although the business appeared to be prosperous, the partners were surprised to find that their cash balance early in 2001 was small. Their books had not been closed during the entire period and their drawings had been charged to their capital accounts.

On March 1, 2001, Frank's capital account showed a credit balance of $440 and Shafer's capital account showed a debit balance of $2,300. On that date, they decided to dissolve the partnership. All the assets, except the fixtures, were sold and trade creditors were paid. As a result, the cash balance on March 1, 2001, amounted to $410. The fixtures originally cost $15,000, on which there was still $2,000 owed on notes.

On April 15, the fixtures were sold for $11,000 and the notes for $2,000 were paid with interest of $16. Legal and accounting fees, amounting to $250, were also paid on that day, as well as additional rent of $600.

Prepare separate Capital Accounts for both partners in detail. Your accounts should show clearly each partner's interest on March 1, 2001, and on April 15, 2001. Show all computations (ignore depreciation).

END OF EXAMINATION

EXPLANATORY ANSWERS

1. (A)

S. MARRON
Balance Sheet
December 31, 2001

Assets			Liabilities and Capital	
Cash		$ 3,020	Liabilities—None	
Merchandise		3,400		
Furniture and Fixtures	$9,000		S. Marron, Capital	$14,520
Accumulated Depreciation	900	8,100		
Total Assets		$14,520	Total Liabilities and Capital	$14,520

Provable as follows:		
Original investment		$15,000
Additional investment		3,000
		18,000
Deduct: Drawings	$6,500	
Car purchase	2,380	8,880
		9,120
Add: Profit per statement below		5,400
Capital, December 31, 2001		$14,520

S. MARRON
Profit and Loss Statement
Year Ending December 31, 2001

Sales		$121,600
Deduct: Cost of Goods Sold		
Purchases	$92,500	
Less Dec. 31 inventory	3,400	89,100
Gross Profit		$ 32,500
Deduct: Operating Expenses		
Rent	$ 4,200	
Salaries	20,800	
Depreciation	900	
Other Expenses	1,200	27,100
Net Profit for Year		$ 5,400

Since Mr. Marron deposited cash from sales reflecting a markup of more than 36 percent over cost, as compared to the stated 33 ⅓ % for the trade, the sales are not too likely to have been understated relative to purchases.

(B) S. Marron's cash account for 2001:

Jan. 1	Balance	$ 15,000	Fixtures	$ 9,000
	Sales	121,600	Drawings, wkly	6,500
	Bonds cashed	3,000	Rent	4,200
			Salaries	20,800
			Expenses, other	1,200
			Drawings, car	2,380
			Mdse. purchases	92,500
		139,600		136,580
			Dec. 31 Balance	$ 3,020
1/1/00	Balance	$ 3,020		

2. **EMPIRE MANUFACTURING COMPANY**
Surplus Account, 2001

4/10/01	Dividends	$ 8,000	12/31/00	Balance	$ 31,500
6/30/01	Income tax res.	12,000	6/30/01	6 mos. profit	42,100
	Balance	53,600			
		73,600			73,600
7/10/01	Dividends	8,000	7/1/01	Balance	53,600
10/10/01	Dividends	8,000	12/31/01	Write-off, tax res.	12,000
12/31/01	6 mos. loss	97,400		Balance	47,800
		113,400			$113,400
1/1/02	Balance	$ 47,800			

Two comments deserve inclusion by the candidate in his solution to this problem:

a) Since the December 31, 2001, balance sheet does not show the $12,000 reserve for federal income taxes, its reversal as of the end of the year has been assumed and shown as part of the activity in the Surplus account.

b) The format of the balance sheet causes an overstatement of both assets and net worth by showing the deficit on the asset side. The deficit should be shown on the capital side as a negative surplus item to show that the net worth is $752,200, which would balance the statement at a more proper total asset value of $1,296,200, rather than the $1,344,000 shown. The deficit is not collectible from anyone, and therefore its appearance as an asset is misleading.

3. Since the cost of goods sold for the period was $720,000 (sales of $1,040,000 minus $320,000 gross profit), the cost of goods manufactured (that is, completed during the period) must have been $460,000 according to the following standard formula:

Cost of Goods Manufactured	$ 460,000
Add: Beginning Finished Goods Inventory (Jan. 1)	540,000
Finished Goods Available for Sale	$1,000,000
Deduct: Closing Finished Goods Inventory (Mar. 19)	280,000
Cost of Goods Sold	$ 720,000

This permits us to work back to goods in process values as follows:

SIMMONS MANUFACTURING COMPANY
Statement of Cost of Goods Manufactured
January 1–March 19, 2001

Material: Inventory, January 1, 2001	$ 900,000	
Purchases during period	240,000	
Available for use	1,140,000	
Deduct March 19, 2001 Inventory	660,000	$ 480,000
Direct Labor	200,000	
Manufacturing Expenses		140,000
Costs added to goods in process during period		820,000
Add January 1 goods in process inventory	(a)	720,000
Cost of goods in process available for completion		1,540,000
Deduct March 19 goods in process inventory	(b)	1,080,000
Cost of goods manufactured (completed) during period		$ 460,000

(a) and (b) values were determined in $ thousands by the formula:

Since (b) is stated to be 50% greater than (a), using (a) as x:
$820 + x = 460 + 1.5x$; or $820 - 460 = 1.5x - x$; or $360 = .5x$; or $720 = x$

4. The required accounts and their postings are:

CASH

Investment—Kantor	$ 20,000	Purchases—Kantor	$ 18,000
Investment—Samuels	30,000	Purchases—Samuels	34,000
Receivables collections	59,000	Drawings—Samuels	4,000
		Salaries & exp.—Samuels	3,200
		Check to Kantor	12,500
(Dr. Bal. 37,300)	$109,000		$ 71,700

ACCOUNTS RECEIVABLE

Kantor's turnover	7,140	Samuels—collections	60,040
Samuels—credit sales	72,000		
(Dr. Bal. 19,100)			

SALES

Kantor	$57,000
Samuels	72,000
(Cr. Bal. 129,000)	

PURCHASES

Kantor	$28,000
Samuels	34,000
(Dr. Bal. 62,000)	

EXPENSES

Sales discounts—Kantor	$ 860
Salaries, etc.—Kantor	4,600
Sales discounts—Samuels	1,040
Salaries, etc.—Samuels	3,200
(Dr. Bal. 9,700)	

	OTHER INCOME		
	Purchase discount—Kantor		$ 400
	KANTOR, CAPITAL		
	Investment		$20,000
	KANTOR, DRAWINGS		
Retained sales receipts	$40,400	Purchases paid for	$ 9,600
Drawings, 4 mos. × 1,000	4,000		
Check from firm	12,500		
(Dr. Bal. 47,300)			
	SAMUELS, CAPITAL		
	Investment		$30,000
	SAMUELS, DRAWINGS		
Drawings, 4 mos. × 1,000	4,000		

A quick trial balance (as scratch work) will show that the debit and credit balances of these accounts are equal at $179,400. Using the $3,700 ending inventory not yet on the books as a reduction of purchases, the following profit and loss statement can then be drawn off:

Sales		$ 129,000
Cost of Goods Sold:		
Purchases (net after discount)	$61,600	
Deduct: Ending Inventory	3,700	$ 57,900
Gross Profit		71,100
Deduct: Partnership Expenses		9,700
Profit to be Distributed		61,400
Allowance for salaries and expenses of partners		8,000
To be distributed per original investment ratio		$53,400

Kantor's share (40% of $53,400) is	$21,360
Plus salary distribution of Net Profit	4,000
It would appear that since the excess of Kantor's drawings over original investment is	27,300
Samuels has already <u>over</u>paid Kantor by	$ 1,940

5. Correction entries:

	Dr.	Cr.
(1) Accounts Payable (control account only)	73	
Miscellaneous Expense		73
To correct unbalanced December 31 footing of disbursements journal by transferring the out-of-balance difference that had been erroneously charged off to Miscellaneous Expense		
(2) Sales Discount	4	
Accounts Payable (Fried)	46	
Accounts Receivable (Fried)		50
To correct the distribution of December 6 check for $74 to Fried		

		Dr.	Cr.
(3)	Purchases	10	
	Accounts Payable (Englander)		10
	To correct understatement of November purchase		
(4)	Accounts Receivable	82	
	Accounts Payable		82
	To correct controlling accounts only for refund from Berman properly posted in the Payables ledger but debited in error to Accounts Receivable		
(5)	Notes Payable	350	
	Interest Expense	5	
	Accounts Payable (Abbott)		355
	To properly record payment of a note, incorrectly entered and posted on December 27 as a payment on account		
(6)	Accounts Payable (Walter)	120	
	Accounts Payable (White)		120
	To support transfer of $120 return from White's account to Walter's. Original entry in December was posted in error to White's account.		

The Accounts Payable control account and supporting creditors' ledger balances would appear as follows after the above corrections were made:

ACCOUNTS PAYABLE

Correction (1)	$ 73		Balance before correction	$7,086
" (2)	46		Correction (3)	10
" (4)	82		" (5)	355
" (6)	120		" (6)	120
Corrected balance forw'd	7,250			
	$7,571			$7,571
			Corrected balance	$7,250

Corrected Schedule of Creditors' Ledger, December 31, 2001:

Abbott	$ 700
Berman	910
Englander	—
Fried	—
Walter	90
White	470
All other creditors	5,080
	$7,250

6. The partners' capital accounts should show:

FRANK, CAPITAL

Drawings, 2000–2001	$11,560		2/15/00	Investment	$12,000
3/1/01 Balance Forw'd	8,075		3/1/01	Profits	7,635
	19,635				19,635
4/15/01 Losses & Expenses	$ 2,433		3/1/01	Balance	$ 8,075

(This leaves Frank with a credit balance and claim of $5,642 on cash)

SHAFER, CAPITAL

Drawings, 2000–2001	$11,800	2/15/00	Investment	$ 9,500
3/1/01 Balance forward	5,335	3/1/01	Profits	7,635
	17,135			17,135
4/15/01 Losses & expenses	$ 2,433	3/1/01	Balance	$ 5,335

(This leaves Shafer with a credit balance and claim of $2,902 on cash)

The March 1, 2001, information stated in the problem can be reflected in the following balance sheet as of that date:

Assets: Cash	$ 410	Liabilities: Notes Payable	$ 2,000
Fixtures	15,000	Capital: Frank	440
		Shafer (dr. bal.)	(2,300)
		Operating account cr. bals.	15,270
Total Assets	$15,410	Liabilities and Capital	$15,410

The net credit balance of $15,270 in operating accounts represents undistributed profits, which were then reflected by distribution equally on March 1 to the capital accounts. The April 15 sale of assets and payment of expenses increased cash by $8,134 ($11,000 – $2,000 – $16 – $250 – $600) to $8,544, balancing the notes payable and fixtures accounts and establishing losses and additional expenses of $4,866 ($4,000 loss on fixture sale plus $16, $250, and $600) to be distributed equally. The distribution reflected in the capital accounts as of April 15 leaves the credits in the partners' capital accounts adding up to the debit balance in the cash account, and the cash would be distributed accordingly.

**ANSWER SHEET
FOR
SAMPLE PRACTICE EXAMINATION V**

1. ________	11. ________	21. ________	31. ________
2. ________	12. ________	22. ________	32. ________
3. ________	13. ________	23. ________	33. ________
4. ________	14. ________	24. ________	34. ________
5. ________	15. ________	25. ________	35. ________
6. ________	16. ________	26. ________	36. ________
7. ________	17. ________	27. ________	37. ________
8. ________	18. ________	28. ________	38. ________
9. ________	19. ________	29. ________	39. ________
10. ________	20. ________	30. ________	40. ________

SAMPLE PRACTICE EXAMINATION V

The time allowed for the entire examination is 4 hours.

Answer questions 1 and 2 on the basis of the information given below.

On March 1, 2001, Mr. Jones opens up a small shop for his son by investing $12,000. Mr. Jones draws nothing for himself. Fixtures are bought and paid for amounting to $3,000. All sales are made for cash. At the end of the year, you secure the following information:

Accounts Payable	$ 2,400
Inventory, December 31, 2001	2,000
Sales for the year	90,000
Expenses paid in cash	29,500

Cost of goods sold is 70% of the selling price. Disregarding depreciation on the fixtures,

1. What was the net worth of the business on December 31, 2001?

2. What was the cash balance on December 31, 2001?

3. At the beginning of the year 2001, on the books of H. Altman, the account "Prepaid Insurance" had a balance of $350. During the year 2001, the firm received bills for insurance amounting to $960 and paid $800 of these bills. At the end of the year, the accountant estimated that the Prepaid Insurance amounted to $425. How much insurance expense should be expected on the Income Statement?

4. At the beginning of the year 2001, the account "Wages Payable" had a balance of $480. At the end of the year, after closing the books, the balance in this account "Wages Payable" stood at $360. The item in the Income Statement for "Wages" for 2001 was $48,780. How much cash was paid for Wages during the year 2001?

5. At the end of the year, the Balance Sheet of a firm had an item of Unearned Rental Income of $270. The Income Statement showed Income from Rents for the year of $6,030. What was the Trial Balance figure for Income from Rents before adjusting the books?

6. At the beginning of the year 2001, the account Prepaid Advertising had a balance of $500. During the year $7,500 was paid for advertising. At the end of 2001, the accountant entered $6,100 as the advertising expense in the Income Statement. How much did he enter on the Balance Sheet as Prepaid Advertising at the end of 2001?

7. A company had an inventory of $37,500 on January 1, 2001, and Sales of $364,000 during the year 2001. It purchased $227,400 worth of merchandise during the year. Its inventory on December 31, 2001, was $46,500. What was the merchandise turnover?

Answer questions 8 and 9 on the basis of the information given below.

The following accounts appeared in the ledger of the Smith Co.:

EQUIPMENT

2000		2002	
Jan. 1 Balance	$28,000	Jan. 2 Allowance	$1,500
2002			
Jan. 2	3,200		

Accumulated Depreciation

		2000	
		Jan. 1 Balance	$7,000
		2000	
		Dec. 31	2,800
		2001	
		Dec. 31	2,800

This company depreciates its equipment at the uniform rate of 10% per year. On January 2, 2002, the company bought a new piece of equipment for $3,200 to replace an older piece, which had been bought on January 2, 2000, for $2,400. There was a trade-in allowance of $1,500 made on the old piece of equipment and the bookkeeper made the above entries on the equipment account and credited cash for $1,700.

8. What should be the correct balance in the Equipment account on Jan. 2, 2002, after the transaction?

9. What should be the correct balance in the Accumulated Depreciation account on Jan. 2, 2002, after the transaction?

Answer questions 10–12 on the basis of the information given below.

Henry Kraft bought the equipment and inventories of a small factory on March 1, 2001. On December 31, 2001, he furnishes you with the following data:

Inventories	*Raw Materials*	*Work in Process*	*Finished Goods*
Mar. 1, 2001	12,000	4,000	6,000
Dec. 31, 2001	10,000	3,500	9,200

Disbursements from Mar. 1 to Dec. 31, 2001, were as follows:

Purchases of raw materials $22,000, direct labor $15,000, factory overhead $8,800, selling expenses $9,500, administration expenses $5,200.

10. Find the prime cost.

11. Find the cost of goods manufactured.

12. Find the cost of goods sold.

13. From the following figures taken from the books of a firm on December 31, 2001, determine the Working Capital Ratio.

Cash	$ 1,550
Merchandise	2,000
Accounts Receivable	5,000
Notes Receivable	3,000
Furniture & Fixtures	7,000
Building	20,000
Notes Payable	$ 2,000
Accounts Payable	3,000
Mortgage Payable (in 2008)	12,000
Interest Payable on Mortgage	500
Stockholder's Equity	21,050

Answer questions 14 and 15 on the basis of the information given below.

On the Balance Sheet of a certain corporation there appeared the following accounts:

A. Capital Stock (per 100) issued and outstanding	$100,000
B. Retained Earnings	60,000

The company declares and pays a stock dividend of 10% and thereafter declares its regular cash dividend of $2 per share.

14. How much will appear in the Item A after the above transactions? (If there is no change, write the word "Same" on your answer sheet.)

15. How much will appear in Item B after the above transactions? (If there is no change, write the word "Same" on your answer sheet.)

16. The balance in the Stockholders equity accounts of Nova Corp as of 12/1/02 is:

Common stock $100 per (10,000 issued)	$1,000,000
Premium on Common Stock	120,000
Retained Earnings	430,000
Stockholder's Equity	$1,550,000

On Dec. 15th, the Board of Directors declares a dividend of $2.00 per share. What is the balance in Retained Earnings on 12/31/01?

17. On July 1, 2002, the Board of Directors of a corporation authorizes an issue of First Mortgage Bonds of $50,000 bearing interest at 12% payable July 1 and January 1. On August 1, 2002, the company sells half of the bonds at 95 and accrued interest. How much cash does the company get on August 1? (disregard brokerage)

18. A and B are partners sharing profits and losses equally. Their investments were A—$24,000, B—$16,000. On November 15, 2001, they decide to liquidate. Their assets on that day were $60,000 and their liabilities $20,000. They realize $53,600 on their assets and pay the liabilities in full.

What is A's share of the cash to be distributed?

Answer questions 19 and 20 on the basis of the information given below.

C and D are partners having capitals of $15,000 and $10,000. Their partnership agreement provides for sharing profits equally after allowing interest at 12% on their capital. In 2001, the net profit before any adjustments was $8,500.

19. What was C's capital after division of profits?

20. What was D's capital after division of profits?

21. L and M are partners sharing profits in proportion to capital. On December 31, 2001, their assets were $54,000, liabilities $18,000, L, capital $20,000, M, capital $16,000. Mr. Silver wishes to buy into the partnership. How much cash must Mr. Silver invest to acquire a one-third interest in the partnership?

22. Referring to question 21, assume that L and M demand that the Goodwill of the business is worth $12,000 and Mr. Silver agrees to it. There is no Goodwill on the books at present. In that case, how much must Mr. Silver invest in order to acquire a one-third interest?

23. Johnson's net profit for the year 2002 was shown as $4,650. After the books were closed, it was discovered that the entire balance of the insurance account amounting to $360 had been closed to profit and loss despite the fact that it included a payment for a one year policy dated October 1, 2002, on which the premium was $84. The insurance account also did not include a one-year policy dated December 1, 2002, on which the premium was $80 because the payment had not been made. If corrections were made, what would be the net profit for the year?

24. An accountant prepared his working papers for the year 2002 for a certain firm. The columns for assets and liabilities yielded the figure $25,500 as the net profit for the year. A recheck revealed that the balance of the account Allowance for Doubtful Accounts, $1,500, had been listed in the column for assets and had been added in with the total for that column. He makes the necessary corrections. What net profit will the columns now show?

25. A. Hall's net income for the year 2002 was determined to be $18,640 without taking into account the fact that the purchase discounts for the month of July, amounting to $410, had been credited to the sales account. What will be the net income after the correction has been made?

26. Working papers were prepared for 2002 on the firm of Axtell and Walker, Inc. The income and expense columns yielded a net income of $15,800. A check revealed that the balance of the January 1, 2002, merchandise inventory amounting to $4,500 had been entered in the income column; that the balance of merchandise inventory December 31, 2002, amounting to $5,600 had been entered in the expense column; and that the year's purchases amounting to $45,000 had been entered in the expense column. Necessary corrections were made. What was the amount of the corrected net income?

27. At the end of 2002, J. Dill's books were closed and the profit to be reported for income tax purposes was found to be $11,500. In January 2003, a purchase invoice dated December 26, 2002, amounting to $1,200 was entered. Investigation revealed that the merchandise had been received December 29, 2002, and had been included in the December 31, 2002, inventory amounting to $13,000. Correction entries were made. What is the correct net profit for 2002?

28. The net income of a certain firm for 2002 was found by the bookkeeper to be $18,700. Included in the net income was the balance of an account entitled rent received from subtenants amounting to $3,800. An audit revealed that the following facts had been ignored:

    A. In December 2002, one tenant had paid $500 rent for January 2002.
    B. One tenant was in arrears for the two months of November and December. The total due from him was $510.

    Since the books were kept on an accrual basis, the auditors made the necessary corrections. What was the amount of net profit as determined by the auditors?

29. An accountant was preparing a worksheet with two columns for income and two columns for the balance sheet. In distributing the balances of Sales Discount and Purchase Discount, the accountant entered each in the incorrect income column. The balances were Sales Discount $460, Purchase Discount $950. The income columns were totaled and indicated a net income amounting to $18,600. The errors were discovered and were corrected. What was the net profit after these corrections were made?

30. The books of A. Walker, Inc., were closed on December 31, 2002, and the profit transferred to Retained Earnings. This account now had a balance of $15,642. During 2002, the receipt of $210 as a result of bankruptcy proceedings settled the account of L. Wolf, who owed $580 for goods sold to him in 2002. The bookkeeper debited Cash $210 and credited L. Wolf, account for $210. No other record was made. The Allowance for Doubtful Accounts set up at the end of 2001 still had a balance of $145. If the correct entries had been made for L. Wolf, what would be the balance in the Retained Earnings account at the end of 2002?

31. A. Collins kept his books by the single-entry method. He presents the following data to you:

	Jan. 1, 2002	*Dec. 31, 2002*
Cash	$ 500	$1,000
Merchandise	4,000	3,500
Accounts Receivable	5,000	7,000
Equipment	2,000	2,000
Accounts Payable	2,500	1,800
Accrued Expenses	100	200

During 2002, A. Collins drew $250 Cash per month. During the year, the proprietor found it necessary to pay $1,000 of accounts payable out of his personal funds. What was his net income for the year? (Ignore depreciation on the Equipment.)

Answer questions 32 and 33 on the basis of the information given below.

The balance sheet prepared for J. Drew on December 31, 2002, showed total assets $26,500 and total liabilities $14,000. Subsequently, it was found that the Salesmen's Commissions account with a balance of $8,750 had been closed to income summary without taking into account the following:

a. No record had been made of the fact that December Commissions due to John Bell, a salesman, amounted to $410.
b. Advances to S. Town, a salesman, amounting to $250, had been made in anticipation of his future sales. This had been entered as an expense for 2002.

Corrections were made on the books for the above and the balance sheet was corrected.

32. What were the total assets in the corrected balance sheet?

33. What were the total liabilities in the corrected balance sheet?

Answer questions 34 and 35 on the basis of the information given below.

On December 31, 2002, a balance sheet was prepared for Wilton Lewis showing total assets of $45,800 and total liabilities $12,000. Subsequently it was found that the account Commissions Income, with a balance of $500, and the account Interest Income, with a balance of $450, had been closed to income summary without taking into account the following:

a. A 90-day note from a customer for $8,000 dated November 1, 2002, had already earned $80 interest.
b. The balance of the Commissions Income account included $100 commissions collected in advance.

Corrections were made on the books for the above and the balance sheet was revised.

34. What were the total assets in the corrected balance sheet?

35. What were the total liabilities in the corrected balance sheet?

36. On February 3, 2003, John Marron received his cancelled checks and bank statement from his bank for the month of January 2003. At the end of January, his checkbook balance was $4,284.69. The bank statement showed a debit memo of $8.14 for excessive activity for the month. The checks not returned by the bank were #415 for $82.68; #417 for $10.20; #419 (certified) for $510.60; and #426 for $8. A check that Mr. Marron had entered in the checkbook for $78.59 was actually for $87.59 and so charged by the bank. Also, the receipts for January 31, 2003, entered in the checkbook, amounting to $803.52, had not been credited by the bank on the January statement.

What was the cash balance appearing on the statement submitted by the bank at the end of January?

37. In preparing a worksheet for A. Cohen, the accountants arrived at a net loss of $1,400. Upon rechecking, they discovered the account Furniture and Fixtures with a balance of $12,400 had been entered in the Expense column, and that the account Accumulated

Depreciation of Furniture and Fixtures, amounting to $7,500, had been entered in the Income column. The necessary corrections were made.

What was the corrected profit or loss of the firm? (After your answer, write "P" if it is a profit, or "L" if it is a loss.)

Answer questions 38 and 39 on the basis of the information given below.

C. Alexander received his bank statement, dated March 31, showing a balance of $1,652. The following discrepancies between the bank statement and his Cash Book were noted: A deposit of $135, made on March 31, was credited by the bank on April 1. Checks outstanding as of March 31 were #135, $60.70; #137, $25; #141, $33; and #146, $52. Interest for the month credited by the bank to his account amounted to $5.20, but no entry had been made in the Cash Book. The bank's debit for a new printed checkbook amounting to $4 was not entered in the Cash Book. Check #143 for $87.50, issued on March 12, was recorded in the Cash Book as $78.50.

The Cash Book showed total receipts for the month of March of $718.60 and total disbursements of $475.30.

38. What should be the true available Cash Book balance on March 31?

39. What was the Cash Book balance on March 1?

40. You are given the following uncompleted trial balance as of January 31, 2002:

H. Murphy, Capital		$9,000
Cash	—	
Furniture	$7,000	
Accounts Receivable	2,100	
Accounts Payable		4,400
Inventory, Jan. 1, 2002	1,500	
Purchases	14,000	
Expenses Paid	800	
Sales		—

The Inventory on Jan. 31, 2002, was $1,750 and the net income for the month was $2,200. There were no deferred or accrued expenses. (Disregard depreciation of fixed assets.) What were the sales for the month?

ANSWER KEY

1. 9,500
2. 6,900
3. 885
4. 48,900
5. 6,300
6. 1,900
7. 5.2
8. 28,800 or 29,220
9. 12,120
10. 39,000
11. 48,300
12. 45,100
13. 2.1
14. 110,000
15. 47,800
16. 410,000
17. 24,000
18. 20,800
19. 19,550
20. 13,950
21. 18,000
22. 24,000
23. 4,708
24. 22,500
25. 18,640 or same
26. 18,000
27. 10,300
28. 18,780
29. 19,580
30. 15,417
31. 4,600
32. 26,750
33. 14,410
34. 45,880
35. 12,100
36. 3,564.91
37. 3,500 P
38. 1,616.30
39. 1,380.80
40. 1,6750

ANSWER SHEET
FOR
SAMPLE PRACTICE EXAMINATION VI

1. ______	24. ______	47. ______	70. ______
2. ______	25. ______	48. ______	71. ______
3. ______	26. ______	49. ______	72. ______
4. ______	27. ______	50. ______	73. ______
5. ______	28. ______	51. ______	74. ______
6. ______	29. ______	52. ______	75. ______
7. ______	30. ______	53. ______	76. ______
8. ______	31. ______	54. ______	77. ______
9. ______	32. ______	55. ______	78. ______
10. ______	33. ______	56. ______	79. ______
11. ______	34. ______	57. ______	80. ______
12. ______	35. ______	58. ______	81. ______
13. ______	36. ______	59. ______	82. ______
14. ______	37. ______	60. ______	83. ______
15. ______	38. ______	61. ______	84. ______
16. ______	39. ______	62. ______	85. ______
17. ______	40. ______	63. ______	86. ______
18. ______	41. ______	64. ______	87. ______
19. ______	42. ______	65. ______	88. ______
20. ______	43. ______	66. ______	89. ______
21. ______	44. ______	67. ______	90. ______
22. ______	45. ______	68. ______	
23. ______	46. ______	69. ______	

SAMPLE PRACTICE EXAMINATION VI

Directions: Answer all questions. Write answers to questions on your answer sheet in **INK ONLY** (blue or black). Pencils may be used only for scratch work. You are given 40 questions. Do all work on the scratch paper and put your answers on the answer sheet provided. *Note that you will be given credit only for correct answers.* This examination is designed to test your knowledge of accounting principles and your ability to think clearly and quickly. If you make a mistake in the answer, draw a line through it in ink and put the correct answer alongside of it.

The time allowed for the entire examination is 4 hours.

Answer questions 1 and 2 on the basis of the information given below.

H. B. began business early in 2000 with a certain amount of cash. At the end of the year, his records showed that his sales for the period were $51,000; Accounts Receivable, Dec. 31, 2000, $15,000; Accounts Payable $13,000; Cost of Goods Sold $22,600; Inventory, Dec. 31, 2000, $16,800; Expenses Paid in Cash $31,000; Cash Balance, Dec. 31, 2000, $14,200.

1. What were the purchases for the year?

2. How much cash did H. B. invest?

Answer questions 3 and 4 on the basis of the information given below.

A house valued at $80,000 and contents valued at $5,000 were insured for three-fourths of their value. Fire causes a loss of $32,000 to the house. The contents were completely destroyed. The insurance policies contain an 80% coinsurance clause.

3. How much is payable by the insurance company for the damage to the building?

4. How much is payable by the insurance company for damage to the contents?

5. A company marks its goods at 40% above cost. Expenses are 20% of sales. The net profit for one month is $180. Determine the sales for the month.

Answer questions 6 and 7 on the basis of the information given below.

Our checkbook balance on Dec. 31, 2001, was $4,886. On receiving the bank statement, you discover the following checks issued by you are still outstanding: #165 for $76.50; #280 for $452; and #285 for $310. You also discover that one check for $42.89 was entered on the stub of your checkbook as $24.89. The bank also charged $7.62 for service charges. You had not entered this. A deposit of $564 made by you late on the last day of the month did not appear on the bank statement but was entered in the checkbook on Dec. 31, 2001.

6. What balance appeared on the Dec. 31, 2001, bank statement?

7. How much cash do you have available on Jan. 1, 2002?

Answer questions 8 and 9 on the basis of the information given below.

A retail merchant began the year 2001 with a stock of merchandise valued at $75,000 at retail. During the year he made purchases costing $186,000. On Dec. 31, 2001, he found that his stock on hand had a retail value of $58,100. The average gross profit on sales was 40%.

8. What was the cost of the inventory on Dec. 31, 2001?

9. What were the total sales for 2001?

10. The firm of Packer and Jones divides profits in proportion to invested capital. On Jan. 1, 2001, Packer's capital was $15,000 and Jones' capital was $12,000. They decide to admit Davis as a partner with a one-third interest. How much cash must Davis invest?

Answer questions 11 and 12 on the basis of the information given below.

The partnership of Walker and Gaines had a capital, as per books, as follows: Walker $40,000; Gaines $25,000.

11. Nevins was admitted as partner after allowing the old partners Goodwill of $10,000. How much must Nevins invest to acquire a one-quarter interest in the new firm?

12. What will Walker's capital be after making all records necessary to record the admission of Nevins as a partner?

13. Jones and Williams invested $25,000 and $12,000 respectively in a partnership. Their agreement with respect to profits stated, "after allowing each partner 12% interest on invested capital at year end, remaining profits shall be divided equally." During the first year of operations, the net profit before adjustment for interest on partners' capitals was $4,800. Their drawings during the year were Jones $5,000 and Williams $4,000. Determine Jones' capital after closing books at end of year.

14. Paul and David are partners sharing profits and losses in the ratio of 3:2, respectively. After closing the books on Dec. 31, the capital accounts showed balances as follows: Paul $32,500 and David $21,800. They decided to liquidate and sold all assets and paid all liabilities. The firm remained with a cash balance of $20,300. How much of the cash was Paul entitled to?

Answer questions 15 and 16 on the basis of the information given below.

Johnson and Williams are in partnership, sharing profits and losses equally. On Dec. 31, 2001, their capital accounts were:

A. Johnson, Capital
: 2001
: Jan. 1 $8,500

P. Williams, Capital
: 2001
: Jan. 1 6,000

A. Johnson, Personal
2001
Dec. 31 : 3,000

P. Williams, Personal
2001
Dec. 31 : 4,500

On Dec. 31, 2001, the profit for 2001was determined to be $5,800. On Dec. 31, 2001, their assets were Cash $5,000; Merchandise $14,000; and Accounts Receivable $8,400.

15. How much were their liabilities on Dec. 31, 2001?

16. On Dec. 31, 2001, they decided to liquidate and sold the Merchandise and Accounts Receivable for $17,000 cash. How much of the total cash should be paid to P. Williams?

17. A corporation's liabilities were $58,600. The Authorized Stock was $150,000 par value; Unissued Stock was $32,000 par value; Treasury Stock was $15,000 par value; Donated Capital $8,800; Reserve for Sinking Fund $28,000; and Retained Earnings $12,000. The assets were Cash, Merchandise, Equipment, Prepaid Insurance, and Accounts Receivable. What was the total of these five assets?

18. An asset was purchased for $20,000 Jan.1, 2001, with a salvage value of $5,000. The useful life of the asset was expected to be five years. Using the Sum-of-the-Years-Digits method of depreciation, what depreciation expense can be taken for 2001?

Answer questions 19–24 on the basis of the information given below.

Below you will find the Accounts Receivable account taken from the ledger of S. Walker on Dec. 31, 2001, and the schedule of his customer's ledger on Dec. 31, 2001.

Accounts Receivable

2001 :
Dec. 31 Balance ?:
:

Schedule of Customer's Ledger
Dec. 31, 2001

S. Macon	$ 450
B. Johnson	870
W. Jones	655
H. King	380
R. Michaels	590
All other customers (balances correct)	6,400

A check of the bookkeeper's work reveals the following:

a. A note for $300 received from S. Macon on Dec. 28 was not entered.
b. Goods priced at $50 returned by H. King were posted to the account of R. Michaels.
c. A refund of $100 to B. Johnson was entered in the Accounts Payable column of the cash payments book and was posted from there to B. Johnson's account.
d. A check for $202, received from W. Jones for his $200 interest-bearing note, was credited entirely to the account of W. Jones.
e. A payment of $98 was received from R. Michaels for an invoice, less 2% discount. The amount of $98 was posted from the Cash Book to R. Michaels's account because the discount had been ignored when making the entry in the Cash Book.
f. Freight prepaid by U.S. $15 on a shipment to S. Macon, terms F.O.B. shipping point, was posted to the Freight Inward Account.

After adjustments,

19. Determine the correct balance in Macon's account.

20. Determine the correct balance in Johnson's account.

21. Determine the correct balance in Jones's account.

22. Determine the correct balance in King's account.

23. Determine the correct balance in Michaels's account.

24. What was the balance in control account *before* adjustments were made?

25. A firm estimated that an auto purchased on July 1, 2000, would have a salvage value of $400. Depreciation was recorded by the straight-line method. Below are the accounts referring to the auto truck on Dec. 31, 2002, after closing the books.

Auto		
2000	:	
July 1 $4,000	:	

Accumulated Depreciation—Auto		
	:	2002
	:	Dec. 31 Bal. $1,500

What was the estimated life of the truck?

Answer questions 26–53 on the basis of the information given below.

For items 26–53, you are supplied with the working papers of S. Baldwin. (1) Note that the trial balance amounts are arranged in a *single* column. You are to consider the amounts as debit or credit balances according to the way they would normally appear in a trial balance. (2) Note that adjustments and corrections are correctly entered in the adjustment columns. You are to complete the working papers.

For each item, you are to enter in the appropriate space on your answer sheet the amount you would extend to the Income Statement or Balance Sheet columns. Before the amount, you are to place the letter A, B, C, or D that appear at the top of the columns to indicate in which of the four columns the amount would appear. For example, if for a certain item you wish to indicate that you would write $1,000 in the Balance Sheet debit column, then write in the appropriate space of your answer sheet:

C – $1,000

You may, if you wish, write your scrap work in your question booklet. However, you will be rated only on what appears on your answer sheet. Do not fail to put in the letter, in addition to the amount, on your answer sheet for each item.

S. BALDWIN
Working Papers Dec. 31, 2002

Item	Account	Unarranged Trial Balance Amt. 12/31/02	Adjustments Debit	Adjustments Credit	Income Statement A	Income Statement B	Balance Sheet C	Balance Sheet D
26.	Cash	$ 4,025						
27.	Notes Receivable	3,000	750	110				
28.	Accounts Receivable	9,540		750				
29.	Mdse. Invent. 1/1/02	12,500						
30.	Furniture & Fixtures	2,500		200				
31.	Allowance for Doubtful Accounts	125		350				
32.	Accumulated Depr. Fur. & Fix.	800		200				
33.	Accounts Payable	5,300		810				
34.	Notes Receivable Disc.	200	110					
35.	S. Baldwin, Capital	13,000						
36.	Sales Income	65,980	210					
37.	Purchases	42,700	810	15,000				
38.	Sales Returns & Allow	2,100						
39.	Freight In.	1,390						
40.	Rent	2,100	200	400				
41.	Purchase Ret. & Allow	550						
42.	Salaries	8,400	550					
43.	Interest Cost	170	70					
44.	Purchase Discount	980						
45.	Interest Income	290						
46.	S. Baldwin, Personal (Credit Balance)	12,000						
47.	Mdse. Inventory 12/31/02			15,000				
48.	Prepaid Rent			400				
49.	Int. Cost Accrued				70			
50.	Deprec. Fur. & Fixtures			200				
51.	Bad Debts			350				
52.	Salaries Accrued				550			
53.	Sales Tax collected				210			

Answer questions 54–59 on the basis of the information given below.

Indicate the effect of the following transactions on working capital by placing a "N" next to the question number for *no effect,* an "I" for an *increase* in working capital, and a "D" for a *decrease* in working capital.

54. Bought merchandise on account for $5,000.

55. Declared and paid a cash dividend of $2,000.

56. Sold inventory of $4,000 for $6,000.

57. Purchased a truck on account for $12,000.

58. Paid $8,000 on a note payable.

59. Received $500 on account from customers.

Answer questions 60–69 on the basis of the information given below.

A bookkeeper prepared a trial balance of his general ledger on Dec. 31, 2000, and, among other balances, there appeared the following:

Allowance for Doubtful Accounts	$ 910
Rent	8,000
Interest Earned	500
Insurance	750
Merchandise Inventory 1/1/00	14,000
Merchandise Purchases	86,000
Freight In	700
Freight Out	500
Social Security Taxes (debit)	110
Sales Taxes	425
Rent Income	1,750
Accumulated Depreciation of Fur. & Fix.	850
Interest Expense	125
Proprietor's Drawings	7,150
Salaries	16,350

The auditors checked the bookkeeper's trial balance and found it correct. They made adjusting entries and prepared the financial statements. The balance sheet as of Dec. 31, 2000, contained the following:

BALANCE SHEET, Dec. 31, 2000

ASSETS

Accounts Receivable	$10,000	
Less Allowance for Doubtful Accounts	2,000	$ 8,000
Furniture & Fixtures	5,000	
Less Accumulated Depreciation	1,350	3,650
Mdse. Inventory 12/31/00		6,200
Insurance Prepaid		225
Rent Prepaid		150
Interest Receivable		60
Other Assets		17,990
Total Assets		$36,275

LIABILITIES

Accrued Interest Cost	$ 50
Sales Taxes Payable	425
Accrued Soc. Sec. Taxes	25
Rent Income Received in Advance	200
Other Liabilities	12,275
Total Liabilities	$12,975

CAPITAL

Present Worth	23,300
Total Liab. & Capital	36,275

From the information supplied, you are to determine the amounts of the following items as they appeared in the Income Statement prepared for the year 2000.

60. Bad Debt Expense
61. Rent Expense
62. Interest Income
63. Insurance Expense
64. Cost of Goods Sold
65. Social Security Taxes Expense
66. Rent Income
67. Depreciation of Furniture and Fixtures
68. Interest Expense
69. If the net profit for the year was $7,780, what was the net worth on Jan. 1, 2000?

Answer questions 70–74 on the basis of the information given below.

The following accounts appeared on the ledger of J. Brown:

SALARIES

2000			
Dec.	31	Brought for	$16,250
	31	Accrual J 15	560
			16,810
2000			
Dec.	31	Income Statement	16,810
			$16,810
2001			
Jan.	1	Accrual J 17	560

SALARIES PAYABLE

2001			
Jan.	1	J 17	$ 560
2000			
Dec.	31	Accrual J 15	$ 560

70. How much was the total earnings of employees during 2000?

71. What amount was paid out for employees, services during 2000?

72. On the Income Statement for the year 2000, what amount was listed as the expense for salaries?

73. The firm's total capital on Dec. 31 was $22,600 after closing the books. What amount would it have been if the $560 accrual had not been entered?

74. If at the end of 2001 the debits to the salaries account amounted to $17,800, what will the expense for salaries be in the year 2001?

Answer questions 75–78 on the basis of the information given below.

The postings from the sales book to customer's ledger were found to be correct. However, the footing in the sales book was found to be $100 short, and so posted. State whether it is true or false (write T or F on the answer sheet) that as a result of the error:

75. the trial balance will be out $100.

76. the gross profit on sales will be overstated.

77. the Accounts Receivable control account is not affected.

78. the balances of the individual customers' accounts in the Accounts Receivable ledger will be wrong.

Answer questions 79–90 on the basis of the information given below.

Below you will find a list of ledgers accounts with a number before each:

1. Accounts Receivable
2. Bonds Payable
3. Capital Stock Authorized
4. Capital Stock Unissued
5. Cash
6. Discount on Treasury Stock
7. Dividends Payable
8. Goodwill
9. Land and Buildings
10. Notes Payable
11. Organization Expense
12. Profit and Loss
13. Reserve for Contingencies
14. Reserve for Inventory Depreciation
15. Reserve for Sinking Fund
16. Sinking Fund Cash
17. Subscriptions Receivable
18. Retained Earnings
19. Treasury Stock
20. Capital Stock Subscribed

Using the numbers in front of each account, make the following journal entries for the transactions listed below. Do not write the names of the accounts on your answer sheet. Simply indicate in the proper space on the answer sheet the numbers of the accounts to be debited or credited. Always give the number of the account to be debited first, then give the number of the account to be credited. For example, if Cash is to be debited and Accounts Receivable to be credited, write on the answer sheet 5–1.

79. A subscriber to 50 shares of Capital Stock paid an installment when due.

80. All stockholders donated 10% of their stock to the corporation to be used to raise additional working capital.

81. Applications had been previously made to increase the authorized capital stock. Approval has been received for this action.

82. The condition of the corporation was such that it was deemed advisable to eliminate the Reserve for Contingencies.

83. In order to improve the showing made on the financial statement, the Goodwill on the books was reduced by half.

84. Issued 500 shares of stock as the purchase price of a building.

85. Drew a check to deposit cash with the trustee of the Sinking Fund.

86. Purchased 300 shares of stock paying par value.

87. The directors declared a stock dividend payable to stockholders of record two months from today.

88. J. Smith cancelled his subscription of last month for 10 shares of stock. He had paid nothing on his subscription.

89. Interest for the current period was added to the Sinking Fund Cash account.

90. Issued stock in payment of the stock dividend declared and recorded on a previous date.

ANSWER KEY

1. 39,400
2. 35,600
3. 30,000
4. 3,750
5. 2,060 or 2,160
6. 5,134.88
7. 4,860.38
8. 34,860
9. 326,900
10. 13,500
11. 25,000
12. 45,000
13. 23,120
14. 12,100
15. 14,600
16. 1,700
17. 210,400
18. 5,000
19. 165
20. 870 or 770
21. 857
22. 330
23. 638
24. 9,345
25. 6
26. (C) 4,025
27. (C) 3,640
28. (C) 8,790
29. (A) 12,500
30. (C) 2,300
31. (D) 475
32. (D) 1,000
33. (D) 6,110
34. (D) 90
35. (D) 13,000
36. (B) 65,770
37. (A) 28,510
38. (A) 2,100
39. (A) 1,390
40. (A) 1,900
41. (B) 550
42. (A) 8,950
43. (A) 240
44. (B) 980
45. (B) 290
46. (D) 1,200
47. (C) 15,000
48. (C) 400
49. (D) 70
50. (A) 200
51. (A) 350
52. (D) 550
53. (D) 210
54. (N)
55. (D)
56. (I)
57. (D)
58. (N)
59. (N)
60. 1,090
61. 7,850
62. 560
63. 525
64. 94,500
65. 135 or 122.50
66. 1,550
67. 500
68. 175
69. 22,670
70. 16,810
71. 16,250
72. 16,810
73. 23,160
74. 17,240
75. (F or T)
76. (F)
77. (F or T)
78. (F)
79. 5–17
80. 19–18
81. 4–3
82. 13–18
83. 18–8
84. 9–4
85. 16–5
86. 19–5
87. 18–7
88. 20–17
89. 16–12 or 16–5
90. 7–4

SAMPLE PRACTICE EXAMINATION VII

Explanatory Answers are given at the end of this Practice Exam.

The time allowed for the entire examination is 4 hours.

This examination for Accountant is in two parts. The six questions in Part One are of equal weight in scoring the test. The three questions in Part Two are given double weight. Explanatory answers to all questions appear at the end of this test.

1. The books of the Adams Co., Inc., had been closed as of December 31, 2000. In February 2001, you are called in to audit the 2000 records. You discover the following facts about the 2000 records. Show in two-column journal form the entries, if any, you would make to correct the records for each of the following:

   a. Of a purchase made on July 1, 2000, of machinery amounting to \$2, \$600 had been charged to the Repairs account. This machinery had an estimated life of ten years and no residual value.

   b. Accrued rent income amounting to \$275 as of December 31, 2000, had been ignored.

   c. A gain of \$75 on the sale of an office desk in 2000 had been credited to the Profit and Loss account.

   d. Merchandise sent out on consignment and still unsold on December 31, 2000, had been included in the closing inventory at the consigned price of \$2,800. The consigned price is 125% of cost.

   e. Merchandise was purchased for \$1,500 on credit, terms net ninety days, and received on December 24, 2000. This purchase was recorded on and as of January 8, 2001. This merchandise, however, had been included in the inventory of December 31, 2000, at the invoice price.

   f. Depreciation of auto trucks for 2000 had been overstated by \$750.

   g,h. During 2000, employees earned salaries of \$28,000. Deductions for Social Security taxes amounting to \$560 and of withholding taxes amounting to \$1, \$600 were taken from these salaries and the remainder was paid to the employees in 2000. The total taxes deducted from the employees' salaries were credited to an account entitled "Taxes Withheld from Salaries." During the year, payments to the Director of Internal Revenue were made as follows:

	S.S. Taxes	With-holding Taxes
For 1st quarter of 2000	\$280	\$400
For 2nd quarter of 2000	280	400
For 3rd quarter of 2000	280	400

   Payment for the 4th quarter of 2000, amounting to \$280 for social security taxes and \$400 for withholding taxes, was made in January 2001. Each time a payment to the Director of Internal Revenue was made, the entire sum was entered in the account "Taxes Withheld from Salaries." The December 31, 2000, balance of this account was listed on the Balance Sheet for December 31, 2000, as a current liability.

   i. The Adams Co., Inc., had four stockholders until November 10, 2000. On that date, one stockholder who owned 30 shares of common stock (par value \$100) transferred his stock to the other three stockholders, each of whom received 10 shares. In payment, the corporation issued its check for \$4, 200 to the retiring stockholder. The bookkeeper for the corporation debited this \$4,200 to the account "Common Stock Issued and Outstanding," thereby reducing the balance of that account from \$50,000 to \$45,800. The minutes of the corporation made no reference to this transaction, since the arrangement had been made among the four stockholders.

   j. The minutes of the corporation showed that a dividend of \$5 per share of common stock had been declared in December 2000, payable in June 2001. The bookkeeper had made no entries for this transaction, since he preferred to wait until June 2001.

2. In auditing the records of the New York branch of the Chicago Trading Company on June 30, 2001, you find the discrepancies listed below. You are required to do the following, using the information given:

   (1) Prepare journal entries, with explanations, on the books of the branch, in two-column journal form, to adjust the branch office books.
   (2) Set up the Home Office account on the branch books, showing the balance of this account *before* your adjustments.

   a. A credit by the home office for $600 for defective merchandise was entered on the branch books as $660.
   b. The home office charged the branch $210 for office supplies. The branch bookkeeper incorrectly entered the amount as $140.
   c. A charge by the home office of $875 for advertising was entered twice on the branch books.
   d. The branch office incorrectly charged the home office account $370 for cartage. The home office did not enter this transaction.
   e. A charge by the home office of $12.50 for postage was incorrectly entered on the branch books as $125.
   f. The home office spent $510 for wrapping materials and incorrectly charged the branch. The branch office made no record of this transaction.
   g. The home office sent the branch a record of a correction for Item (f.) above. The branch bookkeeper entered a debit to the home office account on June 5, 2001, for this correction.

   On June 30, 2001, the balance of the account with the branch on the books of the home office showed a debit balance of $36,460. At the beginning of 2001 the inter-office accounts were in balance.

3. The following items appeared on the liability and capital side of the balance sheet of the Jaxon Company for June 30, 2001:

<u>Liabilities and Capital</u>

Current Liabilities		$125,650
Bonds Payable		$200,000
Reserve for Sinking Fund		$80,000
<u>Capital Stock</u>		
Common ($100 par value)		
authorized	20,000 shares	
issued and outstanding	8,000 shares	$800,000
Preferred ($100 par value)		
(6% cumulative entitled to		
$120 per share in liquidation)		
authorized	5,000 shares	
issued and outstanding	2,000 shares	
in treasury	200 shares	
		$180,000
Premium on Preferred Stock		$30,000
Premium on Common Stock		$55,600
Earned Surplus		$88,560

Thereafter, in order to provide additional funds for fixed improvements, the company allowed common stockholders to purchase an additional 4,000 shares of common stock at $125 per share. All the holders of common stock availed themselves of this opportunity, and the new stock was issued and paid for.

Compute the book value of one share of common stock after the sale of the additional shares. You must show all steps in your computations in good form.

4. In checking the records for the year 2001 of a retailer who operates his business as a sole proprietorship, you suspect that he has not reported all of his sales as a basis for computing and paying City sales taxes. All of his sales are made for cash. He takes a physical inventory on December 31 of each year. He tells you that no additional investment had been made in 2001. He does not keep a double entry set of books. The only records he keeps are a checkbook and memoranda of his accounts payable.

   He shows you his profit and loss statement for the year 2001. You find that the amount of sales on the profit and loss statement given below agrees with the amount reported as taxable sales for the four quarters of the year 2001.

   Prepare a schedule showing the amount of discrepancy, if any, between the sales reported for sales tax purposes and the actual receipts from sales for the year 2001. You must show all your computations in good form.

PROFIT AND LOSS STATEMENT FOR YEAR ENDED DECEMBER 31, 2001

Sales			$298,000
Inventory 1/1/01	$332,000		
Purchases in 2001	$243,800		
	$275,800		
Less Inventory 12/31/01	28,750		
Cost of Goods Sold			247,050
Gross Profit			$50,950
Expenses			
Salaries of Employees		$9,000	
Rent		4,500	
Taxes on Business		1,750	
Advertising Expense		1,200	
Business Donations		250	
Miscellaneous Expenses		11,500	
Depreciation of Equipment		2,750	
Total			30,950
Net Profit			$20,000

From his checkbook you discover the following:

Checkbook balance 1/1/01	$28,250
Checkbook balance 12/31/01	34,850
Equipment purchased in 2001	16,000
Proprietor drew in 2001	25,000

From the Accounts Payable records you learn the following:

Accounts Payable on 1/1/01	$33,800
Accounts payable on 12/31/01	21,050

5. A and B began business as the A. B. Trading Co., Inc., on March 1, 2001. The corporation was authorized to issue 10,000 shares of stock of no par value. Before April 1, 2001, the corporation had sold a sufficient number of shares at $5 per share to begin operations. They bought $18,000 worth of equipment and with the remaining cash they bought merchandise. Thereafter all purchases were made for credit.

   The sales to the end of 2001 amounted to $320,060. On December 31, 2001, the amounts due from customers were $20,500 and the accounts payable were $31,000. Salaries and expenses paid in cash during the period amounted to $65,700. The average gross profit was 30% of cost. The inventory of merchandise on December 31, 2001, was $27,300 at selling prices. The directors felt they had made sufficient profits during the year, so they declared and paid a dividend totaling $4,100 on the stock outstanding on December 20, 2001. The cash balance on December 31, 2001, was $16,560. In answering this question, you are to ignore depreciation.

   (a) Prepare a Profit and Loss Statement for the period ending December 31, 2001, showing the purchases for the period.
   (b) Prepare a Balance Sheet of December 31, 2001, showing in detail the capital section.

6. During an audit for the period ending December 31, 2001, the bookkeeper gives you the following reconciliation:

<u>RECONCILIATION OF BANK STATEMENT</u>

December 31, 2000

Cash balance per ledger account 12/31/00		$15,270.50
Add: Collections made on the last day of December 2000 — not deposited in December 2000 but entered in the books and charged to cash in bank:		3,312.75
Bank debit memo for a customer's check returned marked "Insufficient Funds." (Check is on hand, but no entry has been made.)		450.00
Bank debit memo for service charges of December 2000		3.50
Deduct: Bank credit memo for note collected for us		$19,036.75
by bank. Not recorded on our books as collected.	$ 860.00	
Our check for an account payable entered on our books as $350 was drawn by us as $550 and paid by bank as $550.	200.00	
Checks drawn by us but not yet paid by bank (see schedule below).	3,074.00	
		4,134.00
		$14,902.75
Unlocated difference		135.50
Balance per bank statement (verified)		$15,038.25

Schedule of Checks Outstanding on 12/31/00	
# 876	$ 434
942	600
1010 (certified)	200
1023	1,840
	$3,074

You are to prepare:

a. A corrected reconciliation in good form, indicating the correct cash balance.
b. Entries in two-column journal form for the items, which should be adjusted before closing the books.

PART TWO

The time allowed for Part Two is 3 hours.

7. The Rex Appliance Company began a cash and installment sales business on January 1, 2001. The company kept separate records for cash sales and for installment sales. In making installment sales, the company required a down payment of 40% of the sales price and 18 equal monthly installments for the balance. An account "Gross Profit Deferred – 2001" was used when adjusting the books at the end of the year. The gross profit percentage for 2001 was 30% of sales. Defaults were handled by transferring the unpaid balance to an account entitled "Expense-Defaults." When repossessed goods were sold, the sales were credited to "Expense-Defaults." At the end of the year, the account was adjusted to show the actual profit or loss. Using the summary of the Rex Appliance Company transactions for 2001 given below, you are to:

   a. Journalize the transactions with explanations.
   b. Set up the ledger account for Installment Accounts Receivable for the year 2001.
   c. Prepare a statement or schedule showing the realized gross profit for the year 2001 on all sales.
   b. Determine the net gain or loss on defaulted contracts for the year 2001. Show all computations in good form.

SUMMARY OF TRANSACTIONS

2001 Sales	
New goods sold on installment (including down payments)	$119,700
New goods sold for cash	14,300
Sales for cash of goods repossessed after defaults	500
2001 Purchases	$122,000
Inventories December 31, 2001	
New goods at cost	$ 28,200
Repossessed goods on hand	70
Collections of cash on installment sales (down payments not included)	$ 31,600
Unpaid balances on defaulted contracts	$ 2,150

8. On December 31, 2000, the Grace Mfg. Co. had $45,000 in common stock outstanding. The assets and liabilities on that date were:

Cash	$ 7,500
Accounts Receivable	15,000
Raw Materials Inventory	6,000
Goods in Process Inventory	3,000
Finished Goods Inventory	9,000
Prepaid Expenses	500
Machinery (net of depreciation)	45,000
Current Liabilities	26,000

During the year 2001, the Surplus account increased 50% as a result of the year's business. No dividends were paid in 2001. Balances of accounts receivable, prepaid expenses, current liabilities, and capital stock were the same on December 31, 2001, as they had been on December 31, 2001. Inventories were reduced by exactly 50% except for the finished goods inventory, which was reduced by one-third. The sales were made at 50% above their cost of $60,000. Direct labor cost was $9,000 and total manufacturing expense was $11,000 including depreciation. General expense and selling expense amounted to 15% and 10% respectively of the gross sales. Depreciation for 2001 was $6,000.

   a. Prepare a Balance Sheet as of December 31, 2000.
   b. Prepare a Statement of Profit and Loss for the year 2001 giving details of Cost of Goods Manufactured in the statement *or* in a separate schedule.

9. In answering this question, use the essay answer paper only. Write legibly. Additional paper may be obtained from the monitor. Your answer will be rated on content, organization of material, and English usage.

   Assume that you are a Senior Accountant in a city agency and that you have been placed in charge of a newly established accounting unit. The staff of the unit is to consist of 12 Accountants and 8 Junior Accountants. There are to be 6 clerical employees who will perform the necessary typing, stenographic, and clerical work of the unit.

   Assume that this unit is to do field and desk audits of business firms, or municipal departments, or public utilities, or any other organizations or activities with which you are familiar. In answering subdivision (a.), (b.), and (c.) of this question, you may also make any other reasonable assumptions that you believe necessary. All such assumptions must be clearly stated in your answer.

a. Describe the methods and procedures you would use in organizing this new unit, and in directing and coordinating its work.
b. Explain the devices and controls you would institute to determine whether the work of the unit is being performed efficiently and accurately.
b. Describe the plans you would make for handling anticipated seasonal peak loads in excess of the capacity of your normal staff of employees.

END OF EXAMINATION

EXPLANATORY ANSWERS

PART ONE

1. Assumed: One objective of the audit is to correct the 2000 closing and prepare a 2000 operating statement reconcilable to the *corrected* 2000 operating accounts. If the 2000 operating accounts had been ruled off after closing and 2001 entries posted, the 2000 corrections below for the starred (*) accounts would be collected in a temporary account, which would be closed into the Earned Surplus account, or the starred items would (less preferably) be posted directly to the Earned Surplus account.

		Debit	Credit
a.	Machinery	$2,600	
	*Depreciation of Machinery	130	
	*Repairs		$2,600
	Accumulated Depreciation – Machinery		130
	To correct entry of July 1 erroneously charging machinery purchase to Repairs, and to record depreciation at 10% annually from July 1 thru Dec. 31		
b.	Rent Income Receivable	$275	
	*Rent Income		$275
	To record asset and income value of Rent earned and unpaid as of Dec. 31, 2000		
c.	No correction required. Any possible Gain or Loss on Fixed Asset Sales account to which this should have been posted would have been closed to Profit and Loss anyway. At worst, the error would only cause a little inconvenience in handling figures on worksheets and statements.		
d.	*Profit and Loss	$560	
	Merchandise Inventory		$560
	To reduce value of consigned goods in closing inventory from $2,800 price to consignee to $2,240 cost price to us		
e.	(1) 2000 correction:		
	*Purchases	$1,500	
	Accounts Payable		$1,500
	To record purchase of goods received 12/24/00, recorded as of January 2001		
	(2) 2001 Correction:		
	Accounts Payable	$1,500	
	Purchases		$1,500
	To reverse 2001 entry of 2000 purchase (see correction entry (e.) (1) to correct as of Dec. 31, 2000)		
f.	Accumulated Depreciation – Auto Trucks	$750	
	*Depreciation of Auto Trucks		$750
	To correct overstatement of 2000 depreciation		
g.	*Payroll Tax Expense		
	Payroll and Withheld Taxes Payable		
	To record employer's share of	$560	
	Social Security taxes for 2000.		$560

	Account	Debit	Credit
h.	Taxes Withheld from Salaries	$120	
	Payroll and Withheld Taxes Payable		$120
	To transfer the credit balance in "Taxes Withheld from Salaries" to the payroll and withholding tax liability account to correctly reflect in it the unpaid fourth quarter 2000 taxes		
i.	Due from Stockholders	$4,200	
	Common Stock Issued and Outstanding		$4,200
	To correct error charging the capital account for check issued to retiring stockholder and to set up the amount of the check as receivable from the stockholders on whose behalf it was issued		
j.	Earned Surplus	$2,500	
	Dividends Payable on Common Stock		$2,500
	To record liability to pay dividend declared in December 2000 of $5 per share on 500 shares of outstanding common stock		

2. Part (1) – Correction entries on branch books:

	Account	Debit	Credit
a.	Purchase Returns and Allowances	$60	
	Home Office		$60
	To correct over-recording of a $600 allowance as $660		
b.	Office Supplies	$70	
	Home Office		$70
	To correct entry recording charge of $210 from home office for office supplies as $140		
c.	Home Office	$875	
	Advertising		$875
	To offset the extra entry of an advertising charge entered twice		
d.	Freight and Cartage In	$370	
	Home Office		$370
	To return to proper expense account an item originally charged back in error to the home office		
e.	Home Office	$112.50	
	Postage		$112.50
	To correct for an item of $12.50 entered as $125		
f.	No entry needed since there was (properly) no entry on branch office books at the time the home office made the erroneous entry; but see (g.) below		
g.	Shipping Supplies	$510	
	Home Office		$510
	To void the correction entered June 5 of an entry that had never been made.		

<u>Part (2)</u> - Home Office account on branch office ledger

Correction (c.)	$ 875.00	June 30	Balance		$36,437.50
" (e.)	112.50		Correction	(a.)	60.00
June 30 corrected bal.	36,460.00		"	(b.)	70.00
			"	(d.)	370.00
			"	(g.)	510.00
	$37,447.50				37,447.50
July 1 Corrected balance					$36,460.00

3. After issue of and payment for the 4,000 shares of common stock at $125, the Common Stock account would have a balance representing 8,000 previously issued and 4,000 newly issued shares at par value of $100 per share.

After issue of and payment for the 4,000 shares of common stock at $125, the Common Stock account would have a balance representing 8,000 previously issued and 4,000 newly issued shares at par value of $100 per share.			$1,200,000
The Premium on Common Stock account balance of $55,600 would be increased by the $25 premium on 4,000 shares	$100,000	to	155,600
The Earned Surplus account shows a balance of but there are two possible restrictions on this:		$88,560	
The $20-per-share over par liquidating value of 1,800 outstanding shares of preferred stock	$ 36,000		
* Preferred treasury stock, 200 shares at $100 par	20,000		
a total restriction of	$ 56,000		
which is only partially absorbed by the Premium on Preferred Stock of	30,000	26,000	
leaving free surplus of only available to common stock for a total book value for 12,000 shares:			62,560
			$1,418,160
or a book value per share of			$118.18

*—The assumption is made here that, at whatever price the 200 shares were bought back by the Jaxon Co., a surplus account was debited or credited for the difference over or under par value.

4. The checkbook balance on December 31, 2000, of remained after the following disbursements:

The checkbook balance on December 31, 2000, of remained after the following disbursements:			$ 34,850
On accounts payable: Balance, 1/1/01	$ 33,800		
For 2001 purchases	243,800		
	$ 277,600		
Deduct unpaid balance, 12/31/01	21,050	$256,550	
Expenses (total expenses of $30,950 minus non-cash item, depreciation, $2,750		28,200	
Equipment purchase		16,000	
Drawings		25,000	325,700
indicating total cash available for 2001 of			$ 360,600
Deducting cash balance at beginning of 2001			28,250
indicates total cash receipts for 2001, presumably all from sales, of			$ 332,350
against reported sales of			298,000
suggesting unreported sales of			$ 34,350

The strategic items here are cash and accounts payable. If set up in account form, they would appear as follows:

CASH

1/1/01 Balance	$ 28,250	Reduction of payables	$256,550
Receipts from sales	332,350	Expenses paid	28,200
		Equipment purchase	16,000
		Drawings	25,000
		12/31/01 Balance Forward	34,850
	360,600		$360,600
1/1/2002 Balance	$ 34,850		

ACCOUNTS PAYABLE

Payments on purchases	$256,550	1/1/01 Balance	$ 33,800
12/31/01 Balance forw'd	21,050	2001 purchases	243,800
	$277,600		277,600
		1/1/02 Balance	$ 21,050

5. Before preparing the statements, we must determine the unstated figures for merchandise purchased and capital stock issued. The latter requires reconstructing the cash account, since this is tied in with the amount of cash originally available.

Since sales were $320,060 and represented 130% of gross cost, cost of goods sold was $\frac{\$320,060}{1.30}$, or $246,200.

Similarly, if ending inventory was $27,300 at sales value, at cost it was $\frac{\$27,300}{1.30}$, of $21,000.

Cash receipts from sales were sales of	$320,060	
minus balances still owed by customers of	20,500	or $299,560
Merchandise purchases were the cost of goods sold,	$246,000	
plus cost of the ending inventory of	21,000	
	$267,200	
but of this, the accounts payable of	31,000	
indicated cash outlays for merchandise of	$236,200	

The cash account, with a known ending balance of $16,560 and the above determinations, can now be set up to reflect the original receipts for stock issued as follows:

Issue of stock	$ 41,000	Equipment purchased	$ 18,000
Sales	299,560	Merchandise purchased	236,200
		Salaries and expenses	65,700
		Dividends paid	4,100
		12/31/01 balance forward	16,560
	340,560		$340,560
1/1/01 Balance	$ 16,560		

We can now prepare:

A. B. TRADING CO., INC.
Profit and Loss Statement
Year Ending December 31, 2001

Sales		$320,060
Deduct: Cost of Goods Sold		
Merchandise Purchases	$267,200	
Deduct: Dec. 31, 2001, inventory	21,000	246,200
Gross Profit on Sales		$ 73,860
Deduct: Salaries and Expenses		65,700
Net Profit		$ 8,160

The balance sheet can be set up as follows:

A. B. TRADING CO., INC.
Balance Sheet
December 31, 2001

Assets		Liabilities		
Cash	$16,560	Accounts Payable		$31,000
Accounts Receivable	20,500			
Merchandise Inventory	21,000	Capital		
Fixed Assets	18,000	8,200 shares no-par stock		
		issued and outstanding		41,000
		Earned Surplus:		
		Profits for year	8,160	
		Dividends paid	4,100	4,060
Total Assets	$76,060	Total Liabilities & Capital		$76,060

6. (a) Corrected RECONCILIATION OF BANK STATEMENT
December 31, 2001

Balance per bank statement			15,038.25	
Add: Deposits not reflected on bank statement			3,312.75	18,351.00
Deduct: Outstanding checks: *	#876	434.00		
	#942	600.00		
	#1023	1,840.00		2,874.00
Adjusted bank statement balance				$15,477.00

Balance per ledger account, 12/31/01		15,270.50	
a. Add: Unrecorded collection of note by bank		860.00	16,130.50
b. Deduct: Under-recorded check ($550 as $350)	$200.00		
c. NSF check not yet deducted on our books	450.00		
d. Bank service charges	3.50		653.50
Ledger account after adjustment for above, (a) through (d)			$15,477.00

*—Note that the certified check, even if still outstanding, *cannot* be included as an adjustment of the bank statement balance because the bank deducts the amount of such a check from the bank balance *at the time of certification,* not when the check clears.

(b) A bank statement in the form above adjusts both bank statement balance and ledger account balance to a corrected checkbook balance. The corrections (a.) through (d.) in the ledger account side of the reconciliation would be the source of the following entries:

	Account	Debit	Credit
a.	Cash in Bank	$860	
	Notes Receivable (no collection expense or interest income indicated)		$860
b.	Accounts Payable	$200	
	Cash in Bank		$200
c.	Accounts Receivable	$450	
	Cash in Bank		$450
d.	Bank Service Charges	$3.50	
	Cash in Bank		$3.50

PART TWO

7. (a) Entries for 2001 transactions

	Account	Debit	Credit
1)	Cash	$14,300	
	Sales		$14,300
	To record cash sales		
2)	Cash	$47,880	
	Installment Accounts Receivable, 2001		$119,700
	Installment Sales		119,700
	Installment Accounts Receivable, 2001		47,800
	To record installment sales and down payments		
3)	Cash	$31,600	
	Installment Accounts Receivable, 2001		$31,600
	To record installment collections		
4)	Purchases	$122,000	
	Cash (or Accounts Payable – not stated in problem)		$122,000
	To record purchases		
5)	Expense–Defaults	$2,150	
	Installment Accounts Receivable, 2001		$2,150
	To transfer unpaid balances on repossessions		
6)	Cash	$500	
	Expense–Defaults		$500
	To record sales of repossessed goods		
7)	Cost of Installment Sales, 2000 (119,700 – 30%)	$83,790	
	Cost of Cash Sales, 2000 (14,300 – 30%)	10,010	
	Merchandise Inventory (at cost)	28,200	
	Purchases		$122,000
	To distribute 2001 purchase costs to cost of sales and ending inventory		
8)	Inventory – Repossessed Goods	$70	
	Expense–Defaults		$70
	To set up inventory value, 12/31/01, of repossessed goods on hand		

	Debit	Credit
9) Installment Sales, 2001	$119,700	
Cost of Installment Sales, 2001		$83,790
Deferred Gross Profit, 2001		35,910
To close the installment sales and cost of sales accounts and set up the deferred gross profit for the year		
10) Deferred Gross Profit, 2001	$23,844	
Realized Gross Profit, 2001		$23,844
To record realized gross profit at 30% of down payment cash of $47,880 and installment collections of 31,600 a total of $79,480		
11) Deferred Gross Profit, 2001	$645	
Expense–Defaults		$645
To write off deferred gross profit lost, at 30% of defaulted contract balances of $2,150 and reduce the debit (see entry 5) from sales value to cost		
12) Profit and Loss	$1,075	
Expense–Defaults		$1,075
To close the account showing losses on defaults of installment accounts		

7. (b)

INSTALLMENT ACCOUNTS RECEIVABLE, 2001

a. 2) Sales	$119,700	a. 2) Down payments	47,880
		a. 3) Installment receipts	31,600
		a. 5) Defaults written off	2,150
		12/31/01 Balance forward	38,070
	$119,700		$119,700
1/1/02 Balance	$ 38,070		

(c)

REX APPLIANCE COMPANY
Statement of Realized Gross Profit for the
Year Ending December 31, 2001

Sales—Regular			14,300	
Deduct: Cost of Goods Sold				
Purchases		122,000		
Deduct, 12/31 Inventory	$28,200			
Cost of Installment Sales	83,790	111,990	10,010	
Gross Profit on Regular Sales				3,290
Sales—Installment			119,700	
Deduct: Cost of Goods Sold			83,790	
Deferred Gross Profit			35,910	
Unrealized Gross Profit:				
30% of installments not due of	$38,070	11,421		
30% of defaults written off of	2,150	645	12,066	
	$40,220			

Realized on down payments and collections of	79,480 at 30%	23,844
Realized gross profit on all 2001 sales		$27,134

(d) The debit balance in the "Expense–Defaults" account below would be shown on the Profit and Loss statement as an expense below the gross profit line. The debit balance is closed to Profit and Loss by entry a. 12.

a. 5) Write-off of defaults	2,150	a . 6) Sales, repossessed goods	500
a. 8) Ending inventory–repossessed goods	70	a. 11) Reducing a. 5 to cost	645
		a. 12) To Profit and Loss	1,075
	2,220		2,220

8. To prepare a December 31, 2001, balance sheet, the two unstated figures of cash and surplus at that date must be computed. A quick addition of the December 31,

2000, figures shows total assets of	$ 86,000
and liabilities and capital stock of	71,000
indicating a surplus of	$ 15,000
The stated increase of 50% in surplus from 2001 profits,	7,500
then results in a 12/31/01 surplus of	$ 22,500

Taking the remaining data as stated, and keeping in mind that the problem leaves a suggestion that cash must have been increased, we must work back to this changed figure as follows:

Income from sales (all cash, no change in receivables) was 50% more than the $60,000 cost of sales, or		$ 90,000
There were noncash items of		
Inventory decreases of	$7,500	
and depreciation of	6,000 or $13,500	
which would bring the cash cost of sales to		46,500
for a total increase in available cash of		$ 43,500
to meet general and selling expenses, which		
together were 25% of the $90,000 gross sales, or		22,500
leaving a net increase in cash of		$ 21,000
over the December 31, 2000, balance of		7,500
for a December 31, 2001, balance of		$ 28,500

(a)

GRACE MANUFACTURING COMPANY
Balance Sheet
December 31, 2001

Assets		
Currents Assets: Cash	$ 28,500	
Accounts Receivable	15,000	
Inventories: Raw Materials	3,000	
Goods in Process	1,500	
Finished Goods	6,000	
Prepaid Expenses	500	$54,500
Fixed Assets: Machinery (net of depreciation)		39,000
Total Assets		$93,500

Liabilities and Capital		
Current Liabilities		$26,000
Capital Stock Outstanding	$ 45,000	
Surplus	22,500	
Total Capital and Surplus		67,500
Total Liabilities and Capital		$93,500

(b) A quick reconstruction of the inventory accounts, based on stated cost of sales and 2001 ending inventories, provides data for the Profit and Loss Statement as follows:

FINISHED GOODS

12/31/00 Balance	$ 9,000	12/31/01 To Cost of Sales	$60,000
12/31/01 From Goods in Process	57,000 *	12/31/01 Balance forward	6,000
	66,000		66,000
12/31/01 Balance	$ 6,000		

GOODS IN PROCESS

12/31/00 Balance	$ 3,000	12/31/01 To Finished Goods	$57,000
12/31/01 Raw Materials	35,500 *	12/31/01 Balance forward	1,500
Direct Labor	9,000		
Mfg. Expense	11,000		
	58,500		$58,500
12/31/01 Balance	$ 1,500		

RAW MATERIALS

12/31/00 Balance	$ 6,000	12/31/01 To Goods in Process	$35,500
12/31/01 Purchases	32,500 *	12/31/01 Balance forward	3,000
	38,500		$38,500
12/31/01 Balance	$ 3,000		

*— The starred figures in each of the three inventory accounts were computed in the order given, to arrive at the 12/31/01 balances stated in the problem.

GRACE MANUFACTURING COMPANY
Profit and Loss Statement
Year Ended December 31, 2001

Income from Sales		$90,000
Deduct: Cost of Goods Sold (per attached schedule)		60,000
Gross Profit		$30,000
Deduct: Selling Expenses	$13,500	
General Expenses	9,000	22,500
Net Profit		$ 7,500

GRACE MANUFACTURING COMPANY
Cost of Goods Sold Schedule
Year Ended December 31, 2001

Raw Materials Used:			
Inventory, December 31, 2000	$ 6,000		
Add Purchases	32,500	$38,500	
Deduct: Inventory, December 31, 2001		3,000	$ 35,500
Direct Labor			9,000
Manufacturing Expense			11,000
Cost of Goods placed in Process during year			$ 55,500
Add: Goods in Process, December 31, 2000			3,000
Cost of Goods Available for Completion during year			$ 58,500
Deduct: Goods in Process, December 31, 2001			1,500
Cost of Goods Manufactured (completed) during year			$ 57,000
Add: Finished Goods, December 31, 2000			9,000
Cost of Goods Available for Sale during year			$ 66,000
Deduct: Finished Goods, December 31, 2000			6,000
Cost of Goods Sold during year			$ 60,000

9. *Note:* There can be no provably "correct" answer to this question. As indicated, two of the three bases for rating the answer are organization of material and English usage. Content will depend on the choice of assumptions available as to fields of activity audited and other relevant assumptions, all of which require clear statement in the answer given. The following suggestions are made concerning factors to be considered as to content in the answer to the specific areas of the question:

A. In this area, consider among other things:

(1) the applicability of the accountants and junior accountants working in permanently assigned teams;

(2) the comparative merits of assigning accountants on a regularly recurring basis to specific clients versus rotation of accountants on a given client's audits; and

(3) the assignment of clerical and stenographic help to specific accountants versus the clerical–stenographic "pool" arrangement.

B. For evaluation of efficiency of performance, consider the possibility of setting standards for audit time spent based on volume of activity, nature of audit, past experience, and likelihood and frequency of special problems, as applied to each functional audit area (e.g., cash, receivables, purchase verification) and comparison of actual time spent with the standard time set up for planning purposes.

For checks on accuracy, consider:

(1) the matters of Accountant understanding of uses of controls;

(2) the necessity of checking arithmetic on all reports prior to release to client and other recipients; and

(3) the determination of what functional type of employee is to do what checking (e.g., Senior Accountant on policy or interpretation of policy, Accountant on control coordination, Junior Accountant or clerk on arithmetical checks, stenographers on proofreading).

C. Here some factors to be considered:

(1) the availability of qualified temporary help;

(2) the overtime costs for nonexempt employees; and

(3) the possible compensatory time-off plans for exempt employees.

Final Sample Practice Examination

ANSWER SHEET
FOR
FINAL SAMPLE PRACTICE EXAMINATION

1 Ⓐ Ⓑ Ⓒ Ⓓ	11 Ⓐ Ⓑ Ⓒ Ⓓ	21 Ⓐ Ⓑ Ⓒ Ⓓ	31 Ⓐ Ⓑ Ⓒ Ⓓ
2 Ⓐ Ⓑ Ⓒ Ⓓ	12 Ⓐ Ⓑ Ⓒ Ⓓ	22 Ⓐ Ⓑ Ⓒ Ⓓ	32 Ⓐ Ⓑ Ⓒ Ⓓ
3 Ⓐ Ⓑ Ⓒ Ⓓ	13 Ⓐ Ⓑ Ⓒ Ⓓ	23 Ⓐ Ⓑ Ⓒ Ⓓ	33 Ⓐ Ⓑ Ⓒ Ⓓ
4 Ⓐ Ⓑ Ⓒ Ⓓ	14 Ⓐ Ⓑ Ⓒ Ⓓ	24 Ⓐ Ⓑ Ⓒ Ⓓ	34 Ⓐ Ⓑ Ⓒ Ⓓ
5 Ⓐ Ⓑ Ⓒ Ⓓ	15 Ⓐ Ⓑ Ⓒ Ⓓ	25 Ⓐ Ⓑ Ⓒ Ⓓ	35 Ⓐ Ⓑ Ⓒ Ⓓ
6 Ⓐ Ⓑ Ⓒ Ⓓ	16 Ⓐ Ⓑ Ⓒ Ⓓ	26 Ⓐ Ⓑ Ⓒ Ⓓ	36 Ⓐ Ⓑ Ⓒ Ⓓ
7 Ⓐ Ⓑ Ⓒ Ⓓ	17 Ⓐ Ⓑ Ⓒ Ⓓ	27 Ⓐ Ⓑ Ⓒ Ⓓ	37 Ⓐ Ⓑ Ⓒ Ⓓ
8 Ⓐ Ⓑ Ⓒ Ⓓ	18 Ⓐ Ⓑ Ⓒ Ⓓ	28 Ⓐ Ⓑ Ⓒ Ⓓ	38 Ⓐ Ⓑ Ⓒ Ⓓ
9 Ⓐ Ⓑ Ⓒ Ⓓ	19 Ⓐ Ⓑ Ⓒ Ⓓ	29 Ⓐ Ⓑ Ⓒ Ⓓ	39 Ⓐ Ⓑ Ⓒ Ⓓ
10 Ⓐ Ⓑ Ⓒ Ⓓ	20 Ⓐ Ⓑ Ⓒ Ⓓ	30 Ⓐ Ⓑ Ⓒ Ⓓ	40 Ⓐ Ⓑ Ⓒ Ⓓ

FINAL SAMPLE PRACTICE EXAMINATION

Directions: Each question has four suggested answers, (A), (B), (C), and (D). Decide which one is the best answer, and on the answer sheet find the question number that corresponds to the answer that you have selected and darken the area with a soft pencil.

The time allowed for the entire examination is four and one-half hours.

1. The independent auditor's primary objective in reviewing internal control is to provide

   (A) assurance of the client's operational efficiency.
   (B) a basis for reliance on the system and determination of the scope of the auditing procedures.
   (C) a basis for suggestions for improving the client's accounting system.
   (D) evidence of the client's adherence to prescribed managerial policies.

2. If there is an increase in work-in-process inventory during a period,

   (A) cost of goods sold will be greater than cost of goods manufactured.
   (B) cost of goods manufactured will be greater than cost of goods sold.
   (C) manufacturing costs (production costs) for the period will be greater than cost of goods manufactured.
   (D) manufacturing costs for the period will be less than cost of goods manufactured.

Answer questions 3 and 4 on the basis of the information given below.

The Rand Company purchased 800 of the 1,000 outstanding shares of the Apex Company's common stock for $80,000 on January 1, 2002. During 2002, the Apex Company declared dividends of $8,000 and reported earnings for the year of $20,000.

3. Using the equity method, the investment in Apex Company on the Rand Company's books should show a balance at December 31, 2000, of

   (A) $89,600
   (B) $86,400
   (C) $80,000
   (D) $73,600

4. If, instead of using the equity method, the Rand Company uses the cost method, the balance at December 31, 2002, in the investment account should be

   (A) $96,000
   (B) $86,400
   (C) $80,000
   (D) $73,600

Answer questions 5 and 6 on the basis of the information given below.

The Main Corporation has 50,000 shares of $10 par value common stock authorized, issued, and outstanding. The 50,000 shares were issued at $12 per share. The retained earnings of the company are $60,000.

5. Assuming that the Main Corporation reacquired 1,000 of its common shares at $15 per share and the par value method of accounting for treasury stock was used, the result would be that

   (A) stockholders' equity would increase by $15,000.
   (B) capital in excess of par would decrease by at least $2,000.
   (C) retained earnings would decrease by $5,000.
   (D) common stock would decrease by at least $15,000.

6. Assuming that the Main Corporation reissued 1,000 of its common shares at $11 per share and the cost method of accounting for treasury stock was used, the result would be that

   (A) book value per share of common stock would decrease.
   (B) retained earnings would decrease by $11,000.
   (C) donated surplus would be credited for $5,500.
   (D) a loss on reissue of treasury stock account would be charged.

7. On January 31, 2002, when the Oregon Corporation's stock was selling at $36 per share, its capital accounts were as follows:

Capital Stock (par value $20; 100,000 shares issued)	$2,000,000
Premium on Capital Stock	800,000
Retained Earnings	4,550,000

If the corporation declares a 100% stock dividend and the par value per share remains at $20, the value of the capital stock would

(A) remain the same.
(B) increase to $5,600,000.
(C) increase to $4,000,000.
(D) decrease.

8. In a conventional form of the statement of sources and application of funds, which one of the following would *not* be included?

(A) Periodic amortization of premium of bonds payable
(B) Machinery, fully depreciated and scrapped
(C) Patents written off
(D) Treasury stock purchased from a stockholder

Answer questions 9–11 on the basis of the balance sheet shown below for the Arco, Zayre, and Bett partnership.

Cash	$ 20,000
Other Assets	180,000
Total	$200,000
Liabilities	$ 50,000
Arco Capital (40%)	37,000
Zayre Capital (40%)	65,000
Bett Capital (20%)	48,000
	$200,000

9. If George is to be admitted as a new 1/6 partner without recording goodwill or bonus, George should contribute cash of

(A) $40,000
(B) $36,000
(C) $33,333
(D) $30,000

10. Assume that Bett is paid $51,000 by George for his interest in the partnership. Which of the following choices shows the correct revised capital account for each partner?

(A) Arco $38,500; Zayre $66,500; George $51,000
(B) Arco $38,500; Zayre $66,500; George $48,000
(C) Arco $37,000; Zayre $65,000; George $51,000
(D) Arco $37,000; Zayre $65,000; George $48,000

11. Assume that George had not been admitted as a partner but that the partnership was dissolved and liquidated on the basis of the original balance sheet. Noncash assets with a book value of $90,000 were sold for $50,000 cash. After payment of creditors, all available cash was distributed. Which of the following choices most nearly shows what each of the partners would receive?

(A) Arco $ -0- ; Zayre $13,333; Bett $ 6,667
(B) Arco $ -0- ; Zayre $ 3,000; Bett $17,000
(C) Arco $6,667; Zayre $ 6,667; Bett $ 6,666
(D) Arco $8,000; Zayre $ 8,000; Bett $ 4,000

12. Which one of the following should be restricted to only one employee in order to assure proper control of assets?

(A) Access to safe deposit box
(B) Placing orders and maintaining relationship with a principle vendor
(C) Collection of a particular past due account
(D) Custody of the petty cash fund

13. To assure proper internal control, the quantities of materials ordered may be omitted from that copy of the purchase order that is

(A) sent to the accounting department.
(B) retained in the purchasing department.
(C) sent to the party requisitioning the material.
(D) sent to the receiving department.

14. The Acme Corporation has an inventory of raw materials and parts made up of many different items, which are of small value individually, but of significant total value. A basic control requirement in such a situation is that

(A) perpetual inventory records should be maintained for all items.
(B) physical inventories should be taken on a cyclical basis rather than at year end.
(C) storekeeping, production, and inventory record-keeping functions should be separated.
(D) requisitions for materials should be approved by a corporate officer.

15. In conducting an audit of plant assets, which of the following accounts must be examined in order to ascertain that additions to plant assets have been correctly stated and reflect charges that are properly capitalized?

    (A) Accounts Receivable
    (B) Sales Income
    (C) Maintenance and Repairs
    (D) Investments

16. Which one of the following is a control procedure that would prevent a vendor's invoice from being paid twice (once upon the original invoice and once upon the monthly statement)?

    (A) Attaching the receiving report to the disbursement support papers
    (B) Prenumbering of disbursement vouchers
    (C) Using a limit or reasonable test
    (D) Prenumbering of receiving reports

17. A "cut-off" bank statement is received for the period December 1 to December 10, 2002. Very few of the checks listed on the November 30, 2002, bank reconciliation cleared during the cut-off period. Of the following, the most likely reason for this is

    (A) kiting.
    (B) using certified checks rather than ordinary checks.
    (C) holding the cash disbursement book open after year end.
    (D) overstating the year-end bank balance.

18. "Lapping" is a common type of defalcation. Of the audit techniques listed below, the one most effective in the detection of "lapping" is

    (A) reconciliation of year-end bank statements.
    (B) review of duplicate deposit slips.
    (C) securing confirmations from banks.
    (D) checking footings in cash journals.

19. Of the following, the most common argument against the use of the negative accounts receivable confirmation is that

    (A) cost per response is excessively high.
    (B) statistical sampling techniques cannot be applied to selection of the sample.
    (C) client's customers may assume that the confirmation is a request for payment.
    (D) lack of response does not necessarily indicate agreement with the balance.

Answer questions 20 and 21 on the basis of the information in the Payroll Summary given below. This Payroll Summary represents payroll for a monthly period for a particular agency.

PAYROLL SUMMARY

		Deductions				
Employee	*Total Earnings*	*FICA*	*Withhold. Tax*	*State Tax*	*Other*	*Net Pay*
W	$ 450.00	$26.00	$ 67.00	$18.00	$ 6.00	$333.00
X	235.00	14.00	33.00	8.00	2.00	178.00
Y	341.00	20.00	52.00	14.00	5.00	250.00
Z	275.00	16.00	30.00	6.00	2.40	220.60
Totals	$1,301.00	$76.00	$182.00	$46.00	$15.40	$981.60

20. Based on the data given above, the amount of cash that would have to be available to pay the employees on payday is

(A) $1,301
(B) $981.60
(C) $905.60
(D) $662.60

21. Based on the data given, the amount required to be deposited with a governmental depository is

(A) $334
(B) $182
(C) $158
(D) $76

Answer questions 22 and 23 based on the information given below.

Assume a $1,020 imprest fund for cash expenditures is maintained in your agency. As an audit procedure, the fund is counted and the following information results from that count:

Unreimbursed bills properly authorized	$ 345.00
Check from employee T. Jones	125.00
Check from Supervisor R. Riggles	250.00
I.O.U. signed by employee J. Sloan	100.00
Cash counted – coins and bills	200.00
Total	$1,020.00

22. A proper statement of cash on hand based upon the data shown above should show a balance of

    (A) $1,020
    (B) $1,000
    (C) $545
    (D) $200

23. Based upon the data shown above, the account reflects improper handling of the fund because

    (A) vouchers are unreimbursed.
    (B) the cash balance is too low.
    (C) employees have used it for loans and check cashing purposes.
    (D) the unreimbursed bills should not have been authorized.

Answer questions 24 and 25 based on the information given below.

The following information was taken from the ledgers of the Future Space Corporation:

Common stock had been issued for $6,000,000. This represented 400,000 shares of stock at a stated value of $5 per share. 50,000 shares are in the treasury. These 50,000 shares were acquired for $25 per share. The total undistributed net income since the origin of the corporation was $3,750,000 as of December 31, 2002. 10,000 of the Treasury stock shares were sold in January 2002 for $30 per share.

24. Based only on the information given above, the total stockholders' equity that should have been shown on the balance sheet as of December 31, 2002, was

    (A) $2,000,000
    (B) $6,000,000
    (C) $8,500,000
    (D) $9,750,000

25. Based only on the information given above, the Retained Earnings as of December 31, 2003, will be

    (A) $2,000,000
    (B) $3,750,000
    (C) $3,800,000
    (D) $4,050,000

Answer questions 26–29 on the basis of the information given below.

A statement of income for the Harvard Corporation for the 2002 fiscal year follows:

Sales	$89,000	
Cost of Goods Sold	55,000	
Gross Margin		$34,000
Expenses		20,000
Net Income before Income Taxes		$14,000
Provision for Income Taxes (50%)		7,000
Net Income		$ 7,000

The following errors were discovered relating to the 2002 fiscal year:

(1) Closing inventory was overstated by $2,100.
(2) A $3,000 expenditure was capitalized during fiscal year 2002 that should have been listed under Expenses. This was subject to 10% amortization taken for a full year.
(3) Sales included $3,500 of deposits received from customers for future orders.
(4) Accrued salaries of $850 were not included in Cost of Goods Sold.
(5) Interest receivable of $500 was omitted.

Assume that the books were not closed and that you have prepared a corrected income statement. Answer questions 26–29 on the basis of your corrected income statement.

26. The gross margin after accounting for adjustments should be

    (A) $37,500
    (B) $35,400
    (C) $31,900
    (D) $27,550

27. The adjusted income before income taxes should be

    (A) $5,350
    (B) $9,550
    (C) $15,000
    (D) $15,850

28. The adjusted income after provision for a 50% tax rate should be

(A) $7,925
(B) $7,500
(C) $4,500
(D) $2,675

29. After making adjustments, sales to be reported for fiscal year 2002 should be

(A) unchanged.
(B) increased by $3,500.
(C) decreased by $3,500.
(D) reduced by $2,100.

Answer questions 30–33 based on the following budget for the Worth Corporation for 2002:

Sales	$550,000
Cost of goods sold	320,000
Selling expenses	75,000
General expenses	60,000
Net income	95,000

30. If sales are actually 12% above the budget, then actual sales will be

(A) $550,000
(B) $562,000
(C) $605,000
(D) $616,000

31. If actual costs of goods sold exceed the budget by 10%, then the cost of goods sold will be

(A) $294,400
(B) $320,000
(C) $345,600
(D) $352,000

32. If selling expenses exceed the budget by 10%, the increase in the selling expenses will be

(A) $750
(B) $3,750
(C) $7,500
(D) $8,333

33. If general expenses are under budget by 5%, they will amount to

(A) $3,000
(B) $57,000
(C) $60,000
(D) $63,000

Answer questions 34 and 35 on the basis of the information given below.

A certain company began business on January 2, 2003. During the first month, credit sales totaled $100,000. During February, credit sales totaled $125,000. 70% of credit sales are paid during the month of sale, and the balance is collected during the following month.

34. During the month of January, cash collections on credit sales totaled

(A) $70,000
(B) $95,000
(C) $100,000
(D) $125,000

35. During the month of February, cash collections on credit sales totaled

(A) $70,000
(B) $87,500
(C) $117,500
(D) $125,000

Answer questions 36–38 on the basis of the following information taken from the balance sheet of the Z Corporation:

Common Stock $200 par	$1,400,000
Premium on Common Stock	115,000
Deficit	50,000

36. The number of shares of common stock outstanding is

(A) 200
(B) 700
(C) 7,000
(D) 14,000

37. The total equity is

(A) $50,000
(B) $115,000
(C) $1,400,000
(D) $1,465,000

38. The book value per share of stock is most nearly

(A) $160
(B) $200
(C) $209
(D) $312

Answer questions 39 and 40 based on the following statement:

You are examining the expense accounts of a contractor and you discover that, although his payroll records show proper deductions from employees, he has never provided for the payroll tax expenses for these employees.

39. As a result of the oversight described in the above statement, the Costs of Construction in Progress as given on the balance sheet will be

(A) understated on the balance sheet.
(B) overstated on the balance sheet.
(C) unaffected on the balance sheet.
(D) omitted from the balance sheet.

40. As a result of the oversight described in the above statement, the balance sheet for the firm will reflect an

(A) overstatement of liabilities.
(B) understatement of liabilities.
(C) overstatement of assets.
(D) understatement of assets.

ANSWER KEY

1. B	9. D	17. C	25. B	33. B
2. C	10. D	18. B	26. D	34. A
3. A	11. D	19. D	27. A	35. C
4. C	12. D	20. B	28. D	36. C
5. B	13. D	21. A	29. C	37. D
6. A and D	14. C	22. D	30. D	38. C
7. A and C	15. C	23. C	31. D	39. A
8. B	16. A	24. C	32. C	40. B

PART FIVE

Career Information Resources

HOW TO FIND A GOVERNMENT JOB

Very often, finding a job is a combination of luck and direction. In many instances, you may just happen to stumble upon an opening that seems perfect for you. But if you don't know where to look for those openings, you won't have much luck in finding what you want. You should start by contacting various accounting and auditing firms in your area. Don't stop there, though. Below are a variety of sources you can contact in your search for employment.

FEDERAL JOBS

For federal jobs, the place to start is the Office of Personnel Management (OPM). The OPM's Federal Employment Information System is the official source for federal employment information and contains job listings as well as some state, local government, and private sector listings.

Many job seekers fear the perceived complexities of finding a federal job. The process has been made user-friendly through a Web site established by the OPM called USAJOBS. This is basically made up of three user-friendly components for conducting your personal job search. By using USAJOBS, you have access to federal job listings and some state and local government as well as private sector listings. USAJOBS provides current information, updated daily, and is available 24 hours a day, 7 days a week. Here is a guide to making your federal job search easier:

STEP 1: USE ANY OF THE AUTOMATED COMPONENTS OF THE FEDERAL EMPLOYMENT INFORMATION SYSTEM

USAJOBS, the Federal Government's Employment Information System, is easily accessible federal employment information. USAJOBS provides worldwide job vacancy information, employment information fact sheets, and job applications and forms and has online resume development and electronic transmission capabilities. In many instances, job seekers can apply for positions on line. USAJOBS is updated every business day from a database of more than 12,000 worldwide job opportunities. USAJOBS is available to job seekers in a variety of formats, ensuring access for customers with differing physical and technological capabilities. It is convenient, user friendly, accessible through the computer or telephone, and available 24 hours a day, 7 days a week.

USAJOBS consists of:

> **Internet**—The official Web site for jobs and employment information may be accessed at www.usajobs.opm.gov. On the Web site, job seekers can access worldwide current job vacancies, employment information fact sheets, and applications and forms and, in some instances, apply for jobs on line. Complete job announcements can be retrieved from the Web site. The USAJOBS Web site also has an Online Resume Builder feature. Using the resume builder, job seekers can create online resumes specifically designed for applying for federal jobs. Resumes created on the USAJOBS resume builder can be printed

from the system for faxing or mailing to employers and saved and edited for future use. For many of the vacancies listed on the site, job seekers can submit resumes created through USAJOBS directly to hiring agencies through an electronic submission process.

Automated Telephone System— An interactive voice response telephone system that can be reached at 478-757-3000 or TDD 478-744-2299. By telephone, job seekers can access worldwide current job vacancies, employment information fact sheets, and applications and forms and, in some instances, apply for jobs by phone.

Note that USAJOBS can help you develop the kind of resume needed to successfully apply for government jobs. The direct page link to this is www.resume.usajobs.opm.gov.

STEP 2: OBTAINING THE VACANCY ANNOUNCEMENT

Once you have found an opportunity that interests you by using STEP 1, you will need more information on the specific opportunity and appropriate application forms. Use USAJOBS to obtain a copy of the vacancy announcement, which is an important source of information. Most of the questions you may have will be answered as you read through the announcement. For example: closing/deadline dates for applications, specific duties of the position, whether or not a written test is required, educational requirements, duty location, or salary information.

STEP 3: FOLLOW THE APPLICATION INSTRUCTIONS

You may apply for most jobs with a resume, the Optional Application for Federal Employment (OF-612) (see Appendix), or any written format you choose. For jobs that are filled through automated procedures, federal agencies may require that you submit a resume and/or other specialized forms. Jobs with unique requirements may also occasionally require special forms.

Whatever application method you select (or is required), it is essential that you follow the instructions for applying that are given in the vacancy announcement and that your application contains the following:

- **Job Information**—Announcement number, title, and grade
- **Personal Information**—Full name, mailing address (with zip code), day and evening phone numbers (with area code), Social Security number, country of citizenship, veterans' preference, reinstatement eligibility, and highest federal civilian grade held
- **Education**—High school name (city and state), colleges or universities (name, city, and state), majors and type, and year of any degrees received (if no degree, show total credits earned and indicate whether semester or quarter hours)
- **Work Experience**—Job title, duties and accomplishments, employer's name and address, supervisor's name and phone number, starting and ending dates (month and year), hours per week, and salary. Indicate whether or not your current supervisor may be contacted. Prepare a separate entry for each job.
- **Other Qualifications**—Job-related training courses (title and year), job-related skills, job-related certificates and licenses, and job-related honors, awards, and special accomplishments.

You can also obtain job information via touch screen computer kiosks located throughout the nation at OPM offices, federal buildings, and some colleges and universities.

Most federal, state, and municipal units have recruitment procedures for filing civil service positions. They have developed a number of methods to make job opportunities known. The best source for up-to-date listing information on available job opportunities is on the various Web sites established by the federal and state government employers.

Another popular source for job information is the *Federal Jobs Digest*, a biweekly newspaper that lists thousands of government jobs, both in the United States and in other countries. Its Web site also features thousands of job listings at any one time and can be accessed at www.jobsfed.com or by telephone: 800-824-5000 (toll-free).

STATE AND LOCAL EMPLOYMENT

Each state has its own Web site where information is provided about state and local or county government job opportunities. There is usually a standard format for each state' s home page. Sites may change, but currently they are as follows:

State	Web site	State	Web site
Alabama	www.state.al.us	Missouri	www.state.mo.us
Alaska	www.state.ak.us	Montana	www.mt.gov
Arizona	www.state.az.us	Nebraska	www.state.ne.us
Arkansas	www.state.ar.us	Nevada	www.state.nv.us
California	www.state.ca.us	New Hampshire	www.state.nh.us
Colorado	www.state.co.us	New Jersey	www.state.nj.us
Connecticut	www.state.ct.us	New Mexico	www.state.nm.us
Delaware	www.state.de.us	New York	www.state.ny.us
District of Columbia	www.dchomepage.net	North Carolina	www.state.nc.us
Florida	www.state.fl.us	North Dakota	www.state.nd.us
Georgia	www.state.ga.us	Ohio	www.state.oh.us
Hawaii	www.state.hi.us	Oklahoma	www.state.ok.us
Idaho	www.state.id.us	Oregon	www.state.or.us
Illinois	www.state.il.us	Pennsylvania	www.state.pa.us
Indiana	www.state.in.us	Rhode Island	www.state.ri.us
Iowa	www.state.ia.us	South Carolina	www.state.sc.us
Kansas	www.state.ks.us	South Dakota	www.state.sd.us
Kentucky	www.state.ky.us	Tennessee	www.state.tn.us
Louisiana	www.state.la.us	Texas	www.state.tx.us
Maine	www.state.me.us	Utah	www.state.ut.us
Maryland	www.state.md.us	Vermont	www.state.vt.us
Massachusetts	www.state.ma.us	Virginia	www.state.va.us
Michigan	www.state.mi.us	Washington	www.wa.gov
Minnesota	www.state.mn.us	West Virginia	www.state.wv.us
Mississippi	www.state.ms.us	Wisconsin	www.state.wi.us
		Wyoming	www.state.wy.us

Each state typically has a link to the civil service system, the Department of Personnel, or the Department of Human Resources, where online listings are posted. If a computer is not available as a resource, other places where such information may be obtained include:

- **The offices of the State Employment Services**. There are almost two thousand throughout the country. These offices are administered by the state in which they are located, with the financial assistance of the federal government. You will find the address of the one nearest you in your telephone book.
- **Your state Civil Service Commission.** Address your inquiry to the capital city of your state.
- **Your city Civil Service Commission (if you live in a large city).** It is sometimes called by another name, such as the Department of Personnel, but you will be able to identify it in your telephone directory under the listing of city departments.
- **Your municipal building and your local library.**
- **Newspapers carry complete listings.** For example, *The Chief* is published in New York City, and there are many other city and statewide publications devoted to civil service employees. Many local newspapers run a section on regional civil service news.
- **State and local agencies**. They are looking for competent employees and will contact schools, professional societies, veterans' organizations, unions, and trade associations.
- **School Boards and Boards of Education.** They employ the greatest proportion of all state and local personnel and should be asked directly for information about job openings.

SOURCES OF ADDITIONAL INFORMATION

Other sources also provide information about careers in accounting and about aptitude tests administered in high schools, colleges, and public accounting firms.

Careers in certified public accounting and CPA standards and examinations may be obtained from:

> American Institute of Certified Public Accountants, 1211 Avenue of the Americas, New York, NY 10036. www.aicpa.org

CPA licensure requirements by state may be obtained from:

> National Association of State Boards of Accountancy, 150 Fourth Ave. North, Suite 700, Nashville, TN 37219–2417. www.nasba.org

Careers in management accounting and the CMA designation may be obtained from:

> Institute of Management Accountants, 10 Paragon Dr., Montvale, NJ 07645–1760. www.imanet.org

Accredited in Accountancy, Accredited Business Accountant, Accredited Tax Advisor, or Accredited Tax Preparer designations may be obtained from:

> Accreditation Council for Accountancy and Taxation, 1010 North Fairfax St., Alexandria, VA 22314. www.acatcredentials.org

Careers in internal auditing and the CIA designation may be obtained from:

> The Institute of Internal Auditors, 249 Maitland Ave., Altamonte Springs, FL 32701–4201. www.theiia.org

Careers in information systems auditing and the CISA designation may be obtained from:

> The Information Systems Audit and Control Association, 3701 Algonquin Rd., Suite 1010, Rolling Meadows, IL 60008. www.isaca.org

Careers in government accounting and on the CGFM designation may be obtained from:

> Association of Government Accountants, 2208 Mount Vernon Ave., Alexandria, VA 22301. www.agacgfm.org

Obtaining an accounting position with the Federal Government is available from:

> The Office of Personnel Management (OPM) through a telephone-based system. Consult your telephone directory under U.S. Government for a local number or call 478-757-3000; Federal Relay Service: 800-877-8339 (toll-free). The first number is not toll-free, and charges may result. Information also is available from the OPM Internet site: www.usajobs.opm.gov.

APPENDIX

ACCOUNTING AND BOOKKEEPING DEFINITIONS

This is some of the language you're likely to see on your examination. You may not need to know all the words in this carefully prepared glossary, but if even a few appear, you'll be that much ahead of your competitors. Perhaps the greatest benefit from this list is the frame of mind it can create for you. Without reading a lot of technical text, you'll steep yourself in just the right atmosphere for high test marks.

A GLOSSARY FOR TEST TAKERS

ABATEMENT. A deduction or allowance, as a discount given for prompt payment.

ACCOUNT. A detailed statement of items affecting property or claims, listed respectively as Debits or Credits, and showing excess of Debits or Credits in form of a balance. Sufficient explanatory matter should be given to set forth the complete history of the account. There need not be both Debits and Credits nor more than one of either of these. If Debits and Credits or both are made frequently, the account is active. Items held in suspense awaiting future classification or allocation may be charged or credited to an adjustment account. When desirable to keep a separate accounting for specific shipments of goods, it is known as an Adventure Account. If more than one party is interested in such shipment, it is a joint venture account.

Asset Accounts record value owned.

Book Accounts are kept in books and show in formal manner the details regarding transactions between parties. To be of legal effect, the entries must be original, not transferred or posted.

Capital Accounts show the amounts invested in an enterprise either net, as in case of the Capital Accounts of proprietors, partners, and stockholders shown on the liability side of Balance Sheets, or gross, as in case of the Asset Accounts which show both owned and borrowed Capital invested.

Cash Accounts set forth receipts and disbursements of cash as well as balance on hand at beginning and end of period.

Clearing Accounts are employed to collect items preliminary to their allocation to a more detailed classification of the accounts or preliminary to the determination of the accounts to which such items properly belong.

Contingent Accounts are accounts that list liabilities or assets dependent for their validity upon some event which may or may not occur.

Contra Accounts are accounts that offset each other.

Controlling Accounts are accounts that summarize and afford an independent check upon detailed accounts of a given class, which are usually kept in a subordinate ledger. The controlling accounts are kept in the General Ledger. The balance of the controlling account equals the aggregate of the balances of the detailed accounts when all postings affecting these accounts are completed.

Current Accounts are open or running accounts not balanced or stated.

Deficiency Accounts supplement statements of affairs of an insolvent enterprise, showing what items comprise the deficiency of assets subject to lien for payment of unsecured creditors.

Depreciation Accounts are expense accounts that are charged periodically with the amounts credited to the respective Depreciation Reserve Accounts.

Depreciation Reserve Accounts are credited periodically with the amounts charged to contra depreciation expense accounts. Depreciation Reserve Accounts are valuation accounts because they supplement or evaluate the asset accounts for the ultimate replacement of which they are intended.

Discount Accounts are accounts that are charged with discounts allowed to customers or credited with discounts secured from creditors, accounts that are charged with amounts paid to have Notes Discounted, or accounts that are carried unamortized differences between par of Bonds sold and the amounts realized at time of sale, such amounts realized being less than the par of the Bonds.

Dividend Accounts are credited with amounts declared payable as dividends by boards of directors. These accounts are charged for amounts disbursed in payment—the charge being made either at time checks are sent out and for full amount of dividend or for the amounts of the individual checks as they are returned for payment.

Impersonal Accounts record expenses and revenues and assets and liabilities, but do not make reference to people in their titles.

Income Accounts show sources and amounts of operating revenues, expenses incurred for operations, sources and amounts of non-operating revenues, fixed charges, net income and disposition thereof.

Investment Accounts record property owned but not used for operating purposes.

Liability Accounts record value owed.

Merchandise Accounts are charged with cost of buying goods and crediting with sales, thus exhibiting Gross Profit when opening and closing inventories are taken into consideration.

Nominal Accounts are accounts that, during the accounting period, record changes which affect proprietorship favorably or unfavorably.

Open Accounts are accounts not balanced or closed.

Personal Accounts are accounts with individuals, usually customers and creditors.

Profit and Loss Account is an account into which all earnings and expenses are closed.

Real Accounts record Assets and Liabilities.

Revenue Accounts are equivalent to nominal accounts, showing income and expense.

Sales Accounts are rendered by agents to principals in explanation of consigned goods sold.

Sinking Fund Accounts record periodic installments paid into sinking funds and interest accretions added thereto.

Surplus Accounts record accretions to capital from profits.

ACCOUNTING. The science of accounts, their construction, classification, and interpretation.

ACCRUE. Accumulation of wealth or liabilities based on passage of time.

ACCRUED EXPENSE. A liability representing expense that has accrued but is not yet due and payable. It is in reality postpaid expense, and therefore the opposite of prepaid expense, which is an asset.

ACCRUED INCOME. Income that has accrued but is not yet due. It is in reality postpaid income, and therefore, the opposite of prepaid income, which is a liability.

AGENT. One possessing authority to act for another to a more or less limited extent.

ALLOCATION. Determination of the proper distribution of a given sum among a series of accounts.

AMORTIZATION. Extinction of a debt by systematic application of installments to a sinking fund, or reduction of premiums or discount incurred on sale or purchase of bonds by application of the effective interest rate.

ANNUITY. A sum of money payable periodically in installments.

APPRECIATION. Increase in value of assets.

ASSET. Wealth owned. Assets may be classified in various ways. From the point of view of ease of liquidation they are Quick or Fixed in varying degrees.

AUDIT. Verification of the accuracy of account books by examination of supporting vouchers, making tests of postings and computations, and determining whether all entries are made according to correct accounting principles making sure that there are no omissions.

BALANCE. The excess of the sum of the items on one side of an account over the sum of the items on the other side.

BALANCE SHEET. A schedule of Assets and Liabilities so classified and arranged as to enable an intelligent study to be made of the important financial ratios existing between different classes of assets, between different classes of liabilities, and between assets and liabilities. It also enables one to observe the origin of the equity existing in the assets and to determine to whom it belongs.

BOND. A bond is a written promise under seal to pay a certain sum of money at a specified time. Bonds bear interest at a fixed rate, usually payable semiannually. Bonds may be sold either above or below par, in which case, the coupon rate of interest differs from the effective rate when the bonds are sold below par and higher when bonds are sold above par.

BURDEN. Elements of production cost which, not being directly allocable to output, must be distributed on more or less arbitrary basis.

CAPITAL. In accounting, capital is excess of assets over liabilities of a given enterprise.

Fixed Capital consists of wealth in form of land, buildings, machinery, furniture and fixtures, etc.

Floating Capital is capital that can be readily converted into cash.

Nominal Capital is the authorized capital stock of a corporation.

Paid-Up Capital is the amount of capital stock issued and fully paid.

Working Capital is the excess of current assets over current liabilities.

CASH. All forms of exchange media that by custom are received in settlement of debts.

CHARGES. Items debited in accounts.

CHECK OR CHECQUE. See Draft.

COLLATERAL SECURITY. Personal property transferred by the owner to another to secure the carrying out of an obligation.

CONSIGNEE. An agent who receives shipments of goods from his principal to be sold on commission basis, title to goods remaining in the principal or consignor.

CONSIGNMENT. A shipment of goods to another and held by him for account of the principal or consignor.

CONSIGNOR. One who ships goods to an agent or factor that holds them for account of the principal or consignor.

CONSOLIDATION. Unification or affiliation of enterprises engaged in competitive or supplementary undertakings.

CONTINGENT. That which depends upon some happening or an occurrence—doubtful, conditional.

CORPORATION. An artificial person created by law to carry out a certain purpose or purposes.

COST. Cost is the outlay, usually measured in terms of money, necessary to buy or to produce a commodity. The two elements of Cost are Prime Cost and Overhead or Burden. Prime Cost is the outlay on direct labor and raw materials necessary to produce a commodity. Burden includes all elements of Cost other than direct labor and raw materials.

COST ACCOUNTING. Determination, by means of applying accounting principles, of the elements of Cost entering into the production of a commodity or service.

CREDITOR. One who gives credit in business matters or one to whom money is due.

DEBT. An obligation to pay money or that which one owes to another.

DEBTOR. One who owes money.

DEFERRED ASSET OR CHARGE. See Prepaid Expense.

DEFERRED CREDIT & INCOME OR LIABILITY. See Prepaid Income.

DEFICIENCY. Insufficiency of assets to discharge debts or other obligations.

DEPRECIATION. Decline in value of assets resulting from one or more of the following:

1. Wear and tear.
2. Tenure of holding.
3. Permanency or steadiness of industry.
4. Exhaustion of raw materials.
5. Obsolescence.
6. Accidents.
7. Fluctuations in trade.
8. Inadequacy.

DISBURSEMENTS. Cash payments.

DISCOUNT. Deduction from a listed or named figure, usually computed on a percentage basis.

DIVIDEND. Division of profits among stockholders on a pro rata basis.

DRAFT. A draft or bill of exchange is defined by Uniform Negotiable Instrument Law as, "…an unconditional order in writing addressed by one person to another and signed by the person giving it, requiring the person to whom it is addressed to pay on demand or at a fixed or determinable future time a certain sum in money to order or to bearer."

DRAWEE. The person against whom a draft is drawn and who becomes primarily liable upon acceptance.

DRAWER. The maker of a draft or bill of exchange.

ENTRY. Written description of a business transaction or adjustment made in books of accounts.

ESTATE. A right of ownership in property.

FIXED ASSETS. Those assets that are not readily convertible into cash and in the usual routine of business are not so converted.

FRANCHISE. A privilege or liberty given by the Government to certain individuals.

GOOD WILL. Present right to receive expected future superprofits—superprofits being the amount by which future profits are expected to exceed all economic expenditure incident to its production.

IMPREST SYSTEM. Plan used to account for petty cash disbursements whereby the cashier is at intervals reimbursed for the amount disbursed by him through a check drawn to Cash and charged to the accounts against which such disbursements were made.

INCOME. A flow of benefits from wealth over a period of time.

INTEREST. Expense or income resulting from use of wealth over a period of time.

INVENTORY. An itemized list of goods giving amounts and prices.

INVOICE. A statement issued by a seller of goods to the purchaser giving details regarding quantities, prices and terms of payment.

JOURNAL. The book of original entry in double entry bookkeeping.

Cash Journal is a combination cash book and journal, containing columns for both cash and non-cash transactions.

Purchases Journal records purchases made and the names of persons credited therefor.

Sales Journal records sales and the names of persons charged therefor.

LEDGER. A ledger is the book in which transactions are classified according to function. When subordinate ledgers are used, the General Ledger becomes a digest of details kept in subordinate ledgers, as well as the record of all usual ledger accounts.

Accounts Receivable Ledger contains a record of all transactions affecting trade debtors.

Accounts Payable Ledger contains a record of all transactions affecting trade creditors.

LIABILITY. A debt.

Capital Liabilities are liabilities that are incurred in the acquisition of permanent assets and that are usually in form on bonded indebtedness having a maturity date removed more than a year.

Contingent Liabilities are liabilities that may or may not become definite obligations depending upon some event.

Current Liability are liabilities that will fall due within a period of a year.

Deferred Liabilities are income received but not yet due; see Prepaid Income.

Fixed Liabilities are those in form of bonds or long term notes.

NOTES PAYABLE. The sum of all notes and acceptances upon which a concern is primarily liable as maker, endorser or acceptor.

NOTES RECEIVABLE. The sum of all notes and acceptances upon which others are liable to the holding concern.

NOTES RECEIVABLE DISCOUNTED. Contingent Liability for all notes receivable discounted at bank but not yet liquidated by the makers.

OVERDRAFT. A debit balance in a deposit that should normally have a credit balance.

POSTING. Transferring items from journals to ledgers, and making the necessary cross-references in folio columns.

PREMIUM ON BONDS. Amount above par at which bonds are bought or sold.

PREPAID EXPENSE. An asset representing expenditures for services not yet rendered—also known as Deferred Charge or Deferred Asset.

PREPAID INCOME. Income received for services not yet rendered. It is therefore a liability—also known as Deferred Credit or Deferred Liability.

PROFIT. Increase in net worth resulting from business operations.

PROPRIETORSHIP. Equity in assets over and above liability.

QUICK ASSETS. Assets that can ordinarily be readily converted into cash without involving heavy loss.

RESERVE. A segregation of surplus, or a retention of revenues equivalent to losses in asset values. In the former case it is a reserve of surplus, in the latter case, a valuation reserve.

RESERVE FUND. An amount set aside in form of cash or investments for general or special purposes.

REVENUE. Income from all sources.

SINKING FUND. An amount set aside in form of cash or investments for the purpose of liquidating some liability.

STATEMENT. To set forth in systematic form all data with reference to some phase of a business undertaking. To present essential details, subordinate schedules are frequently appended. A statement of Assets and Liabilities:

Balance Sheets set forth the status of a business as of a given date.

Consolidated Balance Sheets set forth the status of affiliated businesses as of a given time.

Consolidated Income Statements set forth the results of operations of affiliated enterprises over a period.

Income Statements set forth the result of operations over a period.

Statement of Affairs set forth the status of an insolvent business as of a given time, the arrangement being such as to show both book value of assets, what they are expected to realize and gross liabilities, how they are expected to rank.

STOCK. Share issued by a corporation, evidenced by formal certificates representing ownership therein. The total amount of such shares is known as the Capital Stock of the corporation.

Common Stock is that upon which dividends are paid only after dividend requirements on preferred stock and interest requirements on bonds are met.

Donated Stock is stock of a corporation which has been given back to be sold at a discount, usually to afford working capital in cases where the stock was originally issued in payment for fixed assets.

Guaranteed Stock is stock that is guaranteed as to principal or interest or both by some other corporation or corporations.

Inactive Stock is that which is seldom traded oh the exchange.

Preferred Stock is that which has prior rights over common stock either as to dividends or assets or both. Various provisions are found relative to the voting power, as for example, the preferred stock may be given control of the corporation if dividends thereon remain unpaid for two consecutive years. In case of cumulative preferred stock, unpaid dividends become a lien upon profits of following years.

Treasury Stock is stock that has been returned to the treasury of the issuing corporation.

Unissued Stock is the excess of Authorized over Issued Stock.

STOCK BONUSES. Gifts of stock offered to furnish incentive to investors to buy some other security of the issuing company.

STOCK RIGHTS. Privileges extended to stockholders to subscribe to new stock at a price below the market value of outstanding stock.

STOCK SUBSCRIPTIONS. Agreements to purchase the stock of a corporation. They become effective only when ratified by the corporation, unless accepted by a trustee in behalf of the corporation.

SURPLUS. In case of corporations having only par value stock, surplus ordinarily measures, excess of net worth or proprietorship over par value of stock outstanding.

Capital Surplus is surplus derived from extraordinary sources, as sale of stock at premium or sale of fixed assets at a profit.

Surplus from Operations is surplus derived from undertakings from the carrying out of which the business was established.

TRIAL BALANCE. A list of balances of all General Ledger accounts made to determine the correctness of postings from books of original entry as well as the correctness of the work of determining these balances.

TURNOVER. Rapidity of replacement of capital invested in inventories, accounts receivable, etc.

VOUCHER. Any document which serves as proof of a transaction.

VOUCHER SYSTEM. A scheme of accounting under which distribution of all expenditures is made on vouchers preliminary to their entry in the voucher register.

WORK IN PROCESS. Materials in process of manufacture, partly finished goods including all material, labor and overhead costs incurred on those goods up to the time of taking inventory.